Haig's Generals

Haig's Generals

Edited by
Ian F.W. Beckett and Steven J. Corvi

Pen & Sword
MILITARY

First published in Great Britain in 2006, reprinted in this format in 2009 by
Pen & Sword Military
An imprint of
Pen & Sword Books Ltd
47 Church Street
Barnsley
South Yorkshire
S70 2AS

ISBN 978 184415 892 8

A CIP catalogue record for this book is
available from the British Library

Printed and bound in England
By CPI

Pen & Sword Books Ltd incorporates the Imprints of Pen & Sword Aviation,
Pen & Sword Family History, Pen & Sword Maritime, Pen & Sword Military,
Wharncliffe Local History,
Pen & Sword Select, Pen & Sword Military Classics, Leo Cooper, Remember
When, Seaforth Publishing and Frontline Publishing

For a complete list of Pen & Sword titles please contact
PEN & SWORD BOOKS LIMITED
47 Church Street, Barnsley, South Yorkshire, S70 2AS, England
E-mail: enquiries@pen-and-sword.co.uk
Website: www.pen-and-sword.co.uk

Contents

Maps

Acknowledgements

Quotations from the Royal Archives appear by gracious permission of Her Majesty the Queen. Those from Crown copyright sources in the National Archives (formerly the Public Record Office) and elsewhere appear by permission of the Controller of Her Majesty's Stationery Office. The editors and authors are indebted for permission to use and/or quote from other archives in the copyright and/or possession of the Trustees of the National Library of Scotland; the Trustees of the British Library Board; the Churchill Archives Centre, Churchill College, Cambridge; the Trustees of the Liddell Hart Centre for Military Archives, King's College, University of London; the Trustees of the Imperial War Museum; the Trustees of the National Army Museum; the Trustees of the Australian War Memorial; the National Library of Australia; the National Archives of Canada; New Zealand National Archives; Liverpool Central Library; Earl Haig; M.A.F. Rawlinson Esq.; David Smith-Dorrien Esq.; Mrs Macfarland; Mrs Denise Boyes; Major A.J. Congreve; Captain Dugald Malcolm; the Countess de Roany; Mrs Eve Horner; and Mrs Maive Impey. Matthew Hughes also wishes to acknowledge the assistance of Dr Paul Harris.

Abbreviations

AAG	Assistant Adjutant General
ADC	aide-de-camp
AIF	Australian Imperial Force
Anzac	Australian and New Zealand Army Corps
BEF	British Expeditionary Force
BGGS	Brigadier General, General Staff
BGRA	Brigadier General, Royal Artillery
CB	Companion of the Order of the Bath
CGS	Chief of General Staff
CIE	Companion (of the Order) of the Indian Empire
CIGS	Chief of the Imperial General Staff
C.-in-C.	Commander-in-Chief
CO	Commanding Officer
CRA	Commander, Royal Artillery
CRE	Commander, Royal Engineers
DAAG	Deputy Assistant Adjutant General
DAQMG	Deputy Assistant Quarter Master General
DSO	(Companion of the) Distinguished Service Order
GAF	Groupe d'Armées des Flandres
GBE	Knight Grand Cross (of the Order) of the British Empire
GCB	Knight Grand Cross (of the Order) of the Bath
GCMG	Knight Grand Cross (of the Order) of St Michael and St George
GCSI	Knight Grand Commander of the Most Exalted Order of the Star of India
GCVO	Knight Grand Cross of the Royal Victorian Order
GHQ	General Headquarters
GOC	General Officer Commanding
GSO1	General Staff Officer, Grade 1
GSO2	General Staff Officer, Grade 2
GSO3	General Staff Officer, Grade 3
KBE	Knight Commander of the Order of the British Empire
KCB	Knight Commander of the Order of the Bath
KCMG	Knight Commander of the Order of St Michael and St George
KCSI	Knight Commander of the Star of India
KCVO	Knight Commander of the Royal Victorian Order
KRRC	King's Royal Rifle Corps

LHCMA	Liddell Hart Centre for Military Archives, King's College, University of London
MCC	Marylebone Cricket Club
MEF	Mediterranean Expeditionary Force
MGGS	Major General, General Staff
MGRA	Major General, Royal Artillery
MVO	Member of the Royal Victorian Order
NCO	non-commissioned officer
QMG	Quartermaster General
RA	Royal Artillery
RFA	Royal Field Artillery
RHA	Royal Horse Artillery
TF	Territorial Force
VC	Victoria Cross

Contributors

Professor Ian F.W. Beckett was formerly Professor of History at the University of Northampton, and Chairman of the Army Records Society. His publications include *Ypres: The First Battle, 1914* (2004), *The Great War, 1914–1918* (2001) and *The First World War: The Essential Guide to Sources in the UK National Archives* (2002).

Dr John Bourne is Director of the Centre for First World War Studies at the University of Birmingham. His publications include *Britain and the Great War, 1914–1918* (1989) and (co-edited with Gary Sheffield) *Douglas Haig: Diaries and Letters* (2004).

Dr Steven J. Corvi is a Professor at the American Military University and is Northeast Area Chairman for Military History in the Popular Culture Association. His specialization is the First World War, especially the military career of Horace Smith-Dorrien. He has published in the *Journal of the Society for Army Historical Research* and *Journal of Popular Culture*.

Dr Nikolas Gardner is Lecturer in History at the University of Salford. His publications include *Trial by Fire: Command and the British Expeditionary Force in 1914* (2003). He is currently working on the siege of Kut-al-Amara.

Dr Matthew Hughes is Senior Lecturer in History at Brunel University and editor of the *Journal of the Society for Army Historical Research*. His publications include *Allenby and British Strategy in the Middle East, 1917–19* (1999) and *Allenby in Palestine* (2004).

John Lee is Treasurer of the British Commission for Military History. His publications include *The Warlords: Hindenburg and Ludendorff* (2005) and *A Soldier's Life: General Sir Ian Hamilton* (2000).

Dr Helen McCartney is Lecturer in Defence Studies, King's College, London, based at the Joint Services Command and Staff College. Her publications include *Citizen Soldiers: The Liverpool Territorials in the First World War* (2005).

Dr Simon Robbins works in the Department of Documents at the Imperial War Museum. His publications include *British Generalship on the Western*

Front, 1914–1918 (2005) and (co-edited with Brian Bond) *Staff Officer: The Diaries of Walter Guinness, 1914–18* (1987).

Professor Gary Sheffield is Professor of Modern History, King's College, London, based at the Joint Services Command and Staff College. His publications include *Forgotten Victory: The First World War – Myths and Realities* (2001) and *The Somme* (2003).

Professor Peter Simkins MBE is Honorary Professor in Modern History at the University of Birmingham and was formerly Senior Historian at the Imperial War Museum. His publications include *Kitchener's Army* (1988).

Introduction

The generals of the First World War, particularly those of the British army, have had a bad press, the collective popular memory of the war in Britain being one of 'lions led by donkeys', in which a 'lost generation' was needlessly sacrificed by the incompetence of the high command. It is a view of long standing. The war correspondent Philip Gibbs recalled in 1920 that he thought at one point of Sir Henry Rawlinson, commander of Fourth Army, in its headquarters château at Querrieu 'scheming out the battles and ordering up new masses of troops to the great assault over the bodies of their dead'. It was inevitable, therefore, in his view that the troops 'should be savage in their irony when they pass a peaceful house where their death is being planned, and green-eyed when they see an Army general taking a stroll in buttercup fields, with a jaunty young ADC slashing the flowers with his cane and telling the latest joke from London to his laughing chief'. J.F.C. Fuller was wont to remark that the GCB customarily awarded to higher commanders stood for 'Great Cretin Brotherhood'. Another manifestation was the index of the last volume of David Lloyd George's *War Memoirs*, published in 1936, the subheadings under 'military mind' including 'narrowness of', 'does not seem to understand arithmetic' and 'regards thinking as a form of mutiny'. In the text itself, in reflecting finally on the experience of war and the perceived detachment of generals from the front, Lloyd George wrote that the 'distance between the châteaux and dugouts was as great as that from the fixed stars to the caverns of the earth'.[1]

Alan Clark's indictment of Haig in 1961 by way of conclusion to his study of the campaigns of 1915, *The Donkeys*, maintained that the army's heroism and devotion was such that after three years of his custodianship 'they could still . . . be brought to final victory'. One Oxford don had remarked to the future Professor Sir Llewellyn Woodward in 1919 that the army had been run by 'pass men'. Woodward's own judgement in the 1960s was that the army was in the hands of a 'custom-bound clique which would never have been permitted to take over the management of any other important department of state or of a great business'. In their differing ways, the play and subsequent film *Oh What a Lovely War* in the 1960s and the immensely successful television comedy series *Blackadder Goes Forth* in 1989 reinforced the traditional image for new generations. Indeed, in November 1998 the *Daily Express* suggested the removal of Haig's statue from Whitehall, asking rhetorically, 'Why do we let this man cast a shadow over our war dead?'[2] Few rushed to defend the reputation of the generals, the most notable exception being John Terraine, who was denounced by one commentator for 'fantastic philistinism' for suggesting that 'generals who presided over the demolition of a whole British generation were something more respectable than idiots'.[3]

Even as accomplished a military historian as Sir John Keegan has not been immune to the trend. He acknowledged on one occasion that British military leadership in the Great War was generally more 'conscious, principled, [and] exemplary' than before or since. He presumably meant junior leadership for, on another occasion, he also referred to 'that hideously unattractive group, the British generals of the First World War whose diaries reveal hearts as flintlike as the textures of their faces'.[4] Subsequently, Keegan wrote of Great War generals that the 'impassive expressions that stare back at us from contemporary photographs do not speak of consciences or feelings troubled by the slaughter over which those men presided'. However, in writing of the comfortable nature of 'château generalship', he was nonetheless at pains to stress the problems of communication and control. As Keegan expressed it, 'Generals were like men without eyes, without ears and without voices, unable to watch the operations they set in progress, unable to hear reports of their development and unable to speak to those whom they had originally given orders once action was joined.'[5] Others with far less understanding of the character of war on the Western Front have been far more critical. The lingering traditions of the 'lions and donkeys' school are especially apparent in such a 'popular' title as the lamentable *British Butchers and Bunglers of World War One*.[6]

In 1914, of course, the army was a small imperial constabulary in which only three serving soldiers had commanded the army's only permanent peacetime corps at Aldershot, namely Sir John French, Sir Douglas Haig and Sir Horace Smith-Dorrien. The lack of command experience in terms of handling large formations was recognized within the army, as was the lack of a fully trained staff. In all, there were just 12,738 regular officers in August 1914, of whom 908 had graduated from the staff colleges at Camberley or Quetta. Staff training was defective in many ways and a continental-style General Staff had emerged in practice in only 1906, though theoretically established two years earlier. In any case, staffs served commanders in the emergent British model, rather than the staff being the real centre of authority as in the German case, so that, for example, the artillery and engineering advisers were just that and without executive authority.[7] Moreover, the army was rigidly hierarchical and had suffered from the variety of petty vendettas and clashes of personality perhaps inevitable in a relatively small institution. Many of these would continue to influence the conduct of operations during the war itself, though it has been argued that the army reflected wider Edwardian society in this regard and that the 'system' within which individuals interacted was more significant than the individuals themselves.[8]

Significant reforms had been instituted in the aftermath of the South African War (1899–1902), in organizational and tactical terms.[9] The army, however, was still in transition at the moment that the Great War began and, like their continental counterparts, British soldiers were compelled to come to terms with new managerial and technical problems in the midst of war. In the British case, adaptation was also required in the midst of a massive wartime expansion which, in terms of officers alone, saw the granting of 229,316 wartime commissions. Indeed, an army expanded from six to seventy-five infantry divisions required approximately as many officers in staff appointments by 1918 – about 12,000 – as in the entire regular officer corps four years earlier. It is popularly assumed that the army failed the challenge, the consequences of the disjointedness between rapid expansion and coming to grips with the strategic and tactical implications of mass modern industrialized warfare being a maladroit management of operations reflected in high casualties and stalemate.

Whatever the popular perception, however, the image of the wartime British army has been transformed by recent scholarship. It is now generally accepted among historians that the army's 'learning curve', though lengthy and painful, resulted in the emergence of a 'modern army' by 1917–18.[10] It remains a matter of debate how far the transformation of the army at the operational level emerged as a result of initiatives from below or from above in the form of Haig and his General Headquarters (GHQ).[11] In many respects the nature of this particular debate has seen the perspective from which operations are viewed driven increasingly down the chain of command to corps and, especially, to divisional level.[12]

Indeed, one recent examination of the command experience of Henry Rawlinson has concluded that he was effectively a spectator on the Somme in 1916 through the communication difficulties, and a spectator again during the 'Hundred Days' campaign in 1918 through the relentless decentralization process concomitant with advances in technology and the re-emergence of semi-mobile warfare. Quite why subordinate commanders were suddenly capable of exercising flexibility and initiative in the summer of 1918 when they had failed to do so as recently as March and April is explained variously as a consequence of the necessity to improvise ad hoc formations during the chaos of the spring retreat, of the sheer weight of Allied material superiority by the summer, and of the Germans being their own worst enemy. One further suggestion is that tactical initiatives emerged because 'a new breed of young, experienced, determined commanders ... conspicuous not only for the traditional virtues of personal courage and a high sense of duty but also for ruthlessness and aggression, took advantage of the opportunities for rapid promotion'. Certainly, much of the tactical innovation derived from the efforts of junior officers and battalion commanders though training had immeasurably improved by 1917–18.[13] If the level of army command was increasingly irrelevant then, of course, it follows that Haig himself can also be seen as a peripheral figure in terms of direct influence over events after 1917 but this, too, is a matter of debate.[14]

Once centre-stage in the critique of British generalship, Haig's army commanders are now a neglected component in the debate on the learning curve characterized in one recent study as the 'forgotten men of the twentieth century'.[15] Accordingly, they remain very much under the shadow of the 'lions led by donkeys' theme. In part, this is because a number of these key figures are actually still relatively unknown or their roles not well understood. Edmund Allenby, Hubert Gough and Herbert Plumer have been the subjects of popular biographies, as has Horace Smith-Dorrien, who commanded an army alongside Haig in 1914–15. The most recent biographies of Smith-Dorrien and Gough, however, date from the 1970s, with those of Allenby and Plumer dating from the early 1990s. Only Henry Rawlinson has been the subject of a recent academic monograph, though Allenby's role in the Middle East has been examined in a similar academic context.[16] Henry Horne and Charles Monro are almost entirely unknown, with no modern biographies, and Julian Byng and William Birdwood known primarily for their performance at corps level with the Canadians and Australians respectively. Birdwood also lacks a modern biography, though Byng was the subject of an adequate biography by a Canadian in the 1980s.[17]

In war some men rise to the challenge of command, some are remiss in their duties, and others become scapegoats for the calamities of war. The keen operational senses required to win battles or wars are not an inherent ability in all commanders. It has been suggested that those who usually succeeded best in army command during the war were of the 'demanding tyrant school', a category that might include both Allenby and Gough. They were equally abrasive in their ways, though, significantly, as Matthew Hughes points out (Chapter 1), Allenby's notorious temper improved markedly once he was in Palestine. As Gary Sheffield and Helen McCartney note (Chapter 4), Gough was certainly a 'hands on' commander whose style was not always appreciated by his subordinates, though there were some wide variations in attitudes towards him and this has been apparent in subsequent assessments.[18]

In fact, neither Allenby nor Gough was that successful in France and Flanders, though Horne was effective since his insistence on efficiency – he was involved in 'degumming' several of his subordinates – was tempered by the recognition, as Simon Robbins comments (Chapter 5), that he drove himself just as hard as his subordinates. Indeed, it has been said of Horne that he was the one British general 'in whose face it is possible to read the personal cost of command'.[19] Nonetheless, Horne was always ready to back those subordinates whom he trusted. Though he was within what might be termed the 'hands off' school, Rawlinson (Chapter 8), as examined by Ian Beckett, displayed little overt compassion towards his men by contrast to others and was seemingly prepared to sacrifice his subordinates to his own ambition.

By contrast to the drivers and thrusters, the more 'kindly' Byng and Plumer both arguably achieved more, not least through their attention to detail, a virtue shared, as John Lee explains, with Birdwood (Chapter 2). Significantly, perhaps, Gough's chief of staff, Neill Malcolm, accused Plumer on one occasion of having a system of command that 'merely appears to be to tell the corps to carry on', though this was prior to the appointment of Charles 'Tim' Harington as Plumer's chief of staff.[20] In fact, as Peter Simkins indicates (Chapter 7), while very loyal and helpful to his subordinates, Plumer was nevertheless a strict disciplinarian, perfectly capable of delivering strong reprimands. Moreover, of course, Plumer and the unassuming and likeable Byng were not immune to failings. For every Vimy or Messines, there was a counterpoint. Nikolas Gardner notes (Chapter 3) the dangers arising from the lack of consistency achieved among Byng's subordinates in face of the German spring offensive in 1918. Indeed, Byng did not respond well to unexpected crises. Similarly, Plumer's legendary meticulousness did not result in any fewer casualties in the closing stages of Passchendaele than Gough's methods in the opening stages, and he acquiesced willingly in continuing operations of diminishing returns. As Steven Corvi shows, Smith-Dorrien, usually a proactive commander (Chapter 9), was also markedly compassionate towards the men who fought under him. It can be noted, in addition, that, whatever the command style, most army commanders were increasingly seen at the front visiting commanders and units as the war continued, Allenby, Byng, Gough, Horne, Plumer and Rawlinson all being active in this regard.[21]

To a large extent, the disparities in command styles reflected that in the understanding of the nature of command itself, perhaps best expressed by Haig's chief of staff in I Corps, Brigadier General John Gough VC, as hitting the 'happy mean' between control and guidance: 'In other words, superior commanders should command in the true sense of the word. The practical difficulty, however, is that some commanders are so anxious to leave subordinates a free hand that they forget their own duty of control and guidance while others go to the opposite extreme and interfere with the methods of their subordinates.'[22] The inconsistency of Haig in this regard – all too apparent in the planning of both the Somme and Third Ypres offensives – has been well remarked, but it was a general problem at all levels throughout the army. In addition, it has been argued that while Haig himself remained torn between control and guidance in operational planning, the general assumption on the part of its officers that GHQ should not interfere reduced its Operational Section to impotence until the summer of 1918: structural, personal and social factors all made GHQ less intellectually flexible than other parts of the army. Indeed, GHQ only began to become effective once Herbert Lawrence became Haig's chief of staff in January 1918, together with other significant personnel changes.[23] Essentially, inconsistency was a product of a lack of a well-articulated doctrine. *Field Service Regulations*, which had been issued while Haig was director of staff duties between 1907 and 1909, implied decentralization but did not define it clearly, and it has been argued that, since it assumed a well trained staff, the massive expansion of the BEF led to its progressive abandonment when new formations were not entirely trusted. Moreover, the functions of neither corps nor armies were absolutely clear in 1914. Sir John French delayed the introduction of an army level of command in 1914 as he believed that it would impose an unacceptable additional level of command between corps commanders and himself, and he preferred adding more divisions to corps. Even when two armies were created, French saw them primarily as administrative structures. By contrast, Haig did not regard an army headquarters as a mere post office, emphasizing in December 1914 that his corps commanders should not deal directly with GHQ on operational matters.[24]

It is clear that, by 1917–18, able younger men were moving into divisional and brigade command but there was a relatively small pool of ability for an army which had expanded so substantially: over 1,200 men held the rank of brigadier general or above on the Western Front between 1914 and 1918, overwhelmingly drawn from regular officers. In passing, it can be noted that 78 were killed or died of wounds or died on active service, with a further 146 wounded or captured.[25] Less is known as yet about corps commanders, an appointment held by 43 men during the war on the Western Front, but it would appear that the apex of their authority came in 1916, more initiative being conceded to divisions by 1918.[26] Undoubtedly, some made an impact at that level, such as Walter Congreve, Herbert Watts, Beauvoir de Lisle, the Earl of Cavan – an advocate of the 'hands off' with respect to his divisional commanders – Claud Jacob, and Ivor Maxse, as well as Birdwood and Byng. Maxse, however, was not as successful at corps level as he had been at divisional level and Congreve was also removed in May 1918.[27]

Overall, despite the popular impression that all general officers were cavalrymen, most were infantrymen, though, of the army commanders, four of the nine who commanded at that level were cavalrymen, namely Allenby, Birdwood, Byng and Gough. Haig, of course, was also a cavalryman, as was his predecessor, French. While there has been some attention paid to the 'degumming' of general officers, much is still unknown about the process of selecting replacements. Haig, however, does not appear to have favoured other cavalrymen for rapid promotion, with the exception of Gough, and while cavalrymen were arguably over-represented at army level, infantrymen dominated corps and divisional commands.[28] In his magnificently malicious way, James Edmonds maintained that Horne 'owed his rise entirely to agreeing with GHQ every time', but it is clear that Haig valued Horne, whom he also saw as a technical expert with respect to artillery, as a safe pair of hands. Haig also protected Byng after the disappointments of Cambrai in November 1917. Rawlinson was also largely dependent upon Haig for his preferment, but the relationship waxed and waned, not least in how far Rawlinson was ready to resist or acquiesce in Haig's operational directions. Rawlinson was also by far the most given to intrigue among the army commanders. Relations with Allenby were especially problematic, though Allenby displayed a 'silent loyalty' and generally followed Haig's direction even when he believed the decisions fundamentally flawed; however, for a while at least, Allenby resisted Haig's suggestions with regard to the artillery plan at Arras in May 1917. Byng, too, was a loyal subordinate, while Monro, with whom Haig had a somewhat ambivalent relationship, as John Bourne notes (Chapter 6), remarked that he would never question the decisions of a superior or refuse any appointment offered, however much he disliked it.

As a fellow army commander with Haig, Smith-Dorrien, of course, was in a rather different category, but was cordially disliked by both French and Haig, both of whom saw him as something of a rival. Plumer, too, was considered for 'degumming' by Haig in early 1916, conceivably as he was also emerging as a potential alternative, and it was Gough rather than Plumer whom Haig chose to undertake the main offensive in Flanders in the summer of 1917. In the event, Haig came to appreciate Plumer's qualities more and more. Other than Allenby, Birdwood appears to have been the one among his army commanders whom Haig most disliked, probably through Birdwood's connections to Kitchener. Birdwood himself was no great admirer of Haig but 'largely unwilling to stand up to his superiors'.[29]

The pattern that emerges is one of very different relationships between Haig and individual army commanders, yet a generally acquiescent group within the context of Haig's alternating detachment from and interference in those areas of operational planning that should have been the province of his subordinates. GHQ was apt to refer to the army commanders as the 'wicked barons', but it has been argued that the latter were collectively 'simply afraid of Haig and were not prepared to question him'.[30] Gough later suggested that there were too few conferences. The assumption that army commanders' conferences were an ineffective forum largely rests on Gough's testimony, though Allenby also found them frustrating affairs. Certainly, they were increasingly less frequent but there were many individual meetings between Haig and his army commanders, suggesting GHQ was less psychologically isolated than sometimes inferred. Nonetheless, Haig and his GHQ staff always brought their own lunch to conferences with army commanders, thus limiting the opportunities for informal discussion.[31]

It has been argued effectively that there was as much a learning curve in higher command relationships within the army as elsewhere, though the process was clearly assisted by the diminishing sphere of real influence on the part of both Haig and his immediate subordinates as the nature of warfare changed in 1918. In terms of the relationship between GHQ and army commanders, the decisive shift in power may have largely resulted from the efforts of Herbert Lawrence.[32] Nonetheless, it is instructive to assess how far individual army commanders themselves appreciated the changes taking place and this is a major focus of this volume. Smith-Dorrien had thought about his profession, had instituted tactical reforms while commanding at Aldershot before the war, and displayed an especially keen tactical sense on the battlefield itself in 1914. He clearly recognized the increased impact of artillery, but his effective removal from the scene in May 1915 prevents any realistic means of assessing how far he might have influenced future developments within the BEF. Byng also saw the value of artillery as well as mechanization and was open to new ideas, but was not himself an innovator, while Birdwood rarely became involved in detailed planning. As already suggested, Allenby and Gough did not really meet the challenges, though Gough performed magnificently in the dark days of March 1918, only to be removed as a scapegoat for the wider debacle, and might have risen well to the challenges of more mobile warfare later that year. Monro had so little opportunity to achieve anything on the Western Front that it is difficult to form a definitive view of his ability or potential.

Horne was certainly innovative, not least in artillery methods, though at one point on the Somme as a corps commander he suggested he did not understand the efficacy of the creeping barrage. However, it was Rawlinson who evolved the most viable operational alternative to prevailing practice through his advocacy of what became known as 'bite and hold'. Unfortunately, however, as Rawlinson himself acknowledged, limited offensives held out little prospect of strategic success in the short or medium term. Moreover, his inconsistency extended to his commitment to his own operational concepts. Gough accepted some aspects of 'bite and hold' in terms of adopting a precise timetable but realized that opportunities had been lost when subordinate commanders were not sufficiently far forward to recognize them as such. His instincts, however, ran ahead of the technology available, not least in terms of communications.[33] It was Plumer who developed 'bite and hold' techniques to their greatest extent. However, as Peter Simkins demonstrates, the conditions in Flanders in 1917 were not really conducive to their success, and the technology and the circumstances in which that technology could really make a difference were not available until the closing months of the war.

In the case of Byng and Birdwood, attention in terms of planning shifts to their staffs, and generally the army commanders cannot be seen in isolation from their immediate circle of advisers. Consequently, therefore, it is apparent from the contributions to this volume that the role of the chief of staff in particular was immensely important. Initially, the lack of trained staff officers meant that commanders often acted in effect as their own chiefs of staff, busying themselves with responsibilities properly those of others. Rawlinson was certainly guilty of this in 1914 and it was also said of Birdwood in 1916. The situation increasingly improved, however, as staff became more experienced. At corps level, Birdwood had the Australian, Brudenell White. At army level, Horne had Hastings Anderson, Rawlinson had Archie Montgomery, Plumer had Tim Harington and Byng had John Vaughan. Neill Malcolm was more controversial as Gough's chief of staff. George Forestier-Walker was not notably efficient as Smith-Dorrien's chief of staff and Plumer did not appreciate the efforts of Jocelyn Percy, who replaced Harington in 1918. Moreover, just as there was a coolness between Smith-Dorrien and Haig so, too, was there between Forestier-Walker and Haig's then chief of staff, John Gough, in 1914, to the detriment of co-operation between I and II Corps in that opening campaign of the war.[34]

It has been remarked that 'few groups in British history have been the subject of such vilification as the Western Front generals of the Great War'.[35] In offering these essays on the army commanders among that group, the authors have been requested to examine in their own way the individual's personality, command experience, relationship with Haig and with his own subordinates, how the war changed (or not) his pre-war expectations, and how far the individual adapted to those technological and other elements of modern battle which were to determine a partial solution to the problem of war on the Western Front. In addition, each concludes with a case study of a particularly significant action for each individual, namely Le Cateau (Smith-Dorrien), Fromelles (Monro), the Somme (Rawlinson), the Ancre (Gough), Arras (Allenby), Passchendaele (Plumer), Cambrai (Byng), the Hundred Days (Birdwood) and the Crossing of the Canal du Nord (Horne). Together these essays provide a new and comprehensive portrait of a highly significant group of individuals too often neglected in the current debate on the 'learning curve'.

IFWB
SJC

Notes

1 Philip Gibbs, *Realities of War* (London: 1920), p. 42; David Lloyd George, *War Memoirs* (London: Ivor Nicholson & Watson, 1936), VI, pp. 3421, 3497.

2 Alan Clark, *The Donkeys* (London: Hutchinson, 1961), p. 186; Sir Llewellyn Woodward, *Great Britain and the War of 1914–1918* (London: Methuen, 1972 edn), pp. xix–xx; Brian Bond, *The Unquiet Western Front: Britain's Role in Literature and History* (Cambridge: Cambridge University Press, 2002), pp. 51–89; Ian F.W. Beckett, *The Great War, 1914–1918* (London: Longman/Pearson, 2001), pp. 462–5; Gary Sheffield, 'Oh What a Futile War! Representations of the Western Front in Modern British Media and Popular Culture', in Ian Stewart and Susan Carruthers, eds, *War, Culture and the Media* (London: Flicks, 1996), pp. 54–74.

3 John Terraine, 'British Military Leadership in the First World War', in Peter Liddle, ed., *Home Fires and Foreign Fields* (London: Brassey's, 1985), pp. 39–51; Terraine, 'The Generals', *Stand To!*, 7 (1983), pp. 4–7; Terraine, *The Smoke and the Fire* (London: Sidgwick & Jackson, 1980), p. 36; B. Page, 'The Gunner's Story', *New Statesman*, 24 August 1979.

4 John Keegan, *The Face of Battle* (Harmondsworth: Penguin, 1978), p. 277; Keegan, 'Whole Stunt Napoo', *New Statesman*, 17 November 1978.

5 John Keegan, *The First World War* (London: Pimlico, 1988), pp. 337–9, 347.

6 John Laffin, *British Butchers and Bunglers of World War One* (Stroud: Alan Sutton, 1988).

7 Ian F.W. Beckett, 'Hubert Gough, Neill Malcolm and Command on the Western Front', in Brian Bond, ed., *'Look to Your Front': Studies in the First World War* (Staplehurst: Spellmount, 1999), pp. 1–12.

8 Tim Travers, *The Killing Ground: The British Army, the Western Front and the Emergence of Modern Warfare* (London: Allen & Unwin, 1987), p. 27.

9 Ian F.W. Beckett, 'The South African War and the Late Victorian Army', in Peter Dennis and Jeffrey Grey, eds, *The Boer War: Army, Nation and Empire* (Canberra: Army History Unit, 2000), pp. 31–44.

10 Gary Sheffield, *Forgotten Victory: The First World War: Myths and Realities* (London: Headline, 2001), pp. 258–63; Sheffield, 'The Indispensable Factor: the Performance of British Troops in 1918', in Peter Dennis and Jeffrey Grey, eds, *1918: Defining Victory* (Canberra: Army History Unit, 1999), pp. 72–95; Paddy Griffith, *Battle Tactics of the Western Front: The British Army's Art of Attack, 1916–18* (New Haven: Yale University Press, 1994), pp. 192–200; Jonathan Bailey, *The First World War and the Birth of the Modern Style of Warfare* (Camberley: Strategic and Combat Studies Institute, 1996), pp. 13–21.

11 Travers, *Killing Ground*, pp. 85–100; Travers, *How the War Was Won: Command and Technology in the British Army on the Western Front, 1917–1918* (London: Routledge, 1992), pp. 32–49.

12 See, for example, John Bourne, 'Major General W.C.G. Heneker: A Divisional Commander of the Great War', in Matthew Hughes and Mathew Seligmann, eds, *Leadership in Conflict, 1914–18* (Barnsley: Leo Cooper, 2000), pp. 54–67; John Lee, 'The SHLM Project: Assessing the Battle Performance of British Divisions', in Paddy Griffith, ed., *British Fighting Methods in the Great War* (London: Frank Cass, 1996), pp. 175–81; Peter Simkins, 'Co-stars or Supporting Cast? British Divisions in the Hundred Days, 1918', in ibid., pp. 50–69.

13 Quoting John Bourne, 'British Generals in the First World War', in Gary Sheffield, ed., *Leadership and Command* (London: Brassey's, 1997), pp. 93–116; also Robin Prior and Trevor Wilson, *Command on the Western Front* (Oxford: Blackwell, 1992), pp. 394–8; Travers, *How the War Was Won*, pp. 149, 175–82; Simon Robbins, *British Generalship on the Western Front, 1914–18: Defeat into Victory* (London: Frank Cass, 2005), pp. 83–114.

14 John Bourne, 'Haig and the Historians', in Brian Bond and Nigel Cave, eds, *Haig: A Reappraisal 70 Years On* (Barnsley: Leo Cooper, 1999), pp. 1–11; Keith Simpson, 'The Reputation of Sir Douglas Haig', in Brian Bond, ed., *The First World War and British Military History* (Oxford: Clarendon, 1991), pp. 141–62.

15 Robbins, *British Generalship*, p. 2.

16 A.J. Smithers, *The Man Who Disobeyed: Sir Horace Smith-Dorrien and His Enemies* (London: Leo Cooper, 1970); Anthony Farrar-Hockley, *Goughie: The Life of General Sir Hubert Gough* (London: Hart-Davis, MacGibbon, 1975); Lawrence James, *Imperial Warrior: The Life and Times of Field Marshal Viscount Allenby* (London: Weidenfeld & Nicolson, 1993); Geoffrey Powell, *Plumer: The Soldier's General* (London: Leo Cooper, 1990); Prior and Wilson, *Command*; Matthew Hughes, *Allenby and British Strategy in the Middle East, 1917–19* (London: Frank Cass, 1999).

17 Jeffrey Williams, *Byng of Vimy: General and Governor General* (London: Leo Cooper, 1983).

18 Beckett, 'Gough, Malcolm and Command', pp. 1–12; Gary Sheffield, 'The Australians at Pozières, 1916', in David French and Brian Holden Reid, eds, *The British General Staff: Reform and Innovation, 1890–1939* (London: Frank Cass, 2002), pp. 112–26; idem, 'An Army Commander on the Somme: Hubert Gough', in Gary Sheffield and Dan Todman, eds, *Command and Control on the Western Front: The British Army's Experiences, 1914–18* (Staplehurst: Spellmount, 2005), pp. 71–96; Jonathan Walker, *The Blood Tub: General Gough and the Battle of Bullecourt, 1917* (Staplehurst: Spellmount, 1998), *passim*; Andy Wiest, 'Haig, Gough and Passchendaele', in Sheffield, *Leadership and Command*, pp. 7–92; Robbins, *British Generalship*, pp. 32–3.

19 Bourne, 'British Generals', p. 109.

20 Beckett, 'Gough, Malcolm and Command', p. 8.

21 Robin Prior and Trevor Wilson, *Passchendaele: The Untold Story* (New Haven: Yale University Press, 1996), pp. 138–9, 159–61, 164, 200; Robbins, *British Generalship*, p. 79.

22 Ian F.W. Beckett, *Johnnie Gough VC* (London: Tom Donovan, 1989), pp. 148–9.

23 Travers, *Killing Ground*, pp. 85–97, 101–18; idem, 'A Particular Style of Command: Haig and GHQ, 1916–18', *Journal of Strategic Studies*, 10/3 (1987), pp. 363–76; Beckett, 'Gough, Malcolm and Command', pp. 1–12; Dan Todman, 'The Grand Lamasery Revisited: General Headquarters on the Western Front, 1914–18', in Sheffield and Todman, *Command and Control*, pp. 39–70; Robbins, *British Generalship*, pp. 119–20.

24 Martin Samuels, *Command or Control? Command, Training and Tactics in the British and German Armies, 1888–1918* (London: Frank Cass, 1995), pp. 47–60; Shelford Bidwell and Dominick Graham, *Fire-Power: British Army Weapons and Theories of War, 1904–45* (London: Allen & Unwin, 1982), pp. 38–58;

Niall Barr, 'Command in the Transition from Mobile to Static Warfare', in Sheffield and Todman, *Command and Control*, pp. 13–38; Andy Simpson, 'British Corps Command on the Western Front, 1914–18', in ibid., pp. 97–118.

25 John Bourne, 'The BEF's Generals on 29 September 1918: An Empirical Portrait with Some British and Australian Comparisons', in Dennis and Grey, *1918*, pp. 96–113; Peter Simkins, 'Building Blocks: Aspects of Command and Control at Brigade Level in the BEF's Offensive Operations, 1916–18', in Sheffield and Todman, *Command and Control*, pp. 141–71; Frank Davies and Graham Maddocks, *Bloody Red Tabs: General Officer Casualties of the Great War, 1914–18* (London: Leo Cooper, 1995), p. 22.

26 See, however, Simpson, 'British Corps Command', pp. 97–118.

27 John Baynes, *Far from a Donkey: The Life of General Sir Ivor Maxse* (London: Brassey's, 1995), pp. 166–212; Travers, *How the War Was Won*, p. 73; Robbins, *British Generalship*, pp. 65–6.

28 Bourne, 'BEF's Generals', pp. 96–113; idem, 'British Divisional Generals during the Great War: First Thoughts', *Gun Fire*, 29 (1987), pp. 22–31; idem, 'British General Officers and the Somme: Some Career Aspects', *Gun Fire*, 39 (1997), pp. 12–25; Robbins, *British Generalship*, pp. 52, 210–17.

29 A.D. Harvey, *Collision of Empires: Britain in Three World Wars, 1793–1945* (London: Hambledon, 1992), p. 343; Peter Simkins, 'Haig and the Army Commanders', in Bond and Cave, *Haig*, pp. 78–97.

30 Travers, *Killing Ground*, p. 104.

31 Simkins, 'Haig and Army Commanders', pp. 94–97; Robbins, *British Generalship*, p. 75.

32 Simkins, 'Haig and Army Commanders', p. 97; Prior and Wilson, *Command*, p. 305; Robbins, *British Generalship*, pp. 129, 135–6.

33 Sheffield, 'Army Commander on the Somme', pp. 71–95; on Horne, see Robin Prior and Trevor Wilson, *The Somme* (New Haven: Yale University Press, 2005), p. 224.

34 Robbins, *British Generalship*, pp. 34–50.

35 Bourne, 'BEF's Generals', p. 97.

Chapter One

Edmund Allenby
Third Army, 1915–1917

Matthew Hughes

On 9 April 1917 General Sir Edmund Allenby's Third Army launched the Battle of Arras. Considerable initial success soon evaporated and by 11 April the British had stalled on the Germans' defence-in-depth system. Allenby's only major offensive as an army commander on the Western Front then became an attritional struggle along either bank of the River Scarpe that continued into May 1917 with heavy casualties for little ground gained. In early June 1917 Britain's War Cabinet relieved Allenby of command of Third Army and sent him to Palestine to take charge of the Egyptian Expeditionary Force. Seeing this move as demotion and proof that he had failed at Arras, a 'desolate' Allenby motored over to see the Hon. Sir Julian Byng – commander of the Canadian Corps and the man who would take charge of Third Army once Allenby had gone – where 'he broke down very badly'.[1] In Palestine, Allenby was so successful, conquering the whole of the Levant region by October 1918, that, at the war's end, he was rewarded with a field marshal's baton, a viscountcy and the high commissioner post in Egypt, and Parliament voted him £50,000. Rather like Byng, who went on to become governor-general of Canada after the war, Allenby is best remembered for what he did outside of the Western Front. The Palestine campaign turned around Allenby's career and made his name. It also overshadows his time in France, where he struggled as commander of Third Army. Without the move to the Middle East, Allenby would probably have ended the war as a prematurely dismissed or castigated commander, someone who had done little except throw away his men's lives for little obvious gain in the later phases of the Battle of Arras.

Born on 23 April 1861, St George's Day, at Brackenhurst Hall in Nottinghamshire, Allenby was the second child and eldest son of six children – three boys, three girls – of Hynman Allenby, a country gentleman, and his wife, Catherine Anne, the daughter of a local clergyman. Brought up the son of a country squire far from the urban sprawl of a rapidly industrializing Britain, Allenby loved nature, a passion that would remain with him all his life. His family background and early years did not suggest a military career. In 1875 he

Chronology

23 April 1861	Edmund Henry Hynman Allenby born at Brackenhurst Hall, Southwell, Nottinghamshire
	Educated at Haileybury and Royal Military College, Sandhurst
10 May 1882	Gazetted Second Lieutenant, 6th (Inniskilling) Dragoons
1884–5	Served in Bechuanaland
10 January 1888	Promoted captain
27 March 1889	Appointed regimental adjutant
30 December 1896	Married Adelaide Mabel Chapman
1896–7	Attended Staff College, Camberley
19 May 1897	Promoted major
29 November 1900	Promoted brevet lieutenant colonel
22 August 1902	Promoted brevet colonel
19 October 1905	Appointed GOC 4th Cavalry Brigade and substantive colonel
10 September 1909	Promoted major general
25 April 1910	Appointed inspector general of cavalry
5 August 1914	Appointed GOC Cavalry Division
10 October 1914	Appointed GOC Cavalry Corps and temporary lieutenant general
8 May 1915	Appointed GOC V Corps
23 October 1915	Appointed GOC Third Army and temporary general
1 January 1916	Promoted substantive lieutenant general
3 June 1917	Promoted substantive general
28 June 1917	Took over as GOC Egyptian Expeditionary Force
29 July 1917	Son killed on Western Front
9 December 1917	Capture of Jerusalem
19 September 1918	Battle of Megiddo
1 October 1918	Capture of Damascus
21 March 1919	Acting special commissioner, Egypt
31 July 1919	Promoted field marshal
October 1919	Created Viscount Allenby of Megiddo and Felixstowe, and appointed high commissioner, Egypt
June 1925	Returned to Britain and retirement
14 May 1936	Died in London (cremated, laid to rest in St George's Chapel, Westminster Abbey, alongside Lord Plumer)

Appointed CB 1902, KCB 1915, GCMG 1918, GCB 1918, GCVO 1934

went to Haileybury College in Hertfordshire, a former training school for the East India Company recently resurrected as a public school. While Allenby showed no remarkable aptitude in either the classroom or sport, his schooling left its mark. The public schools at this time emphasized courage, duty, fortitude, integrity, selflessness, self-control and a 'manly' belief in the virtues of the Christian faith as the vital attributes for 'character' and for a successful career in positions of authority.[2] While there was none of the sense of divine purpose that drove on some of his generation who would rise to high rank – such as Haig – the Anglican faith and tight emotional discipline of Allenby's early years gave him strength and perseverance throughout his life. His childhood and schooling formed a determined rather than an intellectual commander, a practitioner of war rather than a military thinker.

On leaving school, Allenby's first career choice was the Indian Civil Service and he went to several 'crammer' schools to prepare for the entrance exams. These he failed, twice. Only after this setback did he choose a career in the army. As he later recounted in a public speech, he went into the army in 1881 'because he was too big a fool for anything else'.[3] Having passed out of Sandhurst in December 1881, on 10 May 1882 Allenby was gazetted to the 6th (Inniskilling) Dragoons, a not particularly fashionable cavalry regiment. Military life suited him. While not an automaton, he was loyal, accepted orders without question and enjoyed outdoor physical activity. Allenby served his apprenticeship as a subaltern in the 1880s in old-style colonial soldiering in southern Africa in the 1880s. In 1890, when the 6th Dragoons returned home for garrison duties, Allenby settled into a rhythm of hunting, sport, socializing and military duties. He also married. In 1895 he had met Adelaide Mabel Chapman and, in December 1896, the two were married. The marriage was an intensely happy one, lasting until his death in 1936, and Adelaide Mabel, along with Allenby's mother, to whom he wrote regularly until her death in 1922, provided a solid foundation of female support on which Allenby built his reputation as a soldier. The Allenbys had one son, (Horace) Michael, and his death on the Western Front in July 1917 shattered the marmoreal Allenby, who broke down and wept in front of Sir John Shea, one of his divisional commanders in Palestine.[4]

In 1896 Allenby entered the Staff College at Camberley. His cohort at Camberley included Haig and James Edmonds, who would go on to become the official historian of the Great War. Edmonds later recalled that Allenby was 'curiously taciturn' at Staff College and 'rather out of his depth in the very medium company' of 1896–7.[5] While Allenby was neither strikingly intellectual nor garrulous, he was tolerant and flexible, and capable of interesting conversations on a range of topics. In October 1899 Allenby and the Inniskillings shipped out for service in South Africa against the Boers. This would be Allenby's first war. Given temporary command of the Inniskillings in 1900, he emerged at the war's end in 1902 with much credit, a brevet lieutenant colonelcy and useful contacts, and that year was created CB in recognition of his service. Allenby started the South African War as an unknown major; he ended it with a reputation as a competent, reliable leader, and someone marked out for possible promotion. While not a brilliant tactician, he had suffered no major reverses and, physically tough, had proved himself in the field on lengthy, exacting operations during which British columns swept the veldt for Boer commandos. In 1909 he rose to the rank of major general before, the following year, becoming inspector general of cavalry, a post he held until the outbreak of the First World War, when he was put in charge of the Cavalry Division at the head of which he went to France as part of the British Expeditionary Force in August 1914.

Even before the outbreak of war in 1914, Allenby's fiery temper had earned him the nickname 'the Bull'. Sir Hubert Gough, Allenby's chief staff officer when he was inspector general of cavalry, recalled that Allenby had a 'great regard for regulations and all sort of detail' and that if he, when inspecting a unit, saw any neglect of detail or orders he was liable to explode.[6] Cavalrymen who neglected to do up their chinstraps would feel the full weight of Allenby's concern with obeying to the letter all orders. While Allenby had been an easy-going young officer and a good-humoured squadron leader, he was a strict colonel, an irascible brigadier and an explosive general.[7] Field command after 1914 only aggravated his tendency to nit-picking on orders, as one of his officers noted: 'When we arrived in France Allenby paid too much attention to chin straps, number of buttons on uniform sleeves, colour of tie etc. He tended to irritate commanders.'[8] Stories abound of Allenby's explosive temper – some true, many apocryphal – most of which have found their way into the various accounts of his time in France (and Palestine). One officer, on being reproved by Allenby during a visit to the trenches, replied 'very good, sir', to which Allenby barked back, 'I want none of your bloody approbation'.[9] Lieutenant General Sir John Keir of VI Corps, someone willing to stand up to Allenby, was nicknamed 'Toreador', before Allenby dismissed him in 1916.[10] On another occasion, Allenby berated a company commander over the regulation that steel helmets and leather jerkins should be worn at all times in the trenches:

> Allenby: 'Did I or did I not issue an order that no man should go up to the front line without jerkin or helmet?'
> Company commander: 'Yes, sir.'
> Allenby: 'Then why has that man not got them on?'
> Company commander: 'The man is dead, sir.'
> Allenby: 'Did I or did I not ...'[11]

Lieutenant General Sir (James) Aylmer Haldane, one of Third Army's corps commanders, wrote in his diary how he took Allenby on an inspection of the trenches:

> He found fault over trivialities as usual – e.g., because a guard in reserve was a little slow in turning out, and one man had his chin strap at the back of his head. I showed him the veritable rabbit burrow out of which they had to come, with bayonets fixed and at the risk of sticking each other, and my opinion was that they turned out wonderfully quickly. The man is impossible and, to boot, is ignorant, as everyone feels.[12]

Two days later, Haldane recorded:

> He was in one of his most unpleasant moods. He becomes almost comical when he lets himself go as he did today, but if one shows

signs of not taking him lying down he caves in, for he is a prime bully. I pity his poor staff as they have a hard time with him and fortunately for [Lord] Dalmeny [Allenby's military secretary] the Bull is a snob and grovels to anyone senior to him or still better has a title.[13]

While Haldane was not alone in criticizing Allenby, an injustice supposedly committed earlier in the war when Haldane served under Allenby in the Ypres salient might explain his hostility.[14] A more balanced view is that Allenby was shy and socially awkward, and so, struggling with the responsibility and stress of senior command, he responded by becoming a martinet. On a tour of the front line with Allenby, Colonel Spencer Hollond witnessed his GOC bully a subaltern over a rusty rifle barrel:

> As we were driving home he told me how shyness had ruined his life. He had tried desperately to overcome this shyness, but had never succeeded. He described a meeting with Haig. They were both so shy that neither of them could say one word. It was ludicrous but true and so they silently and mutually agreed never to be alone when they met. As he was telling me about this shyness complex, I wondered what the 18-year old officer, who had been crushed in the trenches, would have thought.[15]

For Edmonds, in conversation after the war with Basil Liddell Hart, it was when Allenby reached the rank of major general in 1909 'that he for the first time lost his popularity by his bullying ways, apparently due to feeling he must live up to his rank'. The stresses of war in France exacerbated this temper, which then abated when Allenby left the intrigues of the Western Front to take charge in Palestine. Indeed, on the way to Palestine, Allenby 'admitted his mistake in a private conversation in Egypt, and was determined to shed his nickname of "The Bull".'[16] Philip Chetwode, one of Allenby's corps commanders in Palestine, supports Edmonds, arguing that Allenby never earned his men's affections until he came out to Palestine, a view also held by Colonel Charles Grant, GSO1 in Third Army, who wrote in 1936 how the difficulties of trench warfare in France and 'the endless possibilities of finding things wrong' meant that Allenby was never personally popular among regimental officers as he was in Palestine.[17] Another of Allenby's corps commanders in France, Lieutenant General Sir Thomas D'Oyly Snow, gets some way to the truth, writing how Allenby's 'curious characteristics never failed to puzzle all of us. As I said before, a man of great knowledge and wisdom, he was a curious contradiction; at times subject to almost demoniacal bursts of temper, even in front of tired troops; he was at other times, gentle and kindly, with a grim sense of humour.'[18]

Allenby's experience with the Cavalry Division and V Corps in 1914 and 1915 played a part in developing his abrasive personality and style of command.

In 1914, in charge of the Cavalry Division on the retreat from Mons, Allenby struggled to hold together his oversized four-brigade division. In the chaos of the retreat, Allenby lost control of his brigades, with some of the brigade commanders – notably Hubert Gough, but also Henry de Lisle – preferring independent command to serving under him. In effect, the Cavalry Division disintegrated, something that reflected badly on Allenby.[19] During the confusion of the retreat, Gough detached his unit and joined Haig's corps. Disloyalty – or, as one officer put it, 'open rebellion' – such as this played hard on Allenby and would dog him through the war as Gough, commander of Fifth Army from 1916, had privileged access to Haig, backed up by his good social connections back in Britain.[20] (Gough was, of course, familiar with such behaviour, having been a leading figure in the Curragh mutiny of 1914.) George de S. Barrow was with Allenby on the retreat from Mons and saw first-hand the effect of Gough's actions:

> Allenby, myself, Home and Howard were in a little two room cottage, which had one bed. Allenby lay on the bed and we slept on the floor. Before lying down I saw Allenby for the only time show signs of fatigue. He sat for a short while on a chair, leaning forward with his forehead in his hand, looking physically and mentally utterly tired out. I never saw him like this again. The continuous responsible strain and physical fatigue together with the certain sense of impotence in face of disloyalty of subordinates supported by higher authority which deprived him of the power of acting more vigorously . . . all combined to wear down momentarily even his strong name and spirit.[21]

Allenby remained loyal and straight despite the machinations of those such as Gough who 'never lost an opportunity of indulging in common abuse of Allenby before his staff or any officer no matter how minor . . . Had he not been a persona grata with French and Haig he [Gough] would have been sent straight back to England'.[22] Allenby's determination to ignore the intriguing that went on around him was, for Barrow, his 'greatness of character', the expression also tellingly used by Archibald Wavell as the subtitle for the first of his two-volume biography, *Allenby: A Study in Greatness* (1940). Not once, it seems, did Allenby lose his temper over Gough's behaviour, at least not while there was a war on, as Barrow recalled in the 1930s:

> I was in constant close touch with Allenby all this time, until I left the Cavalry Corps H.Q. and I know how much he felt Gough's behaviour and abuse of which he was well aware. But he never once lost his temper or showed any further resentment than to say 'It's only Gough's funny little way.' Not long before his death, however, he one day let himself go. We were walking home together in London. Gough's name came up, and all the pent up feeling burst out with a

vehemence worthy of his best efforts of earlier days. And what he said of Gough there – quite unrepeatable – is a measure of the self control he showed when greater matters called for his attention.[23]

Hugh Jeudwine, Brigadier General General Staff with V Corps and later GOC of 55th Division, also remembered Allenby's complete obedience to orders, even if he disagreed with what he was being asked to do:

> His silent loyalty to his superiors had the effect of leading his subordinate commanders to believe that the responsibility for a mistaken policy was his own, and you probably know that in certain instances some endeavoured by approach to G.H.Q. behind his back to effect his removal. Allenby was fully aware of this but treated such actions with contempt and never allowed his knowledge to affect his treatment of the culprits.[24]

Allenby's willingness to carry out orders, even if he thought that they were wrong, would be part of the reason that he came unstuck at the Battle of Arras. As was noted in his obituary in *The Times* in 1936, at Arras he 'conscientiously, if clumsily, carried out an operation which, it was recognized, could hardly be decisive, and had been continued mainly with a view to giving the French time in which to recover'.[25] The assessment of Gough, who, as commander of Fifth Army, would himself face the sack following the first Ludendorff offensive in March 1918, was that while Allenby was 'very just' and 'never bore any malice against subordinates who disagreed', he also had 'no ideas and when in France would apply orders rigidly without reasoning'.[26] Moreover, it seemed as if Allenby cared little if there were heavy casualties, as long as his orders were obeyed.[27] One of Allenby's biographers noted that while Allenby had tenacity, aggression and moral stamina, these were, perhaps, poor substitutes for generalship.[28] Similarly, Gough argued that Allenby had very few ideas of his own, 'although he was good at taking them from a subordinate and generous in accepting responsibility for any failure, but he had no grip on the situation in France – partly because his Chief of Staff was John Vaughan who did not supply him with ideas'. Gough wondered whether his success in Palestine was not due mainly to the easier problems he had to deal with.[29]

The difficult experience of command in the Ypres salient in 1914 and 1915 proved to Allenby that he had to take 'personal control' of the battlefield.[30] This helps to explain Allenby's obsession with orders while with Third Army: they were his means of asserting his command and his emotional response to the strains of high command. What Allenby lacked in cerebral brilliance he would make up for with effective preparation and planning, an absolute loyalty to his superiors, and a tight control over his emotions. As a result, he was a rigid commander and someone who, while possessing a wide knowledge on an eclectic range of subjects, was not personable: with subordinates he would ask blunt questions and be easily annoyed by unsubstantiated assertions; with his seniors – such as Haig – he was unable to articulate himself.

In Allenby's defence, with his staff, he could be tolerant, was invariably fair, was happy to delegate and, like Ulysses S. Grant, issued crisp, clear orders.[31] Grant, GSO1 with Third Army, told Wavell after the war how Allenby had been very kind to his staff, leaving them to do their work. All that Allenby asked of his staff was that they devoted themselves to their jobs and did them properly.[32] Another of his staff officers tasked with tackling the question of logistics at Arras recalled that:

> His orders were always very clear, and he left one free to carry them out without fussing or interfering. When I joined the Third Army he was preparing for the battle of Arras. He sent for me to his office, showed me on the map what he wanted me to do in arranging roads etc. and then dismissed me to think it over. A couple of days later he called me in again to hear what I was proposing to do, and having satisfied himself that my plans were right, never again interfered as to that particular operation – though I have no doubt he took care in his visits to corps commanders to ascertain that things were going as intended.[33]

Snow of VII Corps found Allenby to be likeable and someone who maintained contact with all of his staff officers, as opposed to just the senior ones.[34] In return, Allenby's staff were 'devoted' to him: 'Those who like us were in a position to see more of him than outsiders, could appreciate not only his commanding brain and supreme military genius, but also the human side of his character which those who lived further away from him could not. He was often sadly misjudged, merely on the strength of his temper.'[35] Moreover, for Snow, Allenby's thinking was crystal clear, if rather pedantic. Having presented a scheme to Allenby for approval before going to GHQ, Snow found his commander to be agreeable, but:

> This was the first experience I had of placing before the Army Commander a question involving principle rather than routine and in my anxiety and keenness, I had drafted a long letter, explaining the whole scheme and ending by a recommendation couched in unnecessarily forcible terms; my unfortunate final words 'I therefore strongly recommend' brought a deluge upon me. 'How can I strongly recommend?' burst out the 'Bull'. 'I either recommend or I do not recommend. I don't know what the hell you mean by strongly recommend.'[36]

The military correspondent Lieutenant Colonel Charles à Court Repington also had a good opinion of Allenby, as did the war leader David Lloyd George.[37] While Allenby undoubtedly had a foul temper, this was worst when he was serving on the Western Front. He was a kinder, more understandable man than is often allowed for in the literature, he did not bear a grudge, and he was someone who, as will be seen, when given his one big chance at Arras, had to fight a battle in unfavourable circumstances. Moreover, his relationship with Haig was not an easy one.

Allenby's connection to Haig stretched back to the Staff College, where, in 1896, in preference to Haig, fellow officers had elected him to the prestigious position of Master of the Drag Hounds. Whether this incident was the start of the feud is unclear. According to Barrow, Allenby more than once said that Haig was 'infernally jealous' of him.[38] In all fairness to Haig, such pettiness does not seem to have been in his nature, and in Allenby's last interview with Barrow, he denied that there was ever any rift between them.[39] Snow, however, was convinced that GHQ treated Allenby badly:

> I believe that his temper improved enormously when he was Commander in Chief in Palestine, and I have often thought that the intense irritation which gave rise to these outbursts was perhaps due to the way in which he was thwarted by higher authority and which to one of his nature must have been particularly galling. There is no doubt that he was treated badly. It is unnecessary to give instances, but everybody in France at the time, who knew anything, knew this. However, and this was a measure of his greatness, he never mentioned the matter, even to his Chief of Staff, and none of us were ever allowed to criticise G.H.Q.[40]

In a similar vein, Grant observed that Allenby was often 'distressed' by Haig's attitude at army commanders' conferences where he was able to explain what he wanted only if the much-favoured Gough was not present, and that this situation made Allenby lose his temper.[41] Barrow puts it more bluntly:

> Once a week I accompanied my Chief to the Army Commander conferences, presided over by the Commander-in-Chief. These were rather dreary affairs at which each Army commander gave an account of his stewardship during the past week. It struck me as odd that Haig, himself a singularly inarticulate man, should turn a readier ear to the opinions of the vocal commanders of Fourth and Fifth Armies than those of the more reticent, but by no means less capable commanders of the First and Third Armies. But Haig often erred in his judgment of men.[42]

Wavell, who served with Allenby and who would go on to high command in the Second World War, recounts in his biography of Allenby how, at the commanders' conferences, Allenby's opinion carried 'little weight, and received scant attention, especially if Gough, commander of Fifth Army, had a different view. Often Sir Douglas Haig would turn to one of the other army commanders and ask his opinion on some point while Allenby was still speaking'.[43]

Part of the problem was that both Allenby and Haig had poor communication skills, which made for awkward conversations between the two men. Their personalities were antagonistic. At meetings Allenby fumbled for words, while Haig rambled through a series of unfinished sentences, a situation that resulted in 'completely futile' conferences where the finer points of strategy were lost in a mass of garbled conversation.[44] In his diary for 8 April 1917 – one day before the start of the Battle of Arras – John Charteris, Chief Intelligence Officer at GHQ, recorded the following entry that says much about relations between the two men:

> Allenby shares one peculiarity with Douglas Haig, he cannot explain verbally, with any lucidity at all, what his plans are. In a conference between the two of them it is rather amusing. D.H. hardly ever finishes a sentence, and Allenby's sentences, although finished, do not really convey exactly what he means. Yet they understand one another perfectly; but as each of their particular staffs only understands their immediate superior a good deal of explanation of details has to be gone into afterwards and cleared up.[45]

While Haig and Allenby gave an outward appearance of good will – with Allenby giving Haig a horse in January 1916 – there was clearly friction between the two men and a lack of genuine good feeling, not helped by the fact that Allenby was seen as Sir John French's appointee.[46] As a result, the best that the two men could manage when together was a formal, frigid politeness, a situation that, arguably, adversely affected operational planning and execution when Allenby came to launch the Battle of Arras.

The Battle of Arras

Unhappily sandwiched between the Somme and Passchendaele battles, Arras is a 'little-known' battle largely ignored in the literature on the Great War.[47] Indeed, the only part of the Arras battle that has drawn any real attention is the capture of Vimy Ridge, a subsidiary masking operation by the Canadian Corps in First Army north of Third Army's main battle zone. This is despite the fact that the initial gains in the battle were the greatest yet achieved by the British in France, and despite the fact that Arras became an attritional struggle with daily casualty rates greater than any other major British battle on the Western Front. The histories of the war skip from the Somme to Passchendaele and in doing so ignore Allenby's role in the battle, much preferring to concentrate on his exploits in Palestine (if he is discussed at all).

Prior to Arras, Allenby's only experience as an army commander of a major assault was when Haig gave Third Army the unenviable task of taking the fortified village of Gommecourt as a diversionary attack on the opening day of the Battle of the Somme (1 July 1916). Allenby's GSO1 was convinced that his commander was bitter at not being given a bigger role at the Somme battle, and

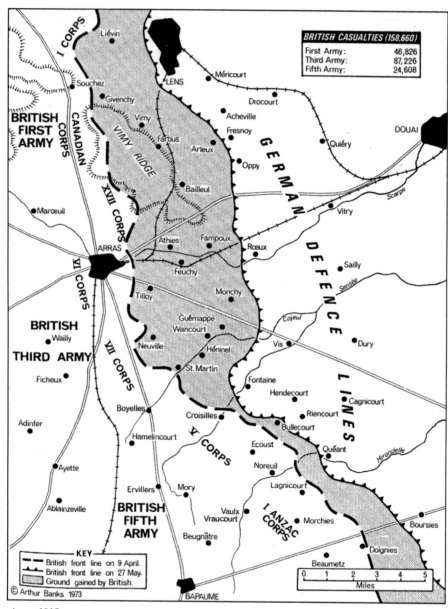

BRITISH CASUALTIES (158,660)	
First Army:	46,826
Third Army:	87,226
Fifth Army:	24,608

KEY
- - - British front line on 9 April.
▲-▲- British front line on 27 May.
░░ Ground gained by British.
© Arthur Banks 1973

Arras, 1917.

that he feared that he was going to be replaced before Third Army's big effort in 1917 at Arras.[48] This uncertainty fed into Allenby's already cautious and methodical approach as, from November 1916, he began to prepare for Arras.

Launched in a driving snowstorm on Easter Monday (9 April), the Battle of Arras was fought alongside the River Scarpe in four phases: the First Battle of the Scarpe, 9–14 April; the Second Battle of the Scarpe, 23–24 April; the

Third Battle of the Scarpe, 3–4 May; and the final stages of the battle, 5–24 May. On 9 April, Third Army dealt one of the heaviest blows ever struck by British arms in France, a credit to Allenby's planning and style of command. Compared to battles before and after, it was a stunning success in terms of ground gained – up to 3½ miles in one day – and one that almost pierced the Germans' defences at Drocourt-Quéant.[49] Allenby was absolutely delighted at his success – 'awfully jolly' in Snow's words – as was Haig.[50] Allenby's meticulous preparations had paid off. He had used various tactical measures to help overcome the deadlock of trench warfare. His men widened and extended the existing network of tunnels and sewers under Arras to create a system of some 11,000 yards of well-lit, airy passages that allowed troops to get to the front line in comfort and safety.[51] In all of this, Allenby's attention to detail was impressive. Thus, Third Army arranged and assembled an eight-day supply of hot food with pack animals to transport it forward to help maintain offensive momentum.[52] Captured German artillerymen attested to the power and effectiveness of the well-prepared and all-important artillery barrage that had given the German gunners 'no chance'.[53] Allenby was so hopeful of achieving a breakthrough that, at 19.40 hrs on 10 April, he issued the order to his men that they were pursuing a defeated enemy and so 'risks must be taken freely'.[54] There was, however, no breakthrough. Instead, after 11 April, Arras became a costly attritional slog along the Scarpe – especially by the fortified village of Monchy-le-Preux south of the Scarpe – that dragged on into May 1917 and which resulted in Allenby's dismissal.

Was this failure Allenby's fault? Firstly, it should be noted that Haig and GHQ interfered with Allenby's preparations and execution of the battle. A good example of this is the shorter artillery fire-plan that Allenby mooted as a means of overcoming the German defences. Allenby and his artillery expert, Major General A.E.A. Holland, wanted a surprise 48-hour 'hurricane' bombardment, followed by a swift, deep advance by the infantry – in effect, the storm-troop tactics of 1918, but a year earlier. Typically, Allenby's shorter fire-plan was the result of careful planning: from late 1916 his gunners had been practising to good effect with rapid rates of fire, seeing if the buffer springs and gun barrels could bear such a bombardment.[55] But when Allenby formally proposed to GHQ the novel 48-hour bombardment on 7 February 1917, GHQ responded negatively on the 12th, Haig much preferring the longer, traditional Somme-style bombardment of up to a week.[56] Haig sent artillery experts such as Major General Noel Birch, in charge of artillery at GHQ and someone who had served under Allenby in 1914, to Third Army to prove to the stubborn Allenby that he needed a longer bombardment. In a letter after the war to the official historian, Birch remembered how awkward this mission had been:

> the battle of Arras caused me deep concern. I was faced with a situation that I knew was wrong. The senior gunner of Allenby's

army [Holland] was senior to me regimentally and no argument would turn him away from his purpose, so first of all I knew that he had to go elsewhere before we could fight the battle of Arras. The second thing was that I was devoted to Allenby, and I was his Chief of Staff when he commanded the Cavalry Corps, and I had to go to him and say that I disagreed with every word he had said since breakfast, no easy task for an acting major-general.[57]

Despite all of this, Allenby strenuously backed what he saw as Holland's innovative plan and refused to yield, even when Haig personally came to visit:

Finally Haig himself came down to see Allenby and talk it over. They were closeted together but after the interview [Allenby] still stood firm. As neither of them was able to speak during the interview, it was not strange that no alteration of plan was decided upon, but I am convinced that Haig could never have persuaded Allenby to alter his plans. G.H.Q. were beat, they didn't know what to do or how to move Allenby.[58]

Stonewalled, GHQ then resorted to the ruse of promoting Holland to command I Corps, replacing him with Major General R. St C. Lecky, someone who agreed with GHQ's views on a longer bombardment.[59] Allenby was then forced to cancel the 48-hour barrage in favour of a five-day one.[60]

While the military thinker J.F.C. Fuller is not alone in thinking that this change in plan handicapped Allenby, it is not obvious that a short, intense bombardment would have worked in early 1917.[61] While the British army was improving rapidly in this period, learning from its successes and failures (such as at the Somme), it still had a long way to go on its learning curve to become the war-winning combined-arms force of 1918. The German defences at Arras were strong and heavily wired, German morale was high, and there were few tanks available and a shortage of instantaneous fuses.[62] Because of this, many of Allenby's corps, divisional and brigade commanders opposed the short fire-plan, arguing that it would not cut the extensive German wire or dent enemy morale, nor would it take account of the generally immature state of British offensive doctrine.[63]

To complicate matters, between 25 February and 5 April 1917 the Germans had withdrawn to their previously prepared defensive positions along the Hindenburg (or Siegfried) Line. This adversely affected what would become the right flank of Third Army's impending battle zone as Fifth Army, to Allenby's south, with miles of ruined communications behind it, would be hard pressed to provide support. Nor would the French be of much help as they dropped the plan to attack north of the River Oise in support of Allenby. This meant that south of Third Army there was a 60-mile gap in which there would be no serious supporting operations to draw off German reserves. This was a far cry from the original Anglo–French plan drawn up in 1916 for a grand joint offensive in 1917.[64] Finally, at the same time as Allenby was preparing for Arras, the Germans were working on new defence-in-depth systems. For instance, south of the River Scarpe, the Germans used an almost imperceptible 12-mile reverse slope to create a flexible defensive zone with 'acres of wire' that could blunt and absorb attacks.[65] To break such a defensive system required 'methodical' and complicated artillery barrages that took time as the guns were brought forward for another stage of the attack.[66]

Arras confirmed the inherent limitations to what an army commander on the Western Front could achieve. On 11 April, just a few days after the initial gains, Allenby's attack 'stuck', the men under his command – many of whom seem to have lacked initiative and good junior leadership – being unable to make the adjustment to mobile warfare.[67] Allenby had defeated the Germans on 9 April but he could not pursue them and break out (although, to be fair, it is not clear that the objective of the battle was a breakout). With offensive momentum rapidly waning, Allenby's order to his men on the evening of 9 April that they were pursuing a defeated enemy was unduly hopeful.[68] The last day for exploitation was 11 April, as Allenby rotated divisions tired from three days' fighting. The worry of Third Army's officers expressed above that the German wire would not be cut was also borne out as, while the first line of wire was destroyed and that on the second line badly damaged, the wire in front of the third defensive line was uncut.[69] Thus, before any infantry advance could go ahead with any chance of success, Allenby's gunners would have to haul their guns forward and tackle this line of wire, all of which required time and effort, not least in terms of the all-important logistical preparation required for any big assault.

Any chance of a successful cavalry attack had also passed by the evening of 9 April. In his history of British cavalry, the Marquess of Anglesey makes much of the possibilities on 9 April, ones that Allenby failed to exploit:

> Brigadier Carton de Wiart (4th Dragoon Guards), who now commanded the 12th Infantry Brigade, on learning that the cavalry was some twelve miles in the rear and could not get up till the next day, told his cavalry liaison officer, 'Tomorrow will be too late'. The commander of a battalion of the 9th Infantry Division at the same time telephoned his brigade headquarters with the same message. He was asked, 'Are the Boches on the run?' He replied, 'Yes'. To 'Is cavalry good business?' he answered, 'Yes, ten thousand times yes, but it must be done *now*.'[70]

While Allenby seems to have wanted to use his cavalry south of the Scarpe and ignored repeated requests from one of his corps commanders, Lieutenant General Sir Charles Fergusson, on 9 April to redeploy the cavalry, it is far from obvious that a mass use of cavalry was viable.[71] Allenby may have erred in his deployment of his cavalry but the River Scarpe divided his lines of advance and hampered what he could do – as did the freezing snowstorms that descended on the battlefield in April 1917.[72] It is unlikely that any cavalry advance would have been more than a minor irritant to the Germans, as Fergusson himself admits: 'I doubt whether one Brigade, let loose on the Douai plain without any definite objective, would have done more than create some temporary discomfort and local confusion.'[73] Similarly, the GOC of the 1st Cavalry Brigade was sure that, on 9 April, 'the "G" in Gap was not there on that day'.[74] However, the question of the use of cavalry at Arras does seem to have had an adverse effect in terms of Allenby's relations with Haig. When Haig came to visit Fergusson on the evening of the 9th, he asked Fergusson about the cavalry:

> I told him that I had represented the opportunity, but that none had been allotted to me. He seemed annoyed, and used my telephone to speak to General Allenby. Of course, it was not till the following afternoon that a Brigade arrived, far too late to be of any use. I am not criticising. There is no doubt that cavalry could have gone through on the evening of the 9th, if they had been on the spot then, but I doubt whether they would have got through next morning. To have been on the spot on the previous evening would only have been possible had the possibility of their use been envisaged early in the day.[75]

The First Battle of the Scarpe was over by 14 April, and that should have been it. The British had had a great success but the last days of the battle (11–14 April) had begun to assume a 'painfully familiar air'.[76] After the initial rush on 9 April, any small gains had been achieved at an ever-increasing cost. Haig, however, was not prepared to admit that the battle had run its course, not least as he was under pressure from the French to keep up the attack. While the British seem to have been unaware (at least at first) of the mutinies in the French army following its failed offensive of 16 April 1917 along the Chemin des Dames, they were supposed to be supporting their ally with the attack at Arras. As Haig told Edmonds in a letter in 1925, at Arras the British 'had to go on attacking in order to prevent Nivelle and Co. from saying that "the British had not held the German Reserves, and the French attack was not successful"'.[77] At a conference of army commanders chaired by Haig on 30 April, the British voiced their concern that the French army was no longer able to conduct large-scale offensive operations.[78] To support the French strategically, the British knew that it was vital to maintain pressure on the Germans by extending Allenby's operations at Arras into May 1917.

Meanwhile, at the operational level, Haig suspected that there had been inadequate co-ordination by Allenby during the first days of the attack.[79] Haig records that in visits to Third Army HQ on 12–13 April, he emphasized the need to substitute shells for men, sparing the infantry as much as possible.[80] On 14 April he wrote in his diary, 'Personally I think the movements of the several divisions want to be better coordinated, especially astride the Scarpe'.[81] Unconvinced that Allenby was up to the task, Haig began to take personal charge of the battle, something that would undermine and eventually unstick Allenby. Ever dutiful, Allenby carried out his orders to continue the attacks as best he could, despite terrible losses among his men as they became tangled in the Germans' defensive lines. As one of Allenby's biographers notes, the poor personal communications between Haig and Allenby played their part in Allenby's decision to continue the attack, as he was left with the impression that he was free to carry on attacking after 11 April.[82] These continued attacks led to protests from three of Allenby's divisional commanders, major generals Wilkinson (50th), de Lisle (29th), and Robertson (17th), who issued a resolution on 15 April registering 'a strong expression of opinion' against isolated operations which exposed the men to flanking fire.[83] The generals made their complaint – which was 'toned down' in the official history – directly to Haig, further damaging Allenby's reputation at GHQ. This was a dramatic event: a collective refusal of an operation Allenby said would present no difficulty, and an act of defiance amounting to a generals' mutiny that seems to have had tacit support at corps level. Moreover, Haig seems to have taken notice of it as he halted major operations for a week.[84]

Allenby was torn between his loyalty to his superiors and the need to take account of the worries of his subordinate commanders in Third Army that continued attacks were futile. At an army commanders' conference on 30 April, Allenby agreed to renew the attack on 3 May; then on 7 May he informed Haig that his men were too tired to attack and would need 10–12 days in which to rest, adding, however, that after this period he would 'like to repeat the attack'.[85] On 7 May, Allenby pointed to the disadvantages of premature attacks by semi-trained troops 'unable to use their rifles properly'.[86] Despite Allenby's worries, Haig pressed for continued operations:

> First, Third and Fifth Army commanders must realize that in the general interest they have to carry on with tired troops and 'cut their coats' accordingly. Their efforts will be regulated with a view to wearing out as many of the enemy's troops as possible, but as our troops available for this purpose must necessarily be tired troops and as reliefs from outside the armies cannot be expected and few drafts will be available, the objectives must be strictly limited.[87]

At the same time, at GHQ, Gough undermined Allenby by, for instance, persuading Haig to change the zero hour for the assault on 3 May at the Third Battle of the Scarpe.[88] Under pressure from above and below, Allenby reached his breaking point in the first week of May, finally protesting to Haig about the futility of the ongoing offensive operations. As Peter Simkins observes: 'It was not a good time for a previously obedient and reliable subordinate to offer criticisms to Haig, who was all too aware of enemies at home and of the current plight of the French army.[89] This action on top of the complaints from Allenby's divisional commanders convinced Haig that the usually tractable Allenby had to go.[90]

Coincidentally, since mid-April the War Cabinet in London had been looking for a new commander for Palestine.[91] The first choice was the South African statesman Jan Smuts, who turned down the offer of command in a peripheral theatre.[92] Lloyd George then lit upon Allenby, out of favour in France and someone that he considered suitable to pursue aggressive operations in Palestine. On 5 June, Haig received a telegram ordering Allenby back to London to take charge of the British-led forces in Palestine.[93] Haldane, who had little regard for Allenby's skills as an army commander, was delighted at the news of Allenby's departure: 'Three days later I and other corps commanders were ordered to go to his headquarters, where we were informed that he had been appointed to command the forces in Palestine. I do not think that anyone regretted the prospect of his departure, and I was delighted to hear that he was to be succeeded by my old friend, Julian Byng.'[94]

It is not clear, however, that any other army commander would have done better than Allenby at Arras. He was having to deal with too many factors outside of his control: the need to support the French, the German withdrawal to the Hindenburg Line, the Germans' defence-in-depth system, and the inchoate state of British artillery and infantry tactics in early 1917. At this stage of the war, a break-in was possible but not a breakthrough and breakout, and nothing that Allenby did or could have done would change this fact. Allenby's mistake was not to insist to Haig on an earlier termination of the Arras offensive – something that went against the grain of his obedient personality – but even this was problematic as the British had to support the flagging French effort to the south. Moreover, he had to conduct operations while looking over his shoulder, knowing that Haig and GHQ were not always fully supportive of his actions. Allenby's straightness of character – rigidity might be a better description – did not fit in well with the machinations on the Western Front, and for this reason the move to Palestine was the best thing that could have happened to him. In Palestine, away from the intrigues surrounding GHQ, away from the all the operational difficulties of trench warfare, and in personal charge of a discrete theatre of war, Allenby shone and made his name as one of the better generals of the First World War.

Bibliography

The starting point for any analysis of the Battle of Arras is Cyril Falls, *Official History of the War. Military Operations: France and Belgium, 1917*, vol. 1 (London: Macmillan, 1940). Readers should also consult the four biographies of Allenby, although Savage's work is largely a hagiography: Raymond Savage, *Allenby of Armageddon* (London: Hodder & Stoughton, 1925); Archibald Wavell, *Allenby: A Study in Greatness*, 2 vols

(New York: OUP, 1941–3); Brian Gardner, *Allenby* (London: Cassell, 1965); and Lawrence James, *Imperial Warrior: The Life and Times of Field Marshal Viscount Allenby* (London: Weidenfeld & Nicolson, 1993). While the general texts on the Western Front only briefly mention Arras, there is some useful discussion in Gary Sheffield, *Forgotten Victory* (London: Headline, 2001) and a complete study in Jonathan Nicholls, *Cheerful Sacrifice: The Battle of Arras, 1917* (Barnsley: Leo Cooper, 1993). Peter Simkins also has a useful chapter on Allenby and Haig entitled 'Haig and his Army Commanders', in Brian Bond and Nigel Cave, eds, *Haig: A Reappraisal 70 Years On* (Barnsley: Leo Cooper, 1999). Robin Neillands also discusses Allenby in his *The Great War Generals on the Western Front* (London: Robinson, 1998).

In terms of memoirs, John Charteris, *At G.H.Q.* (London: Cassell, 1931), gives a sense of daily life at GHQ, and Aylmer Haldane's *A Soldier's Saga: The Autobiography* (Edinburgh and London: Blackwood, 1948) is insightful (if hostile) on Allenby. For Allenby's role in the retreat of 1914, there is a good account in Nikolas Gardner, 'Command and Control in the "Great Retreat" of 1914: The Disintegration of the British Cavalry Division', *Journal of Military History*, 63 (January 1999), pp. 29–54. Allenby's private papers at the Liddell Hart Centre for Military Archives (LHCMA) at King's College, London, have a wealth of relevant material, most of it generated by Wavell when he was writing his biography in the 1930s. There are also some useful insights on Allenby in the post-war conversations that Basil Liddell Hart had with politicians and generals in the Liddell Hart papers at the LHCMA. The Haldane papers at the National Library of Scotland – especially his diary – contain much material relating to Allenby; there is also material in the National Archives at Kew, London. For a relative assessment of Allenby's time in Palestine, see Matthew Hughes, *Allenby and British Strategy in the Middle East, 1917–1919* (London: Cass, 1999) and the introduction to Matthew Hughes, ed., *Allenby in Palestine* (London: Army Records Society, 2004).

Notes

1 Brian Gardner, *Allenby* (London: Cassell, 1965), p. 113; Liddell Hart Centre for Military Archives, King's College, London (hereafter LHCMA), Allenby MSS, 6/7/55–56, Snow to Wavell, 29 April 1937.

2 Lawrence James, *Imperial Warrior: The Life and Times of Field Marshal Viscount Allenby, 1861–1936* (London: Weidenfeld & Nicolson, 1993), p. 6. The other biographies are Raymond Savage's sycophantic *Allenby of Armageddon* (London: Hodder & Stoughton, 1925), Archibald Wavell's *Allenby: A Study in Greatness*, 2 vols (New York: Oxford University Press, 1941–3) and Brian Gardner's *Allenby* (London: Cassell, 1965).

3 Savage, *Allenby of Armageddon*, p. 24.

4 Imperial War Museum London (hereafter IWM), Sound Archive, 4227, General John Shea, typescript of oral recording, 5, pp. 41–2.

5 Gardner, *Allenby*, p. 23.

6 Quoted in Gardner, *Allenby*, p. 62.

7 Wavell, *Allenby*, 1, p. 114.

8 LHCMA, Allenby MSS, 6/6/4, Howell (GSO3 for Cavalry in WO 1910–1914) to Wavell, 20 July [?].

9 National Library of Scotland (hereafter NLS), Haldane MSS, MS 20249, Diary, 8 November 1916. Also told in Aylmer Haldane, *A Soldier's Saga: The Autobiography* (Edinburgh and London: Blackwood, 1948), p. 338.

10 Ibid., Haldane diary, 7 August 1916.

11 James, *Imperial Warrior*, p. 84. This seems to come either from LHCMA, Allenby MSS, 6/7/25–26, Charles Grant (GSO1 Third Army) to Wavell, 21 November 1936, or ibid., 6/1, Edmonds to Wavell, 28 June 1938.

12 NLS, Haldane MSS, MS 20249, Diary, 27 November 1916.

13 Ibid., Diary, 29 November 1916. See also Diary, 7 November 1916.

14 James, *Imperial Warrior*, p. 74; Haldane, *A Soldier's Saga*, pp. 307, 334; NLS, Haldane MSS, MS 20249, Diary, 7 January 1916, 15 January 1916, 24 February 1916, 6 April 1916, 22 July 1916, 7 August 1916; Terry Norman, ed., *Armageddon Road: A VC's Diary, 1914–1916, by Billy Congreve* (London: William Kimber, 1982), p. 143.

15 LHCMA, Allenby MSS, 6/7/30–31, Spencer Hollond to Wavell, n.d. Spencer Hollond (1874–1950) was a brevet colonel in the war and is sometimes confused in the literature with Major General A.E.A. Holland (1862–1927), who was Allenby's chief artillery adviser.

16 LHCMA, Liddell Hart MSS, 11/1934/41, Talk with Edmonds, 7 June 1934.

17 LHCMA, Allenby MSS, 6/6/26, Chetwode to Wavell, 20 June 1938; ibid., 6/7/25–26, Charles Grant (GSO1 Third Army) to Wavell, 21 November 1936.

18 Ibid., 6/7/55–56, Snow to Wavell, 29 April 1937.

19 Nikolas Gardner, 'Command and Control in the "Great Retreat" of 1914: The Disintegration of the British Cavalry Division', *Journal of Military History*, 63 (January 1999), pp. 29–54. See also his *Trial by Fire: Command and the British Expeditionary Force in 1914* (Westport, CT, and London: Praeger, 2003).

20 LHCMA, Allenby MSS, 6/6/26, Chetwode to Wavell, 20 June 1938. For Haig's favouritism towards Gough, see also Tim Travers, *The Killing Ground: The British Army, the Western Front and the Emergence of Modern Warfare, 1900–1918* (London: Unwin, 1990), p. 11.

21 LHCMA, Allenby MSS, 6/6/10, Notes by Barrow, enclosed in letter, Barrow to Wavell, 3 June [1938?]. See also 6/6/20, Wavell to Barrow, 9 July 1938, and 6/6/4, Howell (GSO3 for Cavalry in WO 1910–14) to Wavell, 20 July [?].

22 LHCMA, Allenby MSS, 6/6/10, Notes by Barrow, enclosed in letter, Barrow to Wavell, 3 June [1938?].

23 Ibid., Notes by Barrow, enclosed in letter, Barrow to Wavell, 3 June [1938?].

24 Ibid., 6/7/39, Jeudwine to Wavell, 26 June 1938. See also Robin Neillands, *The Great War Generals on the Western Front* (London: Robinson, 1998), p. 332, and Peter Simkins, 'Haig and his Army Commanders', in Brian Bond and Nigel Cave, eds, *Haig: A Reappraisal 70 Years On* (Barnsley: Leo Cooper, 1999), p. 83.

25 Obituary of Lord Allenby, *The Times*, 15 May 1936, p. 18.

26 LHCMA, Liddell Hart MSS, 11/1935/107, Talk with David Lloyd George and Hubert Gough, 28 November 1935.

27 Neillands, *Great War Generals*, p. 332.

28 James, *Imperial Warrior*, p. 67.

29 LHCMA, Liddell Hart MSS, 11/1935/72, Talk with Sir Hubert Gough, 9 April 1935.

30 James, *Imperial Warrior*, p. 75.

31 Allenby's staff was not always of the highest calibre it seems: LHCMA, Allenby MSS, 6/7/55–56, Snow to Wavell, 29 April 1937; and Liddell Hart MSS, 11/1935/114, Talk with Charles Bonham-Carter, 12 December 1935.

32 LHCMA, Allenby MSS, 6/7/28, Grant (GSO1 Third Army) to Wavell, 29 September 1938. See also ibid., 6/3/3–6, Comments from Barrow on Chapter 3.

33 Ibid., 6/7/40, Kenyon to Wavell, 20 August 1936.

34 Ibid., 6/7/55–56, Snow to Wavell, 29 April 1937.

35 Ibid.

36 Ibid., 6/7/57–58, Snow to Wavell, 25 May 1937.

37 NLS, Haldane MSS, MS 20249, Diary, 5 January 1917; LHCMA, Liddell Hart MSS, 11/1932/42, Talk with Lloyd George, 24 September 1932.

38 LHCMA, 6/3/3–6, Comments from Barrow on Chapter 3.

39 E.K.G. Sixsmith, *Douglas Haig* (London: Weidenfeld & Nicolson, 1976), p. 15.

40 LHCMA, Allenby MSS, 6/7/55–56, Snow to Wavell, 29 April 1937.

41 Ibid., 6/7/25–26, Charles Grant (GSO1 Third Army) to Wavell, 21 November 1936.

42 George de S. Barrow, *The Fire of Life* (London: Hutchinson, 1948), pp. 164–5.

43 Wavell, *Allenby: A Study in Greatness*, 1, p. 170. See also Neillands, *Great War Generals*, p. 332.

44 James, *Imperial Warrior*, pp. 83–84; LHCMA, Allenby MSS, 6/7/33, Spencer Hollond to Wavell, 16 October 1938; Simkins, 'Haig and his Army Commanders', p. 83.

45 John Charteris, *At G.H.Q.* (London: Cassell, 1931), pp. 210–11.

46 Neillands, *Great War Generals*, p. 330; Simkins, 'Haig and his Army Commanders', p. 83; Jonathan Walker, *The Blood Tub: General Gough and the Battle of Bullecourt, 1917* (Staplehurst: Spellmount, 2000), p. 67.

47 Gary Sheffield, *Forgotten Victory. The First World War: Myths and Realities* (London: Headline, 2001), p. 159.

48 LHCMA, Allenby MSS, 6/7/25–26, Charles Grant (GSO1 Third Army) to Wavell, 21 November 1936. See also Jonathan Nicholls, *Cheerful Sacrifice: The Battle of Arras, 1917* (Barnsley: Leo Cooper, 1993), pp. 23–4.

49 Cyril Falls, *Official History of the War. Military Operations: France and Belgium, 1917*, vol. 1 (London: Macmillan, 1940), pp. 201, 253.

50 Imperial War Museum (IWM), Snow MSS, Letters from France, vol. 2, Diary, 12 April 1917. See also LHCMA, Robertson MSS, 7/7/16, Haig to Robertson, 8 April 1917.

51 Nicholls, *Cheerful Sacrifice*, pp. 29–31, 62; NLS, Haldane MSS, MS 20249, Diary, 7 April 1917.

52 Ibid., Diary, 26 March 1917.

53 IWM, Maxse MSS, PP/MCR/C42 (reel 9), Notes received from Captain Hartley, Chemical Adviser Third Army, regarding the effect of counter-battery work carried out on Third Army front, 13 April 1917. See also David Stevenson, *1914–1918: The History of the First World War* (London: Allen Lane, 2004), p. 176.

54 Falls, *Official History*, pp. 258ff; James, *Imperial Warrior*, p. 101.

55 LHCMA, Allenby MSS, 6/7/6–7, R.H. Andrew to Wavell, 13 August 1937.

56 Falls, *Official History*, pp. 177–8.

57 The National Archives (hereafter TNA), CAB 45/116, Noel Birch to Falls, 22 November 1937.

58 LHCMA, Allenby MSS, 6/7/30–31, Spencer Hollond to Wavell, n.d.

59 Falls, *Official History*, pp. 279–80. See also Neillands, *Great War Generals*, p. 335.

60 NLS, Haig MSS, Acc. 3155/97, Diary, 6 April 1917. See also Diary, 2 April 1917.

61 LHCMA, Liddell Hart MSS, 1/11, J.F.C. Fuller, 'How I Remember Allenby', 16 May 1936.

62 London, Royal Artillery Museum (hereafter RAM), Rawlins MSS, 1162/I, 'A History of the Development of the British Artillery in France, 1914–1918', compiled by Col. S.W.H. Rawlins (copy 7).

63 TNA, CAB 45/116, Charles Fergusson to Falls, 14 May 1937.

64 Falls, *Official History*, p. 172. See also RAM, Rawlins MSS, 1162/I, 'A History of the Development of the British Artillery in France, 1914–1918'.

65 Martin Samuels, *Command or Control? Command, Training and Tactics in the British and German Armies, 1888–1918* (London: Cass, 1995), pp. 188–9; TNA, CAB 45/116, Noel Birch to Falls, 22 November 1937. See also RAM, Rawlins MSS, 1162/I, 'A History of the Development of the British Artillery in France, 1914–1918'.

66 TNA, WO 158/311, Record of a conference held at Noyelle Vion at 1100 hrs on 30 April 1917.

67 John Terraine, *Douglas Haig: The Educated Soldier* (London: Hodder & Stoughton, 1963), p. 289; TNA, CAB 45/116, Stanhope to Falls, 27 November 1938, and Twiss to Falls, 18 September 1938.

68 Falls, *Official History*, pp. 258ff.

69 RAM, 1162/I, 'A History of the Development of the British Artillery in France, 1914–1918'.

70 The Marquess of Anglesey, *A History of the British Cavalry, 1816–1919*, vol. 8, *Western Front, 1915–1918: Epilogue, 1919–1939* (London: Leo Cooper, 1997), pp. 74–5.

71 Falls, *Official History*, p. 237; TNA, CAB 45/116, Charles Fergusson to Falls, 14 May 1937.

72 TNA, CAB 45/116, Robert Gordon-Canning to Falls, 9 June 1937.

73 Ibid., Charles Fergusson to Falls, 14 May 1937.

74 Ibid., E. Makins to Falls, 15 December 1937.

75 Ibid., Charles Fergusson to Falls, 14 May 1937.

76 Falls, *Official History*, p. 297. See also Terraine, *Douglas Haig*, p. 290.

77 LHCMA, Edmonds MSS, II/4/39, Haig to Edmonds, 6 August 1925. See also Neillands, *Great War Generals*, p. 334, and Anthony Clayton, *Paths of Glory: The French Army 1914–18* (London: Cassell, 2003), p. 128.

78 TNA, WO 158/311, Record of a conference held at Noyelle Vion at 1100 hrs on 30 April 1917.

79 Falls, *Official History*, p. 297.

80 NLS, Haig MSS, Acc. 3155/112, Diary, 12 and 13 April 1917.

81 Ibid., Diary, 14 April 1917.

82 James, *Imperial Warrior*, p. 102.

83 Falls, *Official History*, p. 378.

84 Simkins, 'Haig and his Army Commanders', p. 84; John Bourne, *Who's Who in World War One* (London: Routledge, 2001), pp. 5, 71; Sheffield, *Forgotten Victory*, p. 165.

85 TNA, WO 158/311, Record of a conference held at Noyelle Vion at 1100 hrs on 30 April 1917.

86 TNA, WO 158/224, Note of proceedings at Army Commanders' Conference, Doullens, 7 May 1917.

87 TNA, WO 158/224, Record of Instructions issued verbally by the Field-Marshal Commanding-in-Chief at the Army Commanders' Conference, Doullens, 7 May 1917.

88 Simkins, 'Haig and his Army Commanders', p. 84.

89 Ibid.

90 James, *Imperial Warrior*, pp. 105–6.
91 NLS, Haig MSS, Acc. 3155/112, Robertson to Haig, 15 April 1917.
92 London, National Army Museum, Rawlinson MSS, 5201–33–27, Diary, 30 May 1917.
93 Robert Blake, ed., *The Private Papers of Douglas Haig, 1914–1919* (London: Eyre & Spottiswoode, 1952), p. 235.
94 Haldane, *A Soldier's Saga*, p. 344. See also NLS, Haldane MSS, MS 202489, Diary, 8 June 1917.

Chapter Two

William Birdwood
Fourth Army, 1918; Fifth Army, 1918

John Lee

When Sir Douglas Haig ordered the reactivation of the Fifth Army in May 1918 and its insertion into the line between Horne's First and Plumer's Second Armies, he had already decided that Sir William Birdwood would have command of it. As the only full general in command of a corps on the Western Front, it had long been determined that 'Birdie' would get the next army command to become available. Haig must have been supremely confident that he was promoting a general with an enormous and proven record of command, and who had led an Australian and New Zealand Army Corps since December 1914 through some of the hardest fighting of the war. At the age of fifty-three, he was the youngest of the army commanders in the field. Only Hubert Gough had been younger when appointed.

William Riddell Birdwood was born on 13 September 1865 in Kirkee, India, where his father was under-secretary to the governor of Bombay. Theirs was a military family: two brothers joined the army and died in service, one in 1894, one with the 4th Gurkha Rifles in Mesopotamia in 1914. After schooling at Clifton College (Haig's old school), Birdwood went to Sandhurst and was commissioned into the Royal Scots Fusiliers before transferring, in 1885, into the 12th Lancers, then serving in India. He met the 'legendary' figure Ian Hamilton on the boat going out, and later wrote how in awe the new young officers were of this 'hero of Majuba'. Their paths would cross many times. His family was not wealthy and, in 1886, he transferred to a less expensive Indian regiment, the 11th Bengal Lancers. He loved India and the Indian Army. He saw service in the Tirah expedition of 1897 and witnessed the Battle of Dargai. A great horseman and sportsman, he enjoyed the life and rose steadily in his profession. He was a captain in 1896, a major in 1900, a lieutenant colonel in 1902 and a full colonel in 1905. He married a niece of Lieutenant Gonville Bromhead VC (of Rorke's Drift fame). In South Africa he served well as a commander of fighting troops, being one of the first of the cavalry to march into a relieved Ladysmith, and came to the attention of Lord Kitchener who, in 1900, made him his DAAG and later his military secretary. He was one of

Chronology

13 September 1865	William Riddell Birdwood born at Kirkee, India
	Educated at Clifton College and Royal Military College, Sandhurst
10 March 1883	Commissioned 4th Battalion, Royal Scots Fusiliers
9 May 1885	Gazetted lieutenant, 12th (Prince of Wales's Royal) Lancers
31 December 1886	Transferred to 11th Bengal Lancers
1891	Served on Black Mountain expedition
1893	Appointed adjutant, Viceroy's Bodyguard
1894	Married Janetta Hope Gonville Bromhead
9 May 1896	Promoted captain
18 December 1897	Appointed provost marshal, Tirah campaign
8 November 1899	Appointed brigade major, Natal Mounted Brigade
28 August 1900	Wounded at Machadodorp
15 October 1900	Appointed DAAG to Lord Kitchener
29 November 1900	Promoted brevet major
5 June 1902	Appointed assistant military secretary to Kitchener
26 June 1902	Promoted brevet lieutenant colonel
9 May 1903	Promoted substantive major
1 September 1904	Appointed AAG and substantive lieutenant colonel
26 June 1905	Promoted colonel
23 December 1905	Appointed military secretary to C.-in-C. India
10 May 1908	Appointed chief staff officer, Mohmand expedition
28 June 1909	Promoted GOC Kohat Independent Brigade
3 October 1911	Promoted major general
17 November 1912	Appointed quartermaster general in India
December 1913	Appointed secretary to the Government of India Military Department
18 November 1914	Appointed GOC Australian and New Zealand Army Corps
12 December 1914	Promoted temporary lieutenant general
25 April 1915	Anzacs land at Anzac Cove
17 October 1915	Appointed temporarily GOC Mediterranean Expeditionary Force
28 October 1915	Promoted substantive lieutenant general
23 November 1915	Appointed GOC Dardanelles army
14 September 1916	Appointed GOC Australian Imperial Force (backdated to 18 September 1915)
23 October 1917	Promoted general
21 February 1918	Appointed GOC Fourth Army
23 May 1918	Appointed GOC Fifth Army
1919	Created baronet
30 October 1920	Appointed GOC, Northern Army, India
20 March 1925	Promoted field marshal
6 August 1925	Appointed C.-in-C. India
May 1930	Retired as C.-in-C. India
1931–38	Master of Peterhouse, Cambridge
1 January 1938	Created Baron Birdwood of Anzac and Totnes
17 May 1951	Died at Hampton Court Palace

Appointed DSO 1908, CIE 1908, CB 1911, KCSI 1915, KCB 1917, GCB 1923, GCSI 1930, GCVO 1937

Kitchener's utterly devoted band of staff officers (along with Frank Maxwell, Victor Brooke and Oswald Fitzgerald).

Birdwood returned to India as Kitchener's military secretary. When this 'Simla darling', as soldiers of the field armies would have seen him, was sent to command the highly rated Kohat Brigade, there were some raised eyebrows. He was junior to just about every commanding officer in the brigade and many expected trouble. But within three months, during which he was chiefly remembered for his passion for gardening and reading the newspapers, he had won the affection and respect of the entire brigade, and demonstrated that quality of leadership for which he would become renowned. Though he was not 'p.s.c.' (i.e. he had not graduated from any staff college) he was AAG India in 1904 and QMG India in 1912.

In 1914 Birdwood was a major general of three years' standing, and serving as secretary to the Indian Army Department in Delhi. On 18 November 1914 he received a telegram from Lord Kitchener offering him command of the two divisions of Australian and New Zealand troops then en route to Egypt. In December 1914 he arrived in Cairo, as a lieutenant general and corps commander.

Originally tasked with overseeing the training and preparation of the Anzacs for use in some future campaign, Birdwood might hope that they would eventually go to France, but feared that they might be retained in the Middle East to defend Egypt. At the beginning of March 1915 he was appointed by Lord Kitchener to command the military side of the Royal Navy's attack on the Dardanelles, which might involve troops landing to clear guns off the Gallipoli peninsula that were interfering with the navy's battle with the Turkish forts in the Narrows. When the French added a corps of troops under a very senior officer, Kitchener was obliged to appoint General Sir Ian Hamilton as commander-in-chief. Personally, Birdwood was delighted to be serving under his old friend, but it cannot be denied that he and his staff were greatly offended by the cool reception they got from Hamilton's staff.

Australia's official historian, Charles Bean, praises Birdwood in lavish terms, recognizing in him a general who was quite perfect for the command of these particular troops:

> In entrusting the Australian and New Zealand troops to Birdwood, Lord Kitchener was acting from a sound knowledge of his personality. For a British officer, Birdwood possessed one surprising quality that was the secret of half his success with these forces. Many an Englishman of the period before the war judged things by the conventional outward signs with which he was familiar. The Australians might have found themselves under a commander who would have summed up a man by the boots he wore, or the roughness of his voice, or the manner in which he parted his hair, and would

have laid a horrified insistence upon the correct manner of saluting or addressing an officer, or upon significant points of dress. To such details of dress and manner British officers ordinarily attached great importance. It was Birdwood's nature to look past the forms at the man himself . . .

From the first day when, strolling around the Zoological Gardens at Giseh, he found many an Australian youngster gazing at the cages, he chatted simply to them, chaffed them, and treated them not as professional soldiers, but as the natural human beings they always were. Moreover he never made the mistake of setting before them low or selfish ideals. His appeal to them from first to last was based upon the highest and most honourable grounds. Sometimes he asked too much of them, but he always asked it for a worthy reason – the general good for which the allies were fighting. And that was always the way to appeal to the Australians. Birdwood was ambitious, but he was a man of intense uprightness. If he realized that a thing was wrong, nothing would induce him to do it. Above all he possessed the quality, which went straight to the heart of Australians, of extreme personal bravery.

All these attributes made Birdwood a rare leader – undoubtedly one of the greatest leaders of men possessed by the British Army during the war. Though of good general sense and ability, he was probably not outstanding as a tactician, nor had he the cast of mind peculiar to an organizer.[1] His delight was to be out in the field among his men, cheering them by his talk, feeling the pulse of them. He would come back from the front apparently far more interested in the spirits and conditions of the men than in the tactical situation. Indeed the importance, which he attached to small things, was constantly a puzzle to outsiders. He wrote personally to every officer who was decorated, and his correspondence with anxious or distressed relations in Australia was enormous. When addressing the men, he constantly concluded, with a smile: 'And, mind, whatever you do, write regularly to your mothers and wives and sweethearts – because, if you don't, they will write to me.' He had his secretary, but the writing of these letters must have cost him many hours weekly.

He chose his assistants well, although, like most Englishmen, he disliked to have around him any who lacked polish. His staff was strongly attached to him, and he leant upon it heavily for all organizing and office work. He wanted to be out of doors, finding out for himself what his men could be asked to do. He knew well how to ask them to do it. His power of leadership sprang from an exceptionally kindly nature, which looked upon men as men. He was really interested in them, and his memory of their affairs, when once he knew them, was extraordinary. Perhaps no commander on the front attached men to him so closely as he did. His possession of these indefinable and attractive qualities that made him a leader of men continually suggested a comparison with that great soldier of the previous generation, Lord Roberts.[2]

It was Birdwood who favoured the pre-daylight landing, without naval bombardment, for his troops at Gallipoli on 25 April 1915. When his generals on the peninsula suggested that they should prepare to evacuate that evening, before a Turkish counter-attack drove in their highly disorganized forces, it was Birdwood who referred the matter immediately to Sir Ian Hamilton. Hamilton famously encouraged them to 'dig, dig, dig' until they were safe and provided just that touch of leadership to restore all to their duty.

In the long weeks of holding on to the perilous foothold on the peninsula in the area now famous as 'Anzac', Birdwood had many opportunities to display his personal courage and win the affection of his troops. His personal interest in cleanliness and hygiene led him to encourage swimming in Anzac Cove. Anything up to 400 men at a time took to the water, as did Birdwood on a daily basis. It was a dangerous spot, often under Turkish fire, but it became a point of honour not to seek shelter. Charles Bean was to comment:

> Under shellfire General Birdwood appeared completely indifferent; if anything, he brightened, probably with a genuine pleasure at having an opportunity of sharing danger with his men. Only once was he known to 'duck', and that was when he was standing in full view of the distant German lines, on a muddy slope near Flers during the winter of 1916, and a shell suddenly shrieked down from the grey sky upon the small group. It fell about five yards away, showering mud over them – and then it was found that everyone in the group had gone down upon his face. 'You ducked that time, General', said his aide-de-camp. 'A sensible thing to do', replied the general shortly.[3]

Birdwood and his then chief of staff, Skeen, independently came up with a scheme to break out of the Anzac perimeter into the difficult but largely unoccupied country to the left. The sudden addition of reinforcements from the UK saw the plan enlarged to take in Suvla Bay and the landing of IX Corps. Birdwood personally briefed the corps commander, Stopford, and his divisional generals on the relatively straightforward task before them. Nothing he did could have foreseen the chaotic lack of leadership that ruined that part of the plan. Neither did he, nor any of his staff, foresee how the bad country at the foot of the Sari Bair Ridge, and the military excellence of Mustapha Kemal, would utterly defeat the attack out of Anzac in August 1915.

When Sir Ian Hamilton was recalled to London in October, Birdwood was placed in command of the Mediterranean Expeditionary Force until Sir

Charles Monro came out to replace Sir Ian. Birdwood, with Brudenell White at his side as chief of staff, was now responsible for three army corps and twelve divisions. When Monro assumed responsibility for Salonika and the eastern Mediterranean, Birdwood was made commander of the Dardanelles Army, and in that capacity he supervised the spectacularly successful evacuation of Anzac in December 1915, and Cape Helles in January 1916.

While in Egypt in January 1916, reorganizing the Gallipoli veterans and absorbing the large numbers of reinforcements there, and creating two more Australian divisions in the process, Birdwood strongly advocated the creation of an Australian and New Zealand Army of five divisions, with its own heavy artillery, mounted troops and air component. This scheme was backed by Sir Archibald Murray and forwarded to the War Office. With its usual antipathy to 'national' armies, the War Office decreed the creation of I and II Anzac Corps, and ordered them both to France forthwith.

Birdwood had the command of I Anzac Corps and retained the services of the incomparable Brudenell White,[4] together with Cunliffe-Owen as CRA and Joly de Lotbinière as CRE. Of the twenty-four officers on the I Anzac staff, twelve were British army, six Australian, four Indian Army, one New Zealander and one French. In France, Birdwood would continue that style of leadership that had won him the affection of his troops in Gallipoli. Charles Bean said of him: 'It is true that Birdwood did not possess the special mind of an organizer; but he was able safely to rely upon those strangely indefinite, yet invaluable, qualities of character that give men the power of leadership.'[5] Bean then quoted an unnamed staff officer serving with 'Birdie' on the Western Front:

> He chose the men whom he thought competent, and then left them absolutely to themselves in running their departments. He never wanted to know how White or we others did our work – he wanted to know the results, of course … but from the first he has never worried about the details in the least degree … Ever since he was a subaltern he has always done his work in the same way, making you puzzle how he does it – sitting reading the newspapers for hours each morning, busying himself about getting a neat set of gardens going; and he has always had the same result … Men were devoted to him. He has a remarkable way of getting through a great deal of work … Lord K. chose Birdwood (for the command of the Australians and New Zealanders) because he knew that he went among men as a man.[6]

Birdwood spent as much time as he could with his troops, where his reputation was one of being very demanding but scrupulously fair and sympathetic. He spoke to soldiers in a soldier's language. During a trench inspection in the autumn of 1916, an Anzac remarked to him in a typically direct and open way, 'These Germans opposite us are good Germans – they don't fire at us'. 'Don't you believe it', was his characteristic reply. 'The only good German is a dead German.'[7] During the grim winter of 1916–17 Birdwood was concerned at the prevalence of trench foot among his infantry and suspected that the junior officers were not inspecting the men's feet regularly. He fired off a circular to all subalterns enjoining each: 'to realise that it was up to him … to put all thoughts for himself, his comfort, and well-being, far in the background, and to determine that his thoughts and efforts should always be to look after his men first and foremost and sacrifice himself completely'.[8] This is, of course, exactly that kind of paternal care on which the entire British army existed, and it is not surprising that Birdwood would seek to imbue his new subalterns with the same ethos.

Conscious that his force was going to France with something of a reputation, fuelled by some parting remarks by Murray, for an overly relaxed attitude to dress, saluting and discipline in general, Birdwood made some warm speeches on the important role of the men 'to uphold the good name of Australia', and appealing to their honour not to tarnish the good name they had won in Gallipoli. This direct appeal to their finer feelings had a good effect, being generally well received, and there was a most pronounced movement within the AIF to improve standards of dress, saluting and general conduct.

These troops, being new to the rigours of the Western Front, were first deployed in the relatively quiet Armentières sector. It did not stay quiet for long, as Birdwood encouraged the natural aggressiveness of his troops and a programme of trench raids was begun. This was in keeping with Sir Douglas Haig's policy of 'wearing out' the enemy and reducing his fighting efficiency, and, while not all the raids were by any means successful, they helped the new arrivals adapt quickly to the new conditions of warfare. It was not long before the relentless demand for fresh troops saw I Anzac Corps moving down to the Somme and into the terrible fighting for the area around the village of Pozières and Mouquet Farm. Three Australian divisions would suffer 23,000 casualties in the sustained attacks on these positions. It is now generally recognized that many of these attacks were pressed home without adequate preparation, and that Birdwood and the Australian divisional commanders seemed overly keen to prove to the British high command that they could do their share of hard fighting. The Australians learnt early to dislike operations under the overall command of General Sir Hubert Gough, Haig's favourite 'thruster', and would suffer further disillusion in 1917 at the same hands. But Bean also voices some criticism of Birdwood, and makes the useful point that he, too, was on the same sort of learning curve as his troops:

> Birdwood also, though still beloved by most of the force, incurred a
> marked loss of popularity in some quarters through the notion that
> he had too readily offered to undertake impossible tasks. His actual
> attitude had been to undertake in earnest what was required by those

directing the British strategy. The effort of White, repeated again and again, had been to secure thoroughness in preparation – and, for that end, almost invariably, more time. He probably felt more deeply than Birdwood the impossibilities of Gough's tactics, and, had he induced the Corps commander to take the strong stand that he adopted on several occasions later in the war, some of the more impracticable operations would probably have been further modified or abandoned. To this extent White and Birdwood, too, shared the responsibility; but in this, their first introduction to the great operations of the Western Front, neither had yet fully attained the self-confidence which afterwards marked their actions.[9]

In part the development of Birdwood's self-confidence had something to do with the odd fact that, while a corps commander, he was also the commander-in-chief of all the Australian forces serving overseas. It is a measure of the great esteem in which he was held in Australia that, after the death of General Bridges, the first commander of the AIF, at Gallipoli, this thoroughly British general was able to suggest that he, as commander of the Australians in the field, should also serve as the administrative chief of all the greatly enlarged Australian forces. All the while he was a combat commander he had a small and efficient extra staff at his headquarters which he used to liaise with the AIF head offices at Horseferry Road, London, and the various AIF base camps in England, France and Egypt, as well as the Australian government. He also clashed occasionally with the policy wishes of his commander-in-chief in the BEF, Sir Douglas Haig, and the powers that be at the War Office. Thus we see him resisting those who sought to break up for reinforcements the newly formed 3rd Australian Division, and, in 1918, supporting the Australian generals in opposing the reduction of their divisions from twelve to nine infantry battalions. He would even intervene at the 'micro' level and protest at the use of an Australian tunnelling company being used as carrying parties for bridging engineers on the Yser River in 1917. Indeed, no sooner had he reported for duty in France in 1916 than he asked for permission for White and himself to leave for London to attend to important matters relating to AIF organization. Haig rather frostily suggested he might care to ask permission from General Plumer, in whose Second Army he was to serve. Plumer said he could spare either Birdwood or White, but not both at once. White was prepared to have a showdown with the imperial authorities over the issue; Birdwood was not and so he went to London alone. Birdwood was actually confirmed as general officer commanding AIF on 14 September 1916 (back-dated to 18 September 1915), and he retained the post for the duration and beyond. Highly political efforts to have him replaced by an Australian when he relinquished command of I Anzac Corps for Fifth Army were swiftly crushed at the highest levels in Australia. Indeed it was widely felt that having a British chief of the AIF actually reduced the degree of personal rivalry between Australian general officers, and left them to get on with the job of fighting the Germans.

We are fortunate to have a lively pen portrait of Birdwood soon after he arrived on the Western Front. The beautiful Château de la Motte au Bois, in the forest of Nieppe, was used throughout the war by a variety of higher formations of the BEF (usually as a corps headquarters), and, in April 1916, I Anzac moved in.[10] On the arrival of General Birdwood, the châtelaine, the Baroness Ernest de la Grange, wrote:

> I found him most agreeable. Short, thin, active, quick, and energetic, with grey-blue eyes full of frank gaiety, this man had organized and disciplined the Australian Army, who, officers and men alike, adore him, knowing how they can count on his fatherly kindness. He has sustained and encouraged them all through the terrible ordeal of Gallipoli. General Birdwood is English, but his Chief of Staff, General White, is an Australian. He is tall and fair, and very distinguished in type ... The officers of the 1st Anzacs are charming people. I find General Birdwood extremely 'sympathique' and we are becoming real friends.[11]

The baroness was told by an Australian war correspondent the many stories of 'Birdie' at Gallipoli that were, by now, a substantial part of the Anzac myth, of his swimming in the sea with Turkish shells dropping close by, and how he was the last to leave the shore, with his faithful Indian standard bearer, Faizullah. But she was soon able to tell from personal observation just how remarkable a commander he was:

> The first up every day, I see him start off in the morning, wearing the big Australian hat out of compliment to his men. He comes back late from his tour of inspection of the trenches, generally having eaten nothing since the morning. Often I gave the A.D.C. chocolate or a sandwich for his Chief, but nearly always General Birdwood makes his junior eat it! Hard on himself as to work and fatigue, he can ask much of his Anzacs, who, seeing him appear unexpectedly at notoriously dangerous corners, are proud to serve under his orders.[12]

In the winter of 1916–17 a trend set in that would bedevil relations between various elements of the BEF, and, we could say, has continued to do so ever since. The Australian divisions were already complaining that they, as 'storm troops', should not be asked to hold the trench lines for long periods between attacks. Apparently this was voiced aloud by troops on leave in London and it was reported back to White by the Australian high commissioner and Keith Murdoch. Birdwood asked Gough, in whose Fifth Army his corps was serving, if the whole corps could be brought out of the line for a rest. Gough, not unreasonably, pointed out what a strain this would put on the rest of the army, but did promise that one division (the 4th) would be relieved immediately for training in the new system of attack that was just then being introduced into the BEF, if the other three divisions could hold the same line more lightly. Sir Douglas Haig also expressed a wish to pull a second division out for training at the earliest possible opportunity.

After the ordeal of the First Battle of Bullecourt in April 1917 (of which more later), Birdwood did get the agreement of Gough to relieve the 1st, 4th and 5th Australian Divisions immediately, to be joined by the 2nd after its turn of duty at Second Bullecourt. When that battle also went badly, and it was suggested that the 5th Australian Division might have to be pulled out of its rest camp and committed to the battle, the protests began to escalate. The divisional commander, Major General J. Hobbs, the senior Australian officer in France, and a man especially sensitive to the feelings of his troops, made the complaint that Australian divisions were getting noticeably less rest than the British divisions they served alongside. Birdwood replied that he did not believe this to be the case and that all divisions were treated the same, getting rest in turn as the opportunity presented itself. Hobbs retorted that his men were camped beside the 11th and Guards Divisions, the former at rest for three months and the latter for seven weeks. White felt so strongly about this that he wrote to Neill Malcolm, MGGS Fifth Army, saying he would never again agree to mobilizing an Australian Imperial Force unless it had a representative at GHQ that could make its point of view known to the commander-in-chief. There was a strong, and largely justified, feeling that British commanders were not properly reporting the feelings of the Australians to GHQ. Birdwood wrote a firm letter to Gough on the issue and this had to be brought to the notice of Haig's chief of staff, Kiggell. It was he who ensured that I Anzac Corps was pulled out of the line for a four-month period of rest and training in the Amiens area.

As soon as Birdwood and White were presented with Gough's scheme for Fifth Army's contribution to the great British offensive in April 1917, which was designed as the precursor to Nivelle's *coup de grâce* on the Chemin des Dames, they both began to raise serious and understandable objections. Gough's 'boyish enthusiasm' for the attack had I Anzac Corps thrusting itself into a dangerous re-entrant between the Bullecourt and Quéant salients. When Gough began to add ever more ambitious objectives, Birdwood absolutely refused to accept them into the plan. He argued so persuasively that the formidable German wire entanglements would require a good deal more cutting that the whole Fifth Army effort was postponed to beyond the 9 April agreed by First and Third Armies. That attack was such a spectacular success that, when Gough offered large numbers of tanks to assist the Bullecourt attack, there was little the Anzac commanders could in all conscience do to delay matters further. Birdwood, obviously a good deal more confident now than he may have been at Pozières in 1916, did continue to criticize the rationale behind attacking such a strong part of the Hindenburg Line in such a purely frontal way. When a last-minute postponement delayed the attack from 10 to 11 April, Birdwood was heard to say that he was very glad it had been postponed and that he did not like the affair at all. Unfortunately the staff work of I Anzac was not all it could have been and they failed to properly notify the neighbouring 62nd Division of the delay. The West Riding Territorials carried out their part of the attack on schedule and suffered 162 casualties before realizing they were entirely on their own. In another lapse from best practice, the Anzac staff failed to transmit orders for massed machine-gun fire to be used to mask the sound of the tanks deploying for the attack, and an alert enemy was able to prepare its response more carefully.

When the tanks were late getting into position, Birdwood made one last attempt to get the attack called off, but this was quashed at the highest levels of the BEF (by Kiggell). That the following battle became a byword for failure, even to the extent that British instructors would hold it up as a lesson in how not to conduct combined infantry and tank attacks, did a great deal to damage relations within the BEF. When Birdwood later addressed 4th Australian Brigade, it is reported that he and the brigadier, Brand, had tears in their eyes as they explained how they had tried to get the attack plan altered.

It was after Bullecourt that Birdwood's most vocal critic in the AIF, 'Pompey' Elliott, really got into his stride. He was the most extreme example of an element within the AIF that poured scorn on most of the British formations with whom they came into contact. This tendency had started in Gallipoli, and became more vocal after the sorry handling of the battles of Fromelles, Pozières and Bullecourt. It has to be said that Elliott, an experienced and competent brigade commander, was a vitriolic character who exasperated almost everyone he came into contact with. He criticized all and sundry, and became so disturbed after the war that he finally committed suicide in 1931.

Thus Elliott would denounce Birdwood for issuing orders of 'plain unvarnished stupidity' and, surprisingly for an Australian, heap opprobrium on White for supporting Birdwood in holding back the promotion of Australian officers. Matters came to a head in the spring of 1918 when Birdwood, as GOC AIF, issued a circular to all his units:

> I urge the restriction of comparison between Dominion and English troops. The Dominion soldier has so established his merits that depreciation of his kith and kin is not necessary for the full acknowledgement of the great work Dominion troops are doing. We are of the same blood, and the creation of friction by criticism is only playing the German game.
>
> I am sure, though, you will at once agree how essential it is that we should, everyone of us, pull together with the one determination to

defeat the Germans, and it must help enormously to do this if we make up our minds to refrain from unkind criticism of others, and to do all in our power not only to make our own men refrain from such, but to try to show all by our example how we are out to help our neighbours whoever they may be, remembering that the trials and difficulties they have been through may often be unknown even to units alongside them.

This might be read as an earnest plea from a British general for imperial unity in the face of an aggressive and dangerous enemy. However, Elliott reacted in a violent manner, denouncing this message as a 'libel', a 'covert sneer' and 'a brazen shameless insult to our men', claiming it would harm discipline throughout the AIF. He only passed it on to his own brigade with a long preamble explaining that all armies have their 'duds' and that the British army, after its huge expansion, must have its fair share of them. When Elliott was subsequently passed over for the command of an Australian division, it confirmed him in his opinion of both Birdwood and White. In a lengthy series of communications with Charles Bean after the war, Elliott's criticism became quite unreasonable. He wrote that Birdwood had 'little idea of infantry tactics', and that White had only 'the theory of the thing'. He used the rather tired argument that, as a cavalry officer, Birdwood failed on the Western Front once he could find no flank for the cavalry to ride around. Elliot wrote to Bean of how impressed he had been with his personal contacts with Field Marshal Sir Douglas Haig and went on, 'I have had many more conversations with General Birdwood and the impression he gave me on the contrary was that he was utterly incapable of understanding the simplest tactical problems let alone strategical movements'.[13]

It should come as no surprise that Birdwood, having as much real combat experience as any soldier on the Western Front, was thoroughly well versed in the realities of the tactical requirements of the day. He and his staff were fully abreast of the constant updating of the fighting techniques of the BEF, made available to all formations through the issuing of training pamphlets and after action reports. Thus on 18 April 1917 he wrote to 1st, 2nd, 4th and 5th Australian Divisions as they prepared to join the great Arras offensive:

Now that we are approaching a period of what may well develop into open warfare, once we have pierced the Hindenburg Line, there is one point which I think we want to impress on all the troops more than has been necessary when confined to trench warfare. This is the fact that the rifle is the soldier's best friend. While we were engaged in trench warfare, we have had to look upon the bomb, rifle grenade and trench mortar as being the more essential, but we cannot lose any time now in making all ranks realize the great part the rifle and machine-gun must play in the open warfare before us.

I have just had the advantage of seeing a report from a brigadier engaged in what was really open warfare on the left of the Third Army. He strongly emphasizes the point that, when troops were advancing across the open, and saw Germans in front of them, it never seemed to strike them that they should, straight away, get all men onto every rifle and machine-gun they could bring to bear – working machine-guns forward and to the flanks as rapidly as possible, and doing everything to kill Germans while they had even a fleeting opportunity of doing so. It seemed difficult to make the men realize that they were not still in trench warfare. No one appeared immediately to grasp the necessity of rifle fire, and evidently all were waiting to get at the enemy with bombs and rifle grenades.

I hope that every division will shortly have an opportunity of rest and training in a back area, and during this I trust that every endeavour will be made to instil this very necessary fact into the minds of every officer, non-commissioned officer and man.[14]

It wasn't just British commanders bemoaning the over-dependence on the hand grenade to the detriment of rifle skills at this stage in the war. Ludendorff would make the same point in his own memoirs about the German army. Birdwood had a practical and sympathetic understanding towards his subordinates and issued another instruction at about the same time: 'I always impress on every commander that I shall never say a word if small posts are overwhelmed by superior numbers, so long as they have arrangements ready for launching a counter-attack at once.'[15] Indeed, it was the careful attention of Birdwood and White to the need for defence in depth, even when moving forward against the enemy, that ensured the defeat of the massive German counter-attack at Lagnicourt in April 1917.

I Anzac Corps moved up to Hazebrouck in late July 1917, in preparation for the series of battles known as Third Ypres. Some staff officers were wounded as the area came under fire from a German 14 inch gun, 'but no one cared to suggest to Birdwood that he should shift his headquarters'. He successfully argued with Plumer that his corps should be restored from three to four divisions, so that he could operate them in pairs through a number of battles. They were fortunate to come wholly under the command of Plumer's Second Army for the battles of the Menin Road Ridge (20 September), Polygon Wood (26 September), and Broodseinde (4 October). These three classic examples of 'bite and hold' operations saw a well-trained and rehearsed infantry attack under the most powerful artillery protection, seize important positions from the enemy and, most significantly, utterly destroy their predictable counter-attacks, inflicting the most enormous losses upon them. If the campaign ended in some difficulty as the weather broke again and turned the salient into a swamp, it did not detract from the awareness of the troops that they had put the enemy under tremendous pressure. In his regular correspondence with his old friend Sir Ian Hamilton, Birdwood wrote of the pleasure it was to serve under Plumer and his chief of staff, 'Tim' Harington, and how confident they all were of victory.

During the winter of 1917–18 the long-awaited plan to unite the Australian divisions in one corps took a major step forward. The 1st, 2nd, 3rd and 5th Divisions served together under Birdwood, and the 4th acted as depot division for what was now officially known as 'The Australian Corps'. II Anzac Corps was re-designated XXII Corps. It also became official policy to replace British commanders with Australians throughout the corps and, though it never quite became 100 per cent 'Australianized', there was a constant drive to appoint Australians where possible and, in the case of senior commanders such as the incomparable Walker of 1st Division and Smyth of 2nd Division, whenever suitable posts became available for them elsewhere in the BEF. It was during this process that Birdwood was informed that he would get the next available command of an army on the Western Front. He was able to guide his corps through their important interventions in finally halting the massive German spring offensives of 1918, culminating in their spectacular recapture of Villers–Bretonneux on 'Anzac Day' (25 April 1918).

The Hundred Days

And so it came to pass that Birdwood had to leave his beloved Australian troops and take command of the reactivated Fifth Army, which was inserted into a quiet part of the front line between Horne's First Army and Plumer's Second Army. He did ask Haig whether the command was an offer or an order. He would forgo the promotion if he could stay with his Australians. Haig's chief of staff, Lawrence, cleverly argued that he was holding up the promotion of Australian generals by staying, and so the army command was accepted. Birdwood did ask if the Australian Corps could join Fifth Army, but was put off with a vague suggestion that he might get 1st Division. He took over the active front on 23 May, with the superb Brudenell White at his side. Their initial task was to secure the area defences astride the River Lys against any renewal of the enemy offensives. The Fifth Army had under command the XI and XIII Corps, both under very experienced corps commanders, Haking and Morland respectively. The divisions were mainly veteran formations, all recuperating in a quiet sector after heavy fighting earlier in the year. The 3rd, 4th, 5th, 46th and 61st Divisions were joined in June by the 74th Division, the 'Broken Spur' division of dismounted yeomanry brought to Flanders from Palestine. The army had its full complement of heavy artillery and all the army troops one might expect, together with 10 Brigade, Royal Air Force. In July they would be joined by the rebuilt 1st Portuguese Division and would carefully nurse it back to some sort of trench-holding efficiency after the disaster of 9 April 1918.

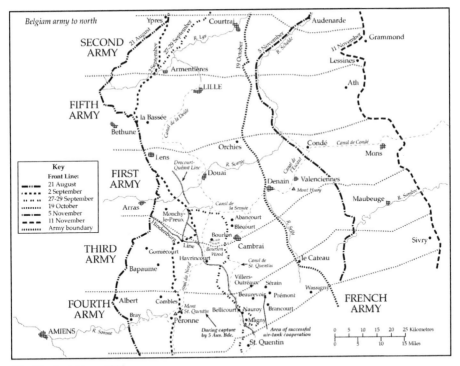

The Hundred Days, 1918.

Throughout June and July 1918 the Fifth Army sector remained relatively quiet, with great attention paid to improving the defences, and keeping up a sustained programme of patrolling and trench raids for the purpose of identifying the enemy formations to their front. The daily reports and weekly summaries submitted by the General Staff of the army detail all land and air activities, even to the daily expenditure of artillery ammunition, listed by type of gun and shell. Something like 20,000 shells would be fired on a 'normal' day (12,000 from field guns, 8,000 from the 'heavies'). When the daily firing rose on 19 and 20 July to 34,000 and 29,000 rounds respectively, we see from the weekly summary that raiders had identified a handover between enemy divisions at that time which was being duly 'interfered with'.

After the French counter-stroke at Soissons on 18 July 1918, all the Allied commanders were alerted to the fact that the overall initiative on the Western Front had irrevocably passed to the Entente powers. Birdwood immediately visited his corps commanders, instructing them to begin planning offensive operations. He wanted estimates of timings, and of troop and material requirements, stressing that plans should aim for surprise and rapidity of attack, without lengthy artillery preparation or obvious concentrations of troops. In under a week he was able to send an attack scheme requiring 10 divisions, 33 brigades of field artillery and 14 brigades of heavy artillery (he had 6, 19 and 8 under command respectively). White alerted the corps to the need to step up both tactical and physical training for the attack:

> The difficulties are realized, but the Army Commander hopes that the Corps Commanders may make it possible to withdraw a battalion at a time and move it to a suitable locality for training for a definite period . . . For success the operation will be largely dependent upon a resolute and rapid advance, and the men must be physically fit for the exertion.[16]

The plans included the provision of an 18-pounder battery allocated to each division to move forward by section or individual gun with the attacking infantry. All the artillery plans included elaborate arrangements for moving the gun lines forward as soon as possible.

Even before the great attack on 8 August, the enemy opposite Fifth Army had begun to evacuate his forward positions, and was followed up closely by the British infantry. This constant probing of the enemy lines went on for some weeks, until enemy resistance began to stiffen. On 23 August, Birdwood received from Sir Douglas Haig the 'clarion call' he had issued the day before to all his army commanders:

> I request that Army commanders will without delay bring to the notice of all subordinate leaders the changed conditions under which operations are now being carried on and the consequent necessity for all ranks to act with the utmost boldness and resolution in order to get full advantage from the present favourable situation. The effect of the two very severe defeats and the continuous attacks to which the enemy has been subjected during the past month has been to wear out his troops and disorganize his plans. Our Second and Fifth Armies have taken their share in this effort to destroy the enemy and have already gained considerable ground from him in the Lys sector of our front. Today the French Tenth Army crossed the Aillette and reports that a Bavarian Division fled in panic carrying back with it another Division which was advancing to its support. Tomorrow the attack of the Allied Armies on the whole front from Soissons to Neuville Vitasse (near Arras) is to be continued. The methods which we have followed hitherto in our battles with limited objectives when the enemy was strong are no longer suited to his present condition. The enemy has not the means to deliver counter-attacks on an extended scale nor has he the numbers to hold a continuous position against the very extended advance which is now being directed upon him. To turn the present situation to account the most resolute offensive is everywhere desirable. Risks which a month ago would have been criminal to incur ought now to be incurred as a duty. It is

no longer necessary to advance in regular lines and step by step. On the contrary each Division should be given a distant objective which must be reached independently of its neighbour and even if one's flank is thereby exposed for the time being. Reinforcements must be directed on the points where our troops are gaining ground, not where they are checked. A vigorous offensive against the sectors where the enemy is weak will cause hostile strong points to fall and in due course our whole Army will be able to continue its advance. This procedure will result in speedily breaking up the hostile forces and will cost us much less than if we attempted to deal with the present situation in a half-hearted manner. The situation is most favourable – let each one of us act energetically and without hesitation push forward to our objective.[17]

A flurry of 'warning orders' went out from Birdwood's headquarters to his units. Mobile advanced guards were formed, with a proper proportion of artillery included in them. Mobile mountings for 6 inch Newton trench mortars were being built as quickly as possible, as they were 'peculiarly suited for employment with vanguards whenever a temporary check is caused by snipers or machine-guns'. All artillery up to the 60-pounder and 6 inch howitzer category was ordered to be ready to advance at the same rate as the forward infantry. Great attention was paid to the need for close personal touch between artillery and infantry commanders, with field guns deployed as far forward as was possible. While warning that ammunition supply for the army did not allow for 'indiscriminate' firing, it did allow for good counter-battery work, support of infantry attacks and 'observed' shooting.[18]

On 2 September 1918 Birdwood held a conference with his corps commanders at which he reinforced the message from Haig. He explained 'the necessity of dissociating ourselves from our old defences' and of pursuing the enemy with mobile and aggressive (if minimal) all–arms advanced guards. They and the follow-on main bodies would have definite objectives and should always be ready to revert to a strong defensive if the enemy should counter-attack. Great stress was laid on getting information back to headquarters, so that troops and artillery assets could be deployed to best effect. Commanders needed to watch the condition of the men and keep them fit. The lines of communication must be advanced in close approximation to the advance of the divisions; bridging equipment would be needed, and studies of the ground to be advanced over with regard to drainage were instituted. All in all, Birdwood showed how completely in tune he was with the requirements of his commander-in-chief, and, if it was really necessary, this should give the lie to critics such as Elliott.

As it happened, almost the whole of September passed fairly quietly on Fifth Army's front, with a slow pressure on the enemy lines conforming to advances by Second and First Armies on either side. Lieutenant General Holland's I Corps (15th, 16th and 55th Divisions) joined the army from First Army late in September, and XIII Corps moved out to Fourth Army. As Second Army prepared its hammer blow that would recover the whole of the Ypres salient area from the enemy, Fifth Army made ready to support it with a powerful use of its artillery assets. As White issued a 'Special Instruction' to the divisions to be alert for a sudden enemy withdrawal, and to have advance guards ready to pursue, the CRA issued 'Artillery Instruction No. 116' calling for a special programme of increased artillery fire, initially for twenty-four hours, later increased to seventy-two hours. Its purpose was solely to inflict casualties and cause disorganization by means of observed counter-battery shoots, by concentrated area shoots on groups of hostile batteries and by the bombardment of known enemy billets and headquarters. Over 115,00 shells were fired off in this organized 'hate', and it contributed to the general dislocation of the whole enemy line in Flanders in late September/early October 1918.

The enemy began to retreat rapidly from the evening of 2 October and Fifth Army followed up closely until resistance stiffened along the line of the Haute Deule Canal. That the daily expenditure of artillery rounds fell to around 4,000, and once even to 1,622, gives an indication of the speed with which the enemy was trying to disengage and fall back to more defensible lines. On 15 October the retreat was so abrupt that contact was lost for most of the day. By now Fifth Army (expanded to three corps and nine divisions) was approaching the environs of the major conurbation of Lille. With a commendable desire to avoid civilian loss of life and damage to 'friendly' property, the British concentrated on working around the city, and restricted artillery shelling to the enemy resisting in the western outskirts, and to closing off exits from the city with gunfire. (With similar forethought to future needs, the artillery was also ordered to avoid the shelling of any water treatment facilities in subsequent advances.) The Germans evacuated Lille on 17 October as the British closed in upon it from flank and rear, and Fifth Army continued to shepherd the retreat towards the Escault (Schelde) River.

On 18 October, a cold and foggy day, only the Royal Air Force was able to track the swift flight of the German army. In common with the whole of the BEF, Fifth Army was learning a new style of warfare from day to day. Each division on the front line was pursuing the enemy along the main roads using all-arms columns, providing their own security. This deployment by 175 Brigade, 58th (2nd/1st London) Division (TF) is typical of the formations used at this time. The advanced guard had one cyclist platoon, an infantry battalion, a section of Royal Engineers and a section of Royal Field Artillery 18-pounders. The main body proceeded in this order: an infantry battalion, a battery of field artillery (minus the forward section), another infantry battalion, brigade headquarters, a machine-gun company, a light trench mortar battery and the rest of a brigade of field artillery (minus the forward battery). Royal

Engineer tunnelling detachments accompanied the main body. Once the advanced guard had made contact with the enemy rearguard, it was able to pin them long enough for the main body to deploy and attack vigorously. The Germans had to fall back before this relentless pressure until they could rally on some strong river/canal defence line well to the rear, and then only for as long as it took the BEF formations to prepare one of their crushing set-piece blows. Germany had nothing left with which to stop this pattern of warfare; the end was only a matter of 'when', not 'if'.

An advanced headquarters opened in Lille on 21 October; besides the usual General Staff and Signals component there was an 'Education Officer' attached, along with French and Belgian liaison officers. Clearly the need for restoring civil government in the liberated areas was an added consideration for army commanders. A formal parade through the city on 28 October was led by the 47th (2nd London) Division, and watched by, among others, the minister of munitions, Mr Winston Churchill. It is typical of 'Birdie' that he remembered to extend an invitation to his old friend the Baroness de la Grange.

Enemy resistance stiffened again towards the end of October; a bridgehead at Tournai was particularly fiercely contested. But Ludendorff's resignation had been accepted by the Kaiser, and there was a growing understanding on all sides that Germany was at the end of its tether. On 1 November, Birdwood warned his formations that a major assault on the Schelde line could be expected before too long. Meanwhile an aggressive programme of 'raids and minor operations' was called for, and no opportunity to seize even a small bridgehead east of the Schelde was to be missed. Very bad weather was delaying the final attack.

In common with all the armies on the Western Front, Fifth Army spent the early part of November preparing another massive blow against the ailing Germans. A major conference was held at army HQ at Lille with Haig, Plumer, Birdwood and Kavanagh all in attendance, to plan the final assault timed for around the 11 November (!). Two divisions (1st and 3rd) of Kavanagh's Cavalry Corps, plus the Household Machine-gun Brigade, were added to Fifth Army's strength on 7 November, for use in a major operation to commence on or after the 10th. Birdwood, the cavalryman, had no illusions about how this force might be used. In a paper setting out future plans, he wrote, 'The opportunity to employ the Cavalry Corps as a whole will therefore not occur at all events until after the passage of the Dendre has been forced'.[19] A cavalry brigade was nominated to co-operate with the infantry, and one of its regiments served with the advanced guards of each of the three corps. The rest of the Cavalry Corps held itself ready to advance on the orders of army HQ, to operate towards Ath and Enghien 'if the necessary conditions occur'.

Instead the final enemy retreat began on 8 November, and it was cycle troops who took up the pursuit before the cavalry had arrived. III Corps was the main force in action, and it received the 42nd Mobile Brigade, Royal Garrison

Artillery, to assist. Once again operations had to take into account the large numbers of civilians living in these relatively unharmed towns, and III Corps was forbidden to bombard any part of Tournai, which it finally liberated on 9 November. The cavalry came into action on 10 November and had difficulty keeping up with the enemy in full flight. Fifth Army captured Ath just as the armistice was announced on 11 November.

While Fifth Army had not engaged in any of the great battles of the 'Hundred Days' offensive from 8 August to 11 November, it had done everything Sir Douglas Haig required of it in keeping up the pressure on the weakening enemy, and linking the efforts of the main offensive group of armies (First, Third and Fourth) with the inter-allied force grouped around Second Army. It was a level of command Birdwood accepted somewhat reluctantly, as it deprived him of those opportunities he preferred of sharing the experiences of his soldiers. But he had seen the war develop from the desperately under-resourced days of 1915 (where lack of men and materials was even worse in Gallipoli than it was in France and Flanders) to the awesome destructive powers of the BEF in 1917 and 1918, and every formation he commanded played its full part in conducting this new, industrialized warfare.

Birdwood was, in every sense of the word, a leader of men. Some have suggested that Haig distrusted his enormous personal popularity, with the hint that he may have played upon it too much for the Field Marshal's liking. Monash would suggest in letters home to his wife that Birdwood was too much of a 'Kitchener man' and that, after the death of his patron in 1916, his career was held back. Only Plumer could rival the personal affection in which he was held by the troops who served under him.

Birdwood toured Australia and New Zealand in 1920 and was mobbed by wildly enthusiastic crowds wherever he went. The genuine affection between the old chief and his soldiers was evident and enduring. He was GOC Northern India from 1920 to 1924, and, duly promoted to field marshal, was GOC India from 1925 to his retirement in 1930. It is widely known that he would have considered an appointment as governor-general of Australia as the fitting end to his career, but the post had to go to an Australian. He was master of Peterhouse College, Cambridge, from 1931 to 1938. He was made a baronet in 1919, and in 1938 was created first Baron of Anzac and Totnes. Between the wars he was the colonel-in-chief of nine regiments in the British, Indian, Australian and New Zealand armies.[20] He died in England on 17 May 1951, and was buried with full military honours.

Bibliography

Birdwood himself wrote two volumes of autobiography, *Khaki and Gown* (London: Ward, Lock & Co, 1941) and *In My Time* (London: Skeffington, 1946). There has been no modern biography and much of the writing on Birdwood has been in the context of wider studies of the Anzacs. On the Anzacs, see E.M. Andrews, *The*

Anzac Illusion (Cambridge: Cambridge University Press, 1993); John Robertson, *Anzac and Empire* (London: Leo Cooper, 1990); and Alistair Thomson, *Anzac Memories: Living with the Legend* (Melbourne: Oxford University Press, 1994). The question of Anzac mythology and the contribution of Charles Bean to its construction has also been the subject of a body of work by Ken Inglis, whose essays are conveniently collected in John Lack, ed., *Anzac Remembered: Selected Writings of K.S. Inglis* (Melbourne: Melbourne University Press, 1998). Among many treatments of Gallipoli, see Nigel Steel and Peter Hart, *Defeat at Gallipoli* (London: Macmillan, 1994); Tim Travers, *Gallipoli, 1915* (Stroud: Tempus, 2001); Jenny Macleod, ed., *Gallipoli: Making History* (London: Frank Cass, 2004); and Jenny Macleod, *Reconsidering Gallipoli* (Manchester: Manchester University Press, 2004). The Hundred Days and the relevant contributions of British and Dominion forces to its successes can be traced in Peter Dennis and Jeffrey Grey, eds, *1918: Defining Victory* (Canberra: Army History Unit, 1999); Gary Sheffield, *Forgotten Victory* (London: Headline, 2001); Tim Travers, *How the War Was Won* (London: Routledge, 1992); and J.P. Harris and Niall Barr, *Amiens to the Armistice* (London: Brassey's, 1998).

Notes

1 This theme recurs in Bean's writing and is discussed later in this chapter. It seems to date from Bean's correspondence with Brigadier General 'Pompey' Elliott in the late 1920s.

2 Charles Bean, *Official History of Australia in the War of 1914–1918*, vol. 1, *The Story of Anzac* (Sydney: Angus & Robertson, 1921), pp. 119–23.

3 Ibid., p. 127.

4 Skeen had been invalided out with enteric fever in September 1915, and White became chief of staff.

5 Charles Bean, *Official History of Australia in the War of 1914–1918*, vol. 3, *The Australian Imperial Force in France, 1916* (Sydney: Angus & Robertson, 1938), p. 186.

6 Ibid., pp. 186–7.

7 Ibid., p. 880.

8 Ibid., p. 956.

9 Ibid., pp. 876–7.

10 Major Jack Churchill, now Birdwood's camp commandant, had been one of the first British soldiers to use the château in 1914, and may have brought it to the attention of his chief in 1916.

11 Baroness de la Grange, *Open House in Flanders, 1914–1918* (London: John Murray, 1929), pp. 181, 184.

12 Ibid., p. 187.

13 Canberra, Australian War Memorial (AWM), Elliott papers, 2 DRL 513, Item 42B.

14 AWM, Operations Files, AWM 26, Box 153, Item 4.

15 Charles Bean, *Official History of Australia in the War of 1914–1918*, vol. 4, *The Australian Imperial Force in France, 1917* (Sydney: Angus & Robertson, 1936), p. 358.

16 The National Archives (hereafter TNA), WO 95/522, Fifth Army General Staff, 26 July 1918.

17 TNA, WO 95/522.

18 TNA, WO 95/522, Artillery Instructions No. 110, HQ Fifth Army, 2 September 1918.

19 TNA, WO 95/522, Special Instruction No. 18, HQ Fifth Army, 7 November 1918.

20 12th Lancers, Royal Horse Guards, 75th AA Regiment RA, King Edward's Own (Probyn's) Horse, 6th Gurkha Rifles, 13th Frontier Force Rifles, 1st New Zealand Mounted Rifles, 3rd Australian Infantry and 16th Australian Light Horse.

Chapter Three

Julian Byng
Third Army, 1917–1918

Nikolas Gardner

Julian Byng was born on 11 September 1862 at Wrotham Park, Hertfordshire. The seventh son and thirteenth child of the second Earl of Strafford, the young Byng was raised with a degree of austerity that did not match his elevated social position. As his biographer, Jeffrey Williams, has observed: 'Most of his clothes were cast-offs and throughout his life his feet were to suffer from wearing the badly fitting boots which his brothers had outgrown.'[1] Julian also followed in the footsteps of his brothers in attending Eton from 1874 to 1878. While he attained few academic or athletic honours, he did acquire the lifelong nickname of 'Bungo', a moniker intended to differentiate Julian, if only slightly, from elder siblings 'Byngo' and 'Bango'. After leaving Eton, he hoped to join the army. With five sons already commissioned, however, the impecunious Strafford was initially unwilling to provide yet another with the allowance necessary to support an officer's lifestyle, and the youngest Byng was forced to join the militia. It was only in 1882 when the Prince of Wales offered Julian a place in his 10th Royal Hussars that his father relented. In January 1883 he became a lieutenant in the most expensive regiment in the British Army.[2]

Byng flourished in his new regimental home. In 1884 he was mentioned in dispatches for his role in the suppression of a native rebellion in Sudan. Two years later he became adjutant. In 1893 he left the regiment to attend the Staff College at Camberley, at the same time as several other senior commanders of the First World War, including Aylmer Haldane, Henry Rawlinson, Thomas Snow and Henry Wilson. During the South African War, Byng commanded the South African Light Horse, a regiment of colonial cavalry. Toward the end of the conflict, he returned to England and married Evelyn Moreton on 30 April 1902. Byng's career gathered momentum in the decade prior to the First World War. Promoted to brigadier general in 1905, Byng commanded the 2nd Cavalry Brigade from 1905 to 1907 and the 1st Cavalry Brigade from 1907 until 1909, when he was promoted to the rank of major general. After commanding the East Anglian Territorial Division for two years, Byng was posted to Egypt in 1912.

Chronology

11 September 1862	Julian Hedworth George Byng born at Wrotham Park, Barnet, Herts
	Educated at Eton
27 August 1879	Commissioned 7th Battalion, King's Royal Rifle Corps
27 January 1883	Transferred as lieutenant to 10th (The Prince of Wales's Own Royal) Hussars
1884	Served in the Sudan
20 October 1886	Appointed regimental adjutant
1893–94	Attended Staff College, Camberley
4 January 1890	Promoted captain
26 October 1897	Appointed DAAG Aldershot
4 May 1898	Promoted major
9 October 1899	Appointed deputy assistant provost marshal, Natal, but then given command of South African Light Horse
29 November 1900	Promoted brevet lieutenant colonel
15 February 1902	Promoted brevet colonel
11 October 1902	Promoted substantive lieutenant colonel
30 April 1902	Married Marie Evelyn Moreton
7 May 1904	Appointed commandant Cavalry School, Netheravon
11 May 1905	Appointed GOC 2nd Cavalry Brigade and substantive colonel
1 April 1907	Appointed GOC 1st Cavalry Brigade
1 April 1909	Went on half pay as major general
9 October 1910	Appointed GOC East Anglian Division
30 October 1912	Appointed GOC Egypt
5 August 1914	Appointed GOC 3rd Cavalry Division
7 May 1915	Appointed GOC Cavalry Corps and temporary lieutenant general
24 August 1915	Appointed GOC IX Corps at Gallipoli
27 February 1916	Appointed GOC XVII Corps
May 1916	Appointed GOC Canadian Corps
3 June 1916	Promoted substantive lieutenant general
9 June 1917	Appointed GOC Third Army and temporary general
23 November 1917	Promoted substantive general
August 1919	Created Baron Byng of Vimy and Thorpe-le-Soken
7 November 1919	Retired from army
August 1920	Appointed governor-general of Canada
1926	Elevated to viscount
June 1928	Appointed chief commissioner of the Metropolitan Police
17 July 1932	Promoted field marshal
6 June 1935	Died at Thorpe Hall, Thorpe-le-Soken

Appointed MVO 1902, CB 1906, KCMG 1915, KCB 1916, GCB 1919, GCMG 1921

Upon the outbreak of the First World War, Byng immediately returned to England, where he assumed command of the newly created 3rd Cavalry Division. Part of Henry Rawlinson's IV Corps, Byng's division joined the British Expeditionary Force in mid–October 1914. Serving under Rawlinson, Edmund Allenby and Douglas Haig in succession, 3rd Cavalry Division contributed to the desperate British defence of Ypres in late October and early November. In May 1915 Byng took over command of the Cavalry Corps, which participated in the Second Battle of Ypres. In August he was sent to Gallipoli to command IX Corps. There he played an integral role in planning the withdrawal of the Mediterranean Expeditionary Force, perhaps the only successful operation of the Gallipoli campaign.

Byng returned to the Western Front in early 1916. After a brief stint at the helm of XVII Corps, he was appointed to command the Canadian Corps in April. It was in this post that he made his reputation as an innovative trainer and commander, as he orchestrated the dramatic Canadian capture of Vimy Ridge on 9 April 1917. Less than two months after the victory at Vimy, he replaced Edmund Allenby as commander of the Third Army, a post that he held until the end of the war. Under Byng, the Third Army conducted the British offensive at Cambrai in November 1917, before suffering heavily as it blunted the desperate German attacks of March 1918. Byng's army recovered, however, to play an important role in the Allied advances of the 'Hundred Days'.

Retiring from the British Army at the end of the First World War, Byng accepted the post of governor-general of Canada in 1920. During their five years at Rideau Hall in Ottawa, he and his wife were popular among Canadians, even after Byng gained a measure of notoriety for refusing to dissolve Parliament at the behest of Prime Minister Mackenzie King in October 1925. In addition to travelling to remote corners of the country, the couple became avid ice hockey fans. In 1925 Lady Byng presented a trophy to the National Hockey League that still recognizes on an annual basis the player best demonstrating sportsmanship in play. After returning to Britain in 1926, Byng became commissioner of the Metropolitan Police in 1928, implementing numerous reforms that did much to restore flagging public confidence in London's law enforcement officers. Failing health forced him to retire from this position in 1931. He died four years later, on 6 June 1935.

In comparison with many senior officers of his era, the details of Julian Byng's personality and private life remain relatively obscure. This is largely a reflection of the lack of documentary evidence he left behind. Unlike many of his colleagues in the upper ranks of the BEF, Byng did not publish memoirs. Nor was he willing to engage in the often acrimonious post-war debates among senior officers regarding the conduct of operations of the Western Front. To ensure that he was not dragged into such controversies posthumously, Byng arranged for the destruction of his personal papers upon his death. His wife followed suit, thus closing a final window that might have illuminated Byng's private side. This situation is frustrating for the historian, since it precludes anything more than a limited acquaintance with Byng as a person. His remarkable reserve is nonetheless revealing, as it suggests a soldier who was reluctant to bolster his own reputation at the expense of those with whom he served in the First World War.

Available evidence supports this assertion, portraying Byng as an unassuming, personable and compassionate individual whose integrity outweighed his ambition. It would be unrealistic to view an officer who reached the uppermost ranks of his profession as lacking in motivation or interest in his own advancement. Indeed, even Byng's decision to attend the Staff College in the 1890s indicates a level of ambition well beyond that of most members of the Victorian officer corps. Byng's interest in his career irritated certain of his colleagues. During the South African War, Hubert Gough criticized Byng in his diary, labelling him 'an extraordinary intriguer', and commenting: 'I hate that way of Byng's of always trying to get the better of others while pretending the most friendly feelings. I have known several instances of this and would not trust him one yard as a friend.'[3]

This opinion, however, does not appear to have been shared by the numerous officers who knew Byng throughout his career. Indeed, Gough's remarks may reveal more about the ambitions and insecurities of their source than they do about Byng himself. The balance of evidence suggests that throughout his career Byng displayed a sense of humanity that earned him the trust of his colleagues. He was popular at Camberley, an environment where single-minded study elicited the bemusement and often the disdain of other students. Even during the First World War his reliability and understated sense of humour earned the respect of other officers. In late 1914 Douglas Haig praised Byng's composure during the First Battle of Ypres. According to Haig: 'By his merry wit and cheerful bearing, he not only encouraged those under his orders, but also all with whom he came in contact, an asset of much value in the circumstances in which we were placed during the fighting around Ypres.'[4] The esteem in which his colleagues held him was also evident in Edmund Allenby's willingness to unburden himself to Byng when the latter replaced him as commander of the Third Army in 1917. As one of Allenby's subordinates related after the war: 'the first thing he did, when he heard the news early in the morning was to get in his car and visit Lord Byng ... They were not friends, but he knew, as everyone did, that he could trust Byng, and at their interview that early morning, he broke down very badly.'[5]

Byng's considerate nature was also evident in his relations with his staff. Describing Byng affectionately in his memoirs, Charles 'Tim' Harington, his chief of staff in the Canadian Corps, related the following anecdote:

> At Abeele once, at the time of the Mount Sorrel fighting, knowing that I was bothered all night by telephone calls, and wanting me to get a good night's rest, he, as Corps Commander, insisted upon going on night duty. He had his bed moved into my office and the telephone put alongside, and he sent me to be in my hut.[6]

Such consideration was not limited to those with whom Byng interacted on a daily basis. According to Jeffrey Williams, the opening months of the First World War took a heavy toll on Byng, as 'he was greatly troubled by the price in lives paid by his soldiers and by the death of so many of his friends'.[7] The extent to which those under his command reciprocated Byng's feelings is evident in the fact that the soldiers of the Canadian Corps retained the collective nickname 'the Byng Boys' until the end of the First World War, reflecting the title of a well known wartime musical revue.

The respect and fidelity that Byng showed his fellow soldiers were magnified in his relationship with his wife, Lady Evelyn Byng. The couple never had children, but they remained married for thirty-three years. Much more than simply a supporter and confidante of her husband, Lady Byng was a strong personality whose public conduct occasionally gave him cause for exasperation. In a letter written to Lady Haig after the Battle of Cambrai, Douglas Haig compared the antics of Lady Byng unfavourably to his wife's formidable discretion. As Haig commented: 'I am eternally grateful to you for not advertising! Ever so many people in my hearing have commented on the silly things Lady Byng has been doing since her husband's success on 20th Nov. And poor old Bungo is quite displeased, I think, at all the vulgarity in the Press.'[8] Lady Byng's behaviour was not always conducive to her husband's professional relationships. Indeed, during Byng's tenure as governor-general of Canada, the mutual dislike between Evelyn and Mackenzie King probably exacerbated tensions between Byng and the Canadian prime minister.[9] Nonetheless, Byng remained devoted to his wife until he died in 1935, even if their relationship ultimately evolved into one of mutual respect rather than adoration. Overall, despite the relative dearth of information regarding Byng's private life, available evidence suggests a trustworthy individual possessed of a genuine affection for his friends and loved ones, as well as a sense of responsibility for those who served under his command. These qualities earned Byng the esteem of his subordinates and superiors alike.

Byng's personality traits influenced his style of command. Throughout his career, he placed a strong emphasis on personal leadership of his troops in battle, often exposing himself to the same hazards that he asked his subordinates to face. In November 1901 Byng commanded a column comprising the South African Light Horse and approximately 450 Imperial Yeomanry. One day, after surprising a party of about twenty mounted enemy troops, the column gave chase with Byng at its head. By the time he caught up with the enemy riders, Byng had left his own force behind. He managed to compel them to throw down their weapons and surrender despite being armed with nothing but a walking stick.[10] It is likely that this willingness to lead from the front was a partial reflection of the cavalry spirit, a philosophy of command that relied on the instinctive decision-making capabilities of the officer at the head of a mounted force. In the cavalry, the importance of such leadership would probably have been impressed on Byng from his days as a junior officer.

An intuitive approach to command grew much less important as Byng evolved from the commander of a cavalry column to the manager of a combined-arms formation comprising thousands of troops. He nevertheless retained his penchant for personal leadership during the First World War. Rather than simply a means of commanding from the front, however, Byng conceived of his presence among his subordinates as a way of inspiring them by example. This was evident in October 1914, when the BEF collided with enemy forces as it attempted to outflank the German army in northern France and Belgium. Toby Rawlinson, brother of Henry Rawlinson and a chauffeur in 1914, observed Byng under fire on 21 October, as his 3rd Cavalry Division encountered substantial German forces. According to Rawlinson:

> On my return to the main road I found that General Byng had gone on in the direction of Neuve Eglise, and I came up with him at a little roadside cafe on the slope commanding the valley between the hill of Kemmel and the village of Neuve Eglise. There was no doubt that the enemy was holding the crest of the opposite hill, and our own line had not yet descended into the valley. The General therefore ordered some coffee in the little cafe, and, to my astonishment, refused to partake of it in the house, but insisted that the table should be brought out into the road. He then sat down to his coffee in full view of both the enemy's line on the opposite hill and of our own men, who were then descending into the valley. This was done with the most complete unconcern in order that he might be able to observe the advance of our line. There was not the least suggestion of bravado, though it was obvious to everyone that he was offering himself as a most exceptionally favourable target to the enemy.[11]

Byng remained a familiar sight to his troops at the front after the emergence of stalemate in France and Belgium at the end of 1914. Despite the relative stability of the front lines, and the omnipresent danger of enemy fire, he inspected the forward positions under his command on a daily basis even after his promotion to corps commander. In 1916 a Toronto newspaper reporter encountered the commander of the Canadian Corps still attired in a helmet and gas mask after visiting an advanced post within 15 yards of German lines.[12] Byng's personal bravery, however, did not translate into a reckless approach to command. While he was willing to take considerable risks with his own safety, he proved far more circumspect with the lives of those under him. Indeed, during his command of IX Corps at Gallipoli in 1915, Byng stood firm in the face of pressure to launch a large-scale attack on Ottoman positions. Citing inadequate artillery ammunition, he resisted the offensive plans of his divisional commanders and his superior, Sir Ian Hamilton. Moreover, the withdrawal from Gallipoli, which Byng had favoured since his arrival at the Dardanelles, was carried out despite opposition from Lord Kitchener.

Thus, while Byng's nonchalant forays to the front were partly an effort to inspire subordinates, they should also be understood as an attempt by a prudent commander to ascertain in as much detail as possible the tactical and operational situation facing his formation. Indeed, throughout the First World War, Byng displayed a painstaking approach to the planning and conduct of operations. This is most evident in his command of the Canadian Corps from April 1916 until June 1917. Upon assuming his new post, Byng launched a thorough reorganization of the corps with the intent of improving its efficiency. He introduced new regulations on seemingly trivial matters such as the maintenance of uniforms and the saluting of officers, while at the same time implementing measures intended specifically to improve tactical efficiency, such as the establishment of a corps school offering instruction in the use of weapons and the conduct of trench warfare. Like the vast majority of the formations that participated, the Canadian Corps suffered heavily in the Somme offensive. Before operations had even concluded, however, Byng ordered corps and divisional staff to conduct detailed studies of Canadian tactics at the Somme. The disclosure in early 1917 that the Canadian Corps would be attacking Vimy Ridge in the spring added impetus to Byng's careful planning. He developed an intelligence organization that used a variety of sources of information to enable a detailed understanding of the German positions at Vimy, extending to the behaviour of specific units occupying them. Behind the front lines, Byng constructed a full-scale replica of the battlefield, even updating it to reflect changes in the enemy's defensive system. Units in reserve practised their assigned tasks in the weeks preceding the battle itself.[13]

The benefits of Byng's meticulous approach were demonstrated clearly by the Canadian success at Vimy Ridge. It must be acknowledged, however, that his skills as a commander did not receive the universal acclaim of his colleagues. After the First World War, the official historian of the British Army, Sir James Edmonds, alleged that 'Byng was the most incompetent of all the Army Commanders'.[14] While Edmonds's post-war evaluations of senior British officers usually tended toward the caustic, his particularly scathing assessment of Byng merits further examination. Byng's organizational skills and his attention to detail are not in doubt. Nonetheless, he seems to have struggled when faced with unexpected crises in the midst of operations. After the war, Hubert Gough contended that Byng had faltered in his response to the sudden German attacks against the British Third and Fifth Armies in March 1918. According to Gough, the commander of the adjacent Fifth Army during the German spring offensives, Byng held the Flesquières salient for too long, and then failed to control the withdrawal of his force from the position, causing a dangerous gap that Third Army ought to have been strong enough to prevent. This allegation was not simply a reflection of Gough's long-standing animosity toward Byng. In post-war discussions with Edmonds and Sir Basil Liddell Hart, several other officers asserted independently that Byng's leadership in March 1918 had been much less effective than that of his counterpart in command of Fifth Army.[15] As will be discussed in more detail below, similar criticisms were levelled at Byng for his conduct of the Battle of Cambrai in late 1917. Thus, while he possessed the courage to lead by example and the conscientiousness essential for the planning and execution of complex operations, Byng appears to have lacked sufficient *coup d'œil* to adapt quickly to unforeseen developments.

Byng's style of command, however, can only be understood fully within the context of his personal relationships with subordinates and superior officers. Despite his meticulous nature, Byng was by no means prone to micro-managing his underlings. Indeed, he recognized the necessity of allowing subordinate officers leeway to exercise command, particularly when their local expertise exceeded his own. Describing Byng's assumption of command of the Canadian Corps in his memoirs, Tim Harington related an incident that took place when he visited the headquarters of one of his subordinates. According to Harington:

> Major-General Mercer turned to the Corps Commander and said: 'Williams and I are going up tomorrow, General, to make that reconnaissance; will you come?' Knowing General Byng's anxiety to see everything to do with the front line at once, I naturally expected to hear him say 'Yes'. Instead, he paused for quite a long time, which surprised me greatly, and then he said: 'No, you and Williams go to-morrow and make your plans, and Tim and I will come up on Saturday.' ... It was a right decision, he had only just met them that day and he did not want to be in their way, or cramp their style.[16]

Byng also proved able to identify and nurture the talent of his subordinates. As commander of the Canadian Corps, he recognized the diligence and per-ceptiveness of one of his divisional commanders, Arthur Currie. A former real estate agent with little military experience prior to 1914, Currie was neither Byng's long-time protégé nor a typical Major General. Byng nonetheless recommended that Currie accompany a British delegation observing French tactics at Verdun, using Currie's observations to help plan his assault on Vimy Ridge in 1917. Following Byng's promotion to command Third Army, he recommended that Currie succeed him.[17] Thus, Byng's preference for personal leadership and his attention to detail were tempered by his willingness to acknowledge the skills and operational jurisdiction of his subordinates.

Such leeway, however, was not always conducive to victory. In order for tactical innovation to occur in the BEF during the First World War, it was necessary that senior commanders such as Byng allow and even encourage experimentation by their subordinates. Nevertheless, the guidance and judgement of the senior commander was also important in differentiating promising tactical ideas from potentially dangerous ones, and in ensuring as much uniformity of practice as possible among subordinate formations. Consistent with his amicable and considerate nature, Byng seems to have erred on the side of leniency, allowing his subordinates considerable freedom to develop new tactics at the expense of consistency among the formations under his command. Nor were the approaches adopted by Byng's subordinates equally effective. A lack of standardized defensive tactics among the corps and divisions of Third Army contributed to its fragility in the face of German attacks in March 1918. As an officer in 4th Division related to Edmonds after the war: 'The 4th Division front consisted of continuous trenches connected by communicating trenches. The XIII Corps on our left adopted the island system. These islands were blotted out at once on the 28th, and the forward system was gone in a few minutes. I hated that island system, as it was utterly useless.'[18]

Different defensive systems proliferated at the divisional level within Byng's army. As another officer explained to Edmonds:

> General Harper commanding 51st Division believed in deep dugouts both for infantry and M.G.s, and deep communication trenches and ordinary front wire. General Bainbridge commanding 25th Division believed in pushing his front wire half way across No Man's Land, and putting his M.G.s in a sort of shell hole in between the lines of trenches where they had very short fields of fire and were mainly useful for counter preparation and barrage fire. I inherited the latter system with which I was not in agreement.[19]

This lack of uniformity should not be attributed solely to Byng's failure to provide adequate direction to subordinate commanders. The disparate approaches employed by separate divisions indicate that the corps commanders under Byng did little to ensure consistency within their formations. In addition, GHQ apparently provided only limited guidance in this respect. Nonetheless, given Byng's habit of visiting the front as frequently as possible, he would almost certainly have been aware of the assortment of defensive tactics employed within his formation. Moreover, it is evident that Byng was reluctant to impose his will on subordinate commanders. In post-war correspondence with Edmonds, J.F.C. Fuller criticized Byng's lack of assertiveness during the Battle of Cambrai. According to Fuller: 'The whole trouble about the tanks was that Byng would not hold any in reserve. I urged him to do so, but all he replied was: "I cannot go against the wishes of my Corps and Div[isiona]l Commanders." He was far too soft to be a good general.'[20]

While Byng often hesitated to restrain his subordinates, he proved quite loyal to his superiors. This was particularly true of Lord Kitchener and Sir Douglas Haig, the two officers most responsible for his progression to the uppermost ranks of the British army. Serving under Kitchener in South Africa and Egypt prior to the First World War, Byng developed a close personal relationship with his superior. Upon their arrival in Cairo in 1912, Byng and his wife resided with Kitchener. Evelyn acted as his hostess at social events even after they found their own accommodation. It is likely that Byng's appointment to command 3rd Cavalry Division in 1914 stemmed at least in part from Kitchener's influence. While he remained in reasonably close contact with the Secretary of State for War in 1914 and 1915, however, Byng's loyalty did not translate into unquestioning obedience. At Gallipoli he recommended withdrawal despite Kitchener's objections, knowingly incurring the wrath of his long-time friend and patron. Although Byng returned to England in early 1916, Kitchener did not attempt to re-establish contact before his death that June.

Even more significant than Byng's relationship with Kitchener was that with Sir Douglas Haig. While Byng and Kitchener drifted apart prior to the latter's sudden death, he and Haig grew closer throughout the First World War. After serving under Haig in South Africa, Byng apparently had little direct contact with him until 1914. Upon joining the BEF in October of that year, Byng did not make a favourable impression. Operating adjacent to Haig's I Corps in the initial stages of the First Battle of Ypres, Byng elicited Haig's criticism by his apparent aversion to heavy casualties. As the I Corps commander remarked in his diary on 21 October 1914: 'Byng had only some 50 casualties in his whole division yesterday. A small number considering the nature of this war and all that is at stake!'[21]

Haig's view of Byng changed, however, during the First Battle of Ypres, an engagement that had a formative influence on the eventual commander-in-chief of the BEF. With I Corps faced with mounting German attacks on the morning of 31 October, Haig directed Byng's adjacent 3rd Cavalry Division to march to his assistance. Byng's division was part of the Cavalry Corps, under the command of Edmund Allenby. By issuing orders directly to Byng, Haig was effectively bypassing Allenby and attempting to appropriate a division from the Cavalry Corps. Moreover, Allenby's force was also under considerable pressure in this period, and consequently, he attempted to countermand Haig's order and retain control of 3rd Cavalry Division. Byng nonetheless continued to go to Haig's assistance, remaining under his command for the duration of the First Battle of Ypres.[22] Whether it was due to Byng's willingness to eschew protocol and aid I Corps on 31 October or to his subsequent performance in defending Ypres, Haig warmed to Byng in the aftermath of the battle. On 30 November 1914 Haig recommended him for promotion, extolling Byng's virtues in a letter to Sir John French, then commander-in-chief of the BEF. Perhaps referring to Byng's assistance of I Corps on 31 October, Haig commented: 'Throughout the operations east of Ypres, he has commanded his division with skill and gallantry and has at all times moved to the support of other arms with great promptitude and often without waiting for orders to do so when the situation was urgent.'[23]

Haig continued to favour Byng upon his return from Gallipoli to the Western Front in 1916. In May he advised the king that Byng would be a popular and capable commander of the Canadian Corps. When Byng proved him correct, the commander-in-chief soon began pushing for his further advancement. Twice prior to Byng's appointment to command Third Army in June 1917, Haig had attempted to secure his promotion to command an army. Perhaps out of modesty, or a genuine affection for his Canadian Corps, Byng had resisted. The commander-in-chief did not favour Byng to the extent that he accepted his subordinate's ideas uncritically. Indeed, he prodded Byng throughout the Battle of Cambrai in late November 1917. Moreover, during the British offensives in the late summer of 1918, Haig criticized Byng's circumspect attack plans, as well as the allowances he attempted to make for his inexperienced troops.[24] Such periodic discord notwithstanding, Haig never soured on Byng. After the disappointing conclusion of the British offensive at Cambrai, he absolved the Third Army commander from blame. Haig continued to support Byng even after Third Army buckled under heavy German attacks in March 1918. This period saw the removal of Haig's long-time protégé, Hubert Gough, whose performance in the face of the German offensive had apparently been superior to that of Byng. The fact that Byng managed to retain his position indicates the extent of the commander-in-chief's faith in him.

This faith undoubtedly resulted in part from Byng's manifest qualities as a commander. Nonetheless, it is likely that it also stemmed from his consistent loyalty to Haig. Byng was neither sycophantic nor spineless in his relationship with the commander-in-chief. Prior to the offensives at Vimy Ridge and Cambrai, he repeatedly pestered GHQ for the extra resources necessary to implement initiatives, despite his recognition of the numerous demands placed on the British army in 1916 and 1917. In the event of a difference of opinion, however, Byng proved willing to accede to Haig's wishes, even when the commander-in-chief intervened in his operational jurisdiction. As will be discussed below, this was the case at Cambrai, where Byng succumbed to pressure from Haig to expand his planned offensive and continue it despite its dwindling returns after the first day. Granted, it would be difficult for any commander in this situation to ignore the opinion of a superior, particularly one as authoritarian and assertive as Haig. Byng's commitment to the commander-in-chief is further demonstrated, however, by the fact that even though Haig's advice produced few additional gains at the cost of heavy British casualties, his loyalty remained unblemished by bitterness or recrimination. In early 1918, Byng maintained: 'Whatever else happens, we must keep D.H. where he is.'[25]

Given the duration and intensity of the war on the Western Front, it was certainly important that Sir Douglas Haig retain the commitment of his subordinates. Steadfast lieutenants like Byng were essential in enabling the commander-in-chief to conduct extended and costly operations, as well as weather enemy offensives. Unwavering devotion, however, was not necessarily conducive to operational and tactical innovation. If new ideas flowed upward during the war, from divisions, corps and armies to GHQ, loyalty such as Byng showed toward Haig could inhibit their progress, as new approaches were suppressed in order to suit the preferences of the commander-in-chief. Thus, the nature of Byng's relationships with his subordinates and with Sir Douglas Haig created a paradoxical situation. His open-minded attitude toward his subordinates gave them the scope to develop new solutions to the stalemate that prevailed on the Western Front, at the expense of tactical uniformity and occasionally military effectiveness in the formations under his command. Byng's devotion to Haig, on the other hand, ensured consistency with the wishes of the commander-in-chief, but probably inhibited the application and diffusion of the innovations that he encouraged in his subordinates.

The scarcity of surviving documentation produced by Byng complicates any attempt to discern the development of his ideas over the course of the First World War. Fortunately, despite this dearth of written words, the evolution of Byng's understanding of warfare in this period is manifest in his deeds. While the nature of his tactical ideas in 1914 remains unclear, Byng's own audacious behaviour under fire suggests that he valued personal bravery and leadership by officers. Such leadership was instrumental to the survival of the British Army in 1914. The opening months of the war, however, took a murderous toll on the original battalions of the BEF. Byng's disquiet over the heavy casualties of 1914 appears to have motivated him to seek less costly methods of fighting the war. By 1915 he had turned to artillery as a way 'to replace blood and muscle with explosive and steel'.[26] Thus, at Gallipoli, he insisted on heavy artillery bombardments prior to any infantry attacks. To the frustration of Byng's subordinates and superiors, sufficient ammunition was not available to meet his requirements, with the result that attacks were repeatedly postponed. As Sir Ian Hamilton complained in September 1915:

> Byng would like to have four days' successive bombardment for an hour and then attack, and speaks of one HE [high explosive] shell per yard as pat as if they were shells we could pick up on the sea shore. I have assured him it is no earthly use; that he shall have his share of what I have got, but that stuff for bombardment is simply not in existence – not here at least.[27]

Byng's ideas undoubtedly continued to evolve following his return to the Western Front and his appointment to command the Canadian Corps. Nonetheless, the extent to which he could implement new concepts was limited throughout 1916. At the Somme, the Canadian Corps formed part of Hubert Gough's 'Reserve' Army. Its operations were conducted within the constraints of an offensive plan developed by Gough and GHQ. Thus, the scale and pattern of artillery bombardment as well as the formation of advancing infantry were dictated from above. In the aftermath of the Somme, however, and particularly following the January 1917 announcement that the Canadian Corps would assault Vimy Ridge in the spring, Byng initiated a wide range of tactical reforms. Consistent with his earlier recognition of the importance of artillery in limiting casualties, Byng increased the number of guns available to his formation. At Vimy the Canadian Corps had one heavy gun for every 20 yards of front and one field gun for every 10, twice the density of artillery available to British forces at the Somme. With the help of Major General Edward Morrison, the corps artillery commander, Byng also improved the effectiveness of the Canadians' artillery fire. Byng and Morrison introduced new fuses to facilitate the destruction of wire, as well as new methods of directing fire in order to neutralize enemy guns and maintain a creeping barrage in close proximity to advancing Canadian infantry.

In addition to his advocacy of firepower, evident since 1915, Byng increasingly emphasized the importance of surprise and initiative. While the Canadian Corps artillery began shelling German positions as early as 20 March, Byng eliminated the intense bombardment that had previously preceded, and often disclosed, British infantry attacks. He also oversaw the implementation of new infantry tactics prior to Vimy. On the basis of Arthur Currie's observations of French practice, he introduced an approach similar to that of the pre-war British army, featuring the advance of small groups of infantry, taking advantage of existing terrain. To facilitate these tactics, he encouraged the use of initiative by officers and non-commissioned officers in platoons. Rather than seeking to maintain a uniform line of advance, Byng emphasized the exploitation of success, directing that if a battalion or larger formation encountered heavy resistance, those units on its flanks should press forward, enveloping the enemy strongpoint in the process.[28]

Byng's ideas continued to develop after his promotion to command Third Army. He discerned the potential of new technology to enhance surprise and resurrect the possibility of breaking through enemy defences on the Western Front. Adapting an idea apparently conceived by J.F.C. Fuller, Byng developed a plan to use tanks to pierce German positions at Cambrai, enabling infantry and cavalry to break through. The attack would be supported by aerial interdiction of enemy batteries and transport facilities. Surprise would be achieved through the 'silent registration' of artillery, which allowed guns to commence firing without conducting a preliminary bombardment that would warn the enemy of an impending attack. By 1918 some of the ideas Byng had developed earlier in the war were beginning to diffuse throughout the BEF. Sir Douglas Haig was sufficiently impressed by the tactical school Byng had originally established to enhance the leadership capabilities of junior officers in the Canadian Corps that he ordered all of the armies of the BEF to follow suit.

Most of the innovations that Byng introduced in the Canadian Corps and Third Army were devised originally by other officers. Nevertheless, throughout the war he demonstrated the ability to recognize and bring together new concepts that offered a potential solution to the tactical stalemate that prevailed on the Western Front. Rather than seeking to win the war at any cost, Byng's goal was to achieve victory while restricting casualties among his own troops. Even in the summer of 1918 he sought to limit losses in Third Army by confining the advance of his infantry to objectives within artillery range, and replacing tired units with fresh troops during battle. Given that this objective remained consistent from 1914 to 1918, it might be argued that his approach to war did not change throughout the conflict. In pursuing victory at the least possible cost, however, Byng proved more than willing to abandon his existing preconceptions and embrace new and occasionally radical ideas.

The Battle of Cambrai
Byng's Third Army initiated the Battle of Cambrai in late November 1917, in the aftermath of the Third Battle of Ypres. Surprising the enemy on the morning of 20 November, British forces broke into the Hindenburg Line south-west of Cambrai, advancing up to 5 miles on a 6-mile front in a single day. Subsequently, however, Third Army struggled to capitalize on its initial success as co-operation between infantry, armour and cavalry deteriorated in the face of stiff German resistance. On 27 November, Byng halted the offensive, having gouged a salient in the enemy line approximately 9 miles wide and 4 miles deep. Three days later, counter-attacking German forces recaptured much of this territory and in some areas forced the British to retire beyond their original positions. When the battle subsided in early December, German gains largely negated Byng's initial advances. Despite the limited duration of the Battle of Cambrai, it provides a valuable window of insight into Byng's strengths and limitations as a commander. While he proved adept at recognizing and integrating new tactics and technologies, Byng struggled to impose his will on the battle under the pressure of time constraints and an assertive commander-in-chief.

The innovative British plan of attack at Cambrai grew from a variety of roots. In late April 1917 Sir Douglas Haig had proposed to his French counterpart, Robert Nivelle, an Anglo-French assault on the Hindenburg Line in the area of Cambrai. This idea was soon overshadowed by planning for the Third Battle of Ypres, but it remained nascent when Byng's Third Army took over the British line opposite Cambrai in early July. The notion gained momentum over the next two months, as novel suggestions for attacking the formidable German defensive system emerged from different sources. In early August the commander of the British Tank Corps, Hugh Elles, and his chief of staff, J.F.C. Fuller, advocated a raid on enemy positions using tanks supported by aircraft. At about the same time, H.H. Tudor, a divisional artillery com-

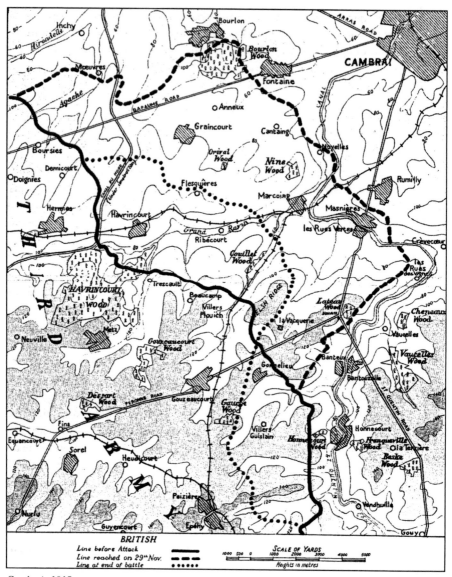

Cambrai, 1917.

mander in Third Army, proposed the use of tanks and the silent registration of artillery to secure surprise in a small-scale attack on the Hindenburg Line.[29]

These proposals found a receptive audience in Julian Byng. Open to the suggestions of subordinate officers by inclination, the Third Army commander was particularly interested in using surprise to break through enemy defences. Consequently, in late August he began to lobby GHQ for the resources to launch an attack at Cambrai based on these ideas. Initially, the novelty of Byng's scheme elicited scepticism. The commander of the Third Army artillery, for example, proved reluctant to abandon the preliminary registration of artillery. Byng encountered even more difficulty persuading Haig and his staff that his plan to achieve surprise would be successful.[30] Moreover, the British commitment to the ongoing Third Battle of Ypres precluded the allocation of considerable resources to a new offensive. After repeated visits to GHQ, however, Byng's persistence paid off. In mid-October, Sir Douglas Haig gave his approval to the plan to attack at Cambrai and ordered Third Army to make preliminary preparations for its initiation.

Byng's force had little time to prepare for the relatively complex operation that he had successfully sold to GHQ. It was 26 October before corps commanders and their staffs learned of Byng's initial plan of battle. Thus, while the Canadian Corps had nearly three months to prepare for its attack on Vimy Ridge, Third Army had less than four weeks to prepare for Cambrai. This period was far from sufficient, as the bulk of the infantry divisions and the three tank brigades assigned to Byng's command for the battle were absorbing new reinforcements in the aftermath of Third Ypres. Moreover, the attack involved close co-operation between infantry and armoured vehicles, a situation with which neither arm had significant experience. The combined training of tanks and infantry did not begin until early November. On the surface, this training resembled Byng's meticulous preparations for the attack on Vimy Ridge. Third Army constructed full-scale models of elements of the Hindenburg Line to familiarize units with the obstacles they would face. Significantly, however, each of the six infantry divisions participating in the attack was allowed only ten days to work with the tanks, leaving individual battalions with only two days of combined training apiece. This left little time for the tanks and infantry to develop co-ordinated tactics. In addition, it seems that Third Army provided little tactical guidance to subordinate formations. Consequently, individual corps, divisions and brigades involved in the attack took different approaches, with some advocating close co-operation between infantry and tanks, while others instructed infantry to follow the armoured vehicles at a distance.[31]

While Third Army hurriedly prepared for the attack, discussions between its commander and Sir Douglas Haig resulted in the expansion of British objectives at Cambrai. Byng had initially conceived of the attack as a diversion to be launched during the Third Battle of Ypres. Even after his decision to conclude the offensive at Ypres, however, Haig envisioned a separate and significant operation at Cambrai. This would maintain pressure on the German army on the Western Front, thereby aiding the Italian army, which was reeling after its recent defeat at Caporetto.[32] Thus, on 13 November, Byng issued a final three-stage plan that reflected Haig's intentions. Tanks and infantry would lead the attack, puncturing the Hindenburg Line, seizing bridges across the St Quentin Canal at Masnières and Marcoing, and capturing the Masnières–Beaurevoir line to the east. Within hours of the beginning of the offensive, the cavalry would initiate the second stage, advancing through the resulting gap in the German line, isolating Cambrai, crossing the Sensée River and capturing Bourlon Wood. Finally, Third Army would clear Cambrai and the area bounded by the St Quentin Canal, the Sensée River and the Canal du Nord. GHQ would then direct any subsequent exploitation of this break-through.

This plan placed high expectations on Byng's force during the opening hours of the offensive. Haig insisted that a full division of cavalry should be through the gap created between Masnières and Marcoing on the first day. He was also adamant that Bourlon Wood, which sat on a ridge on the left of Byng's front overlooking the surrounding territory, should be in British hands by the end of the day. Neither of these objectives was easily achievable. In order to break through between Masnières and Marcoing, the cavalry had to pass along narrow alleyways created by the tanks and infantry through the wire and entrenchments of the Hindenburg defensive system. The mounted troops then had to cross the St Quentin Canal over the few bridges left intact by the enemy.[33] Given that these obstacles would delay the cavalry, the capture of Bourlon Wood would require British infantry units to attack it after first fighting their way through the Hindenburg Line, a difficult task in itself. While Byng apparently expressed his doubts about the feasibility of these objectives, he ultimately submitted to the wishes of the commander-in-chief.[34]

Despite the haste in which the attack was planned, Third Army achieved unprecedented success on 20 November. The silent registration of artillery enabled Byng's force to surprise the enemy, while the tanks broke through German wire, cutting a path for the infantry. As a result, the Hindenburg Line was breached in little more than four hours. Nonetheless, Byng's force did not meet its objectives for 20 November. Not surprisingly, Third Army was unable to force a gap in the German defensive system between Masnières and Marcoing through which the cavalry could advance. This contributed to its failure to secure Bourlon Wood. Believing that these objectives were within his grasp, Byng ordered the attack to continue the following day. On the 21st, however, Third Army retained few tanks after committing the vast majority on the first day of the attack. This shortage, combined with declining co-operation between the remaining tanks and the infantry, sapped Third Army's momentum.

The attack at Cambrai was conceived as a rapid attempt to pierce German defences, rather than a prolonged slugging match. At the outset of the battle, Haig had emphasized to Byng that he would end the offensive if it had not achieved success within forty-eight hours. On the evening of the 21st, however, the commander-in-chief remained hopeful that Third Army could still capture Bourlon Wood. According to the official history, 'it was believed at GHQ on somewhat slender evidence, that the enemy was showing a disposition to retire, whilst the fresh troops he had already put into the battle were reckoned as no more than sufficient to replace his casualties'.[35] Thus, Haig ordered the continuation of attacks against Bourlon Wood on 22 November and subsequent days, despite the inability of Third Army to make substantial gains against increasing numbers of German reinforcements. As one staff officer recalled after the war: 'Douglas Haig was quite obstinate and determined that the battle should go on, when it should have been obvious that the failure to get a footing over the Marcoing [St Quentin] canal made the main objective unobtainable.'[36]

The pressure that the commander-in-chief exerted on Byng as a consequence is manifest in Haig's personal diary for late November 1917. Haig met Byng on 22 November and 'urged capturing Bourlon Wood *tomorrow*'. On the 24th, he instructed his chief of staff, Launcelot Kiggell, 'to inform Byng that he must devote all his strength and if necessary, the reserve divisions at his disposal to establishing our position on the Bourlon ridge, and retaking it if lost'. The next day, with the high ground at Bourlon Wood still in enemy hands, Haig directed Kiggell to telephone the Third Army commander and 'urge him to go *personally into the situation*'.[37] Haig's repeated prodding of his subordinate suggests that Byng did not share his undiminished enthusiasm for the Cambrai offensive after 21 November. It appears, however, that Byng made little attempt to question the orders of his superior, despite the mounting costs and diminishing returns of the offensive. In the words of one officer: 'Bungo was too loyal, if he disagreed, to say so.'[38]

While the continuation of the British offensive resulted largely from the persistence of Sir Douglas Haig, Third Army's significant losses in the face of the German counter-attacks of 30 November can be attributed to Byng's lack of preparation. Intelligence from GHQ in this period suggested that a strong enemy offensive was unlikely. Nonetheless, in the days preceding the attack, Byng's headquarters received information from air and ground observers as well as signals intelligence indicating heightened enemy activity opposite Third Army. On the evening of 28 November, Thomas Snow, commanding VII Corps, requested support in the event of a German attack. As Fuller commented after the war, however: 'Snow knew an attack was coming, but no one at Army Headquarters seemed to worry.'[39] Indeed, although Byng's chief of staff assured Snow that Third Army would provide him with reinforcements, in the words of the official history: 'The Third Army issued no warning order, ordered no movement of reserves, took no steps to ensure that troops in the rear areas should be readily available.'[40]

Thus, despite ample warning, the reserves available to Third Army were poorly positioned to meet the German offensive. Nor did Byng respond effectively once the enemy had attacked. Third Army ordered a counter-attack on the morning of 1 December, but did little to co-ordinate the formations involved. As a result, their efforts had little impact on the enemy. In addition, Byng's force incurred heavy casualties in an unsuccessful and perhaps unjustified attempt to hold its position over the St Quentin Canal. While Third

Army had fought hard for its foothold across the canal, there was little reason for retaining it in the face of heavy enemy attacks. Significantly, Byng clung to the position until 4 December, when GHQ directed that he withdraw the last of his forces to a line that he could hold over the winter.

The disappointing conclusion of the Battle of Cambrai provoked a search for the causes of Third Army's shortcomings. Its commander, however, emerged largely unscathed. Haig rightly accepted responsibility for the continuation of British attacks after 21 November. Byng himself attributed the fragility of Third Army, particularly in the face of German counter-attacks, to inadequately trained officers, NCOs and other ranks. In addition, although he did not publicly criticize the leadership of his senior subordinates, Byng replaced three of his corps commanders, Snow, E.P. Pulteney, and Charles Woollcombe, with younger officers. There were undoubtedly shortcomings in the conduct of the battle at all of these levels. Nonetheless, as Peter Simkins has observed: 'Since neither Byng nor his chief of staff, John Vaughan, were called as witnesses by the Cambrai court of enquiry in January, 1918, it is difficult to escape the impression that there was little intention to probe command problems at the very top.'[41] Indeed, it would appear that Byng's abilities, and perhaps even more so his loyalty to Haig, led the commander-in-chief to overlook any deficiencies in his command of Third Army during the Battle of Cambrai.

There is little to dislike about Julian Byng on a personal level. An unassuming, trustworthy and considerate individual, he gained numerous friends and admirers over the course of his career, both inside and outside the British Army. The aspersions of his relatively few rivals and detractors, such as Hubert Gough or Mackenzie King, are largely undermined by their own personal foibles. Byng's personality contributed significantly to his success as a commander in the First World War. His effective relationships with the vast majority of his colleagues in the upper ranks of the British officer corps facilitated his progression to the command of Third Army. His genuine concern for his subordinates encouraged him to observe personally the conditions under which they fought in order to devise less costly means of victory on the Western Front. His attention to detail enabled the planning and execution of operations based on these means, such as the Canadian assault on Vimy Ridge. Despite his meticulous nature, he was consistently open to new ideas advanced by subordinate officers. While hardly a tactical pioneer himself, he possessed the ability to recognize and integrate new and effective methods of breaking into enemy defences. At Vimy and Cambrai in particular, he oversaw the implementation of inventive tactics that produced significant gains. Thus, as Byng's own ideas about warfare evolved from 1914 to 1918, he also contributed to the evolution of the British army as a whole.

Byng's approach to command was not without its drawbacks. The flip side of his openness to the new ideas of subordinates was an aversion to imposing tactics on them from above. In March 1918 this contributed to the vulnerability of Third Army to German attacks. In addition, Byng's long-standing allegiance to Sir Douglas Haig hindered his implementation of potential solutions to the deadlock on the Western Front. At Cambrai, Haig effectively commandeered the British offensive with little resistance from Byng. Thus, the innovative tactics employed by Third Army were largely squandered in an overambitious and protracted operation. The difficulties of Third Army at Cambrai, however, cannot be laid solely at the feet of Haig. The battle also demonstrates that Byng's knack for recognizing effective new tactics and incorporating them into complex operations was not matched by his ability to exercise command under pressure. In November 1917 and again in March 1918, he struggled to cope with German attacks, although, in the former case, he had ample warning. Byng's limitations, however, were hardly unique. The inconsistency of defensive tactics within Third Army existed elsewhere in the British Army in 1918. Nor was Byng the only senior officer to be cowed by the commander-in-chief. On balance, his contributions as a manager of tactical innovations outweighed his shortcomings. While he was not a battlefield commander in the Napoleonic mould, Julian Byng made a significant contribution to the British army's ultimate victory on the Western Front.

Bibliography

Jeffrey Williams, *Byng of Vimy: General and Governor General* (London: Leo Cooper, 1983), the only biography of Byng, is a well-researched and engrossing account of his life and military career. Williams demonstrates the immense challenges faced by British generals on the Western Front, and explains clearly the innovations introduced by Byng, assailing the 'lions led by donkeys' stereotype well before similar 'revisionist' interpretations gained widespread credence. Although the book tends to skim over his shortcomings, it is still indispensable for an understanding of Byng as a commander and an individual. Paddy Griffith, *British Fighting Methods of the First World War* (London: Frank Cass, 1996) is an important collection of essays examining the development of tactics and the adaptation to new technology within the British Army from 1914 to 1918. While none of the essays evaluates Byng specifically, two in particular shed light on the Battle of Cambrai and the innovations the Third Army commander introduced in this period. J.P. Harris, 'The Rise of Armour', discusses the use of tanks at Cambrai, crediting Byng, rather than J.F.C. Fuller, with the original plan. Stephen Badsey, 'Cavalry and the Development of Breakthrough Doctrine', offers a more critical assessment of the planning for the battle and sheds light on the difficulties experienced by British cavalry. Wilfrid Miles, *Military Operations France and Belgium, 1917: The Battle of Cambrai* (London: HMSO, 1948), published after the deaths of both Haig and Byng, is the final volume of the official history of British operations on the Western Front in 1917. It takes a negative view of their conduct of the battle. Byng in particular is singled out for his misuse of the cavalry and his failure to prepare for the German counter-attacks of 30 November. These criticisms are expressed sharply and succinctly in a preface by Sir James Edmonds. Bill Rawling, *Surviving Trench Warfare: Technology and the Canadian Corps, 1914–1918* (Toronto: University of Toronto Press, 1992), a study of the Canadian Corps, based on archival research, provides a detailed account of tactical reforms implemented under Byng's command, particularly in the crucial period between the Somme and the Battle of Vimy Ridge. Robert Woollcombe, *The First Tank Battle: Cambrai, 1917* (London: Arthur Barker, 1967), written by the grandson of Charles Woollcombe, who commanded IV Corps at Cambrai, is the first archive-based account of the battle. The author is critical of Haig, Byng and the corps commanders of Third Army, with the exception, not surprisingly, of Woollcombe.

Notes

1 Jeffrey Williams, *Byng of Vimy: General and Governor-General* (London: Leo Cooper, 1983), p. 4.

2 Ibid., pp. 5–7.

3 Peter Simkins, 'Haig and the Army Commanders', in Brian Bond and Nigel Cave, eds, *Haig: A Reappraisal 70 Years On* (London: Leo Cooper, 1999), p. 92.

4 Williams, *Byng of Vimy*, p. 84.

5 Liddell Hart Centre for Military Archives (hereafter LHCMA), Allenby MSS, 6/7, A.W. Snow to Archibald Wavell, 29 April 1937.

6 Major General Sir Charles Harington, *Tim Harington Looks Back* (London: John Murray, 1940), p. 50.

7 Williams, *Byng of Vimy*, p. 84.

8 National Library of Scotland (hereafter NLS), Haig MSS, Haig to Lady Haig, 17 December 1917.

9 Williams, *Byng of Vimy*, ch. 15.

10 Williams, *Byng of Vimy*, pp. 44–5.

11 A. Rawlinson, *Adventures on the Western Front: August 1914 – June 1915* (London: Andrew Melrose, 1925), p. 201.

12 Williams, *Byng of Vimy*, p. 127.

13 Bill Rawling, *Surviving Trench Warfare: Technology and the Canadian Corps, 1914–1918* (Toronto: University of Toronto Press, 1992), pp. 87–113.

14 LHCMA, Liddell Hart MSS, 11/1932, 'Talk with Edmonds', 1 November 1932.

15 The National Archives (hereafter TNA), CAB 45/186, E.H. Beddington to Edmonds, 13 August 1934; LHCMA, Liddell Hart MSS, 11/1936/7, 'Talk with Duff Cooper', 18 January 1936; ibid., 11/1935/72, 'Talk with Sir Hubert Gough', 9 April 1935.

16 Harington, *Tim Harington Looks Back*, pp. 47–8.

17 Shane Schreiber, *Shock Army of the British Empire: the Canadian Corps in the Last Hundred Days of the Great War* (Westport: Praeger, 1997), p. 18.

18 TNA, CAB 45/186, Matheson to Edmonds, 21 October 1929.

19 Ibid., Laidler to Edmonds, 7 December 1925.

20 Ibid., CAB 45/118, Fuller to Edmonds, 19 March 1945.

21 NLS, Haig diary, 21 October 1914.

22 Nikolas Gardner, *Trial by Fire: Command and the British Expeditionary Force in 1914* (Westport CT: Praeger, 2003), p. 215.

23 Williams, *Byng of Vimy*, p. 84.

24 Simkins, 'Haig and the Army Commanders', p. 92.

25 Ibid.

26 Rawling, *Surviving Trench Warfare*, p. 107.

27 Williams, *Byng of Vimy*, p. 99.

28 Rawling, *Surviving Trench Warfare*, pp. 95–107.

29 Wilfrid Miles, *Military Operations France and Belgium, 1917: The Battle of Cambrai* (London: HMSO, 1948), pp. 4–7.

30 TNA, CAB 45/118, Basil Brooke to Edmonds, 15 May 1945.

31 Miles, *Military Operations*, pp. 33–5.

32 Robert Woollcombe, *The First Tank Battle: Cambrai, 1917* (London: Arthur Barker, 1967), p. 28.

33 Edmonds, 'Preface', in Miles, *Military Operations*, p. iv; Stephen Badsey, 'Cavalry and the Development of Breakthrough Doctrine', in Paddy Griffith, ed., *British Fighting Methods of the Great War* (London and Portland, OR: Frank Cass, 1996), p. 160.

34 Williams, *Byng of Vimy*, p. 182.

35 Miles, *Military Operations*, p. 115.

36 TNA, CAB 45/118, Gervase Thorpe to E.C. Gepp, 26 April 1945.

37 NLS, Haig diary, 22, 24 and 25 November 1917.

38 TNA, CAB 45/118, Thorpe to Gepp, 26 April 1945.

39 Ibid., Fuller to Edmonds, 14 February 1945. See also ibid., Aylmer Haldane to Edmonds, 14 December 1944.

40 Miles, *Military Operations*, p. 169.

41 Simkins, 'Haig and the Army Commanders', p. 92.

Chapter Four

Hubert Gough
Fifth Army, 1916–1918

Gary Sheffield and Helen McCartney

Hubert de la Poer Gough is among the most controversial of Haig's generals. Noted for his relative youth, Gough rose rapidly through the upper echelons of the British Expeditionary Force. A brigadier at the outbreak of war, just two years later Gough commanded an army. His command of Reserve Army (renamed Fifth Army in October 1916) during the attritional battles of 1916–17 polarized opinion among contemporaries and subsequent historians. The very characteristics on which he founded his success as a commander – energy, drive, ruthlessness – were those that led to deep unpopularity in some parts of the army. Gough's peppery personality – although he was also capable of considerable charm – was another factor in this. Gough also had his admirers, most notably Douglas Haig but also, oddly, Basil Liddell Hart. A balanced verdict was given by an experienced and respected staff officer, Charles Bonham-Carter, who believed that Gough had the potential to be a great commander but was let down by a poor staff, who failed to rein in his natural impatience.[1] Gough's downfall was even more precipitate than his rise. Scapegoated for the success of the German offensive in March 1918, he was dismissed from the command of Fifth Army.

Although Hubert was born in London, he was, as he proudly stated, 'Irish by blood and upbringing'. The Goughs were members of the Protestant ascendancy: Hubert recorded that 'all our relations were anti–Home Rulers'.[2] Hubert's father, General Sir Charles Gough, and his uncle, Sir Hugh Gough, both won the Victoria Cross, Britain's highest award for gallantry. Hubert's brother, Brigadier General 'Johnnie' Gough, was also to win the VC.

Hubert Gough had a conventional education for a Victorian army officer, attending Eton and, in 1888, the Royal Military College, Sandhurst. He was commissioned into the 16th Lancers in 1889; he served in India, and saw active service in the Tirah campaign of 1897. In 1898 he married Nora (known as 'Daisy'), with whom he had four daughters; he married at a somewhat earlier age than many of his peers. The following year Gough's career took a less traditional turn, when he attended the Staff College, Camberley. He did not

Chronology

12 August 1870	Hubert de la Poer Gough born in London
	Educated at Eton and the Royal Military College, Sandhurst
5 March 1889	Gazetted to 16th Lancers
22 December 1894	Promoted captain
1897–98	Served with Tirah Field Force
22 December 1898	Married Margaret Louisa Nora Lewes
9 January 1899	Started at Staff College, Camberley
25 October 1899	Ordered on special service to South Africa
1 February 1900	Appointed CO Composite Regiment of Mounted Infantry
17 September 1901	Captured by and escaped from Boers
July 1902	Appointed Brigade Major, 1st Cavalry Brigade
22 October 1902	Promoted major
23 October 1902	Promoted brevet lieutenant colonel
1 January 1904	Appointed instructor at Staff College, Camberley
11 June 1906	Promoted brevet colonel
18 July 1906	Promoted substantive lieutenant colonel
15 December 1907	Appointed CO 16th Lancers
19 December 1910	Promoted substantive colonel
1 January 1911	Appointed GOC 3rd Cavalry Brigade
20–30 March 1914	Curragh incident
16 September 1914	Appointed GOC 2nd Cavalry Division
26 October 1914	Promoted major general
18 April 1915	Appointed GOC 7th Division
13 July 1915	Appointed GOC I Corps and temporary lieutenant general
4 April 1916	Appointed GOC Reserve Corps
22 May 1916	Appointed GOC Reserve Army
7 July 1916	Promoted temporary general
30 October 1916	Reserve Army designated Fifth Army
1 January 1917	Promoted substantive lieutenant general
28 March 1918	Dismissed from command of Fifth Army
19 May 1919	Appointed head of Allied Military Mission to the Baltic
25 October 1919	Recalled from Baltic
March 1922	Stood unsuccessfully as Independent Liberal at Chertsey
26 October 1922	Retired in the honorary rank of general
June 1940	Appointed zone commander for Chelsea and Fulham Home Guard
August 1942	Retired from Home Guard on grounds of age
18 March 1963	Died in London

Appointed KCB 1916, GCMG 1919, KCVO 1917, GCB 1937

finish the course, departing for South Africa, where the Second Anglo–Boer War had broken out.

In the campaigns across the South African veldt, the mobility of horsed soldiers was a vital asset. Gough made his name as a leader of cavalry, leading the advanced party of the Ladysmith relief force into the town in February 1900. His reputation survived the fiasco at Blood River Poort in September 1901, when, as a brevet lieutenant colonel, attacking without sufficient reconnaissance, he came off very much the worse in an action that led to him and his force being captured by the Boers. After the war Gough served as an instructor at the Staff College (1904–6), where the commandant was Henry Rawlinson, who was to be Gough's fellow army commander in 1916, and one of the students was his brother, Johnnie, a Rifle Brigade officer. Hubert's career continued along the lines that showed he was a high-achieving officer, commanding his regiment, the 16th Lancers, from 1907 to 1910, and then taking command of the 3rd Cavalry Brigade, based at the Curragh, in Ireland. Fearing that the army would be used to coerce Protestant Ulster into accepting Home Rule, in March 1914 Gough and 57 officers of 3rd Cavalry Brigade threatened to resign their commissions rather than carry out such orders if issued. The Curragh incident was eventually defused but at the cost of dividing the army. Some friendships broke down irretrievably, including that of the Gough brothers with Henry Wilson.

Gough took his brigade to France in August 1914, and as early as 16 September he was given command of the newly formed 2nd Cavalry Division as a Major General. Gough did well during the First Battle of Ypres (October–November 1914). Much later, Gough was to reflect that if he had served his 'apprenticeship in India and during the Boer War', during First Ypres the 'Germans gave me my trade test'; however, Gough himself had to determine 'whether I had passed it or not'.[3] Clearly, Gough's superiors had no doubts about him having passed the test, as he was offered first a command in a British force intended for Salonika, which he declined, and then, in April 1915, he took over 7th Infantry Division, vice its wounded commander. Gough was Haig's protégé, but this is not enough to entirely explain his rapid rise, as he then became commander of I Corps in July 1915, some five months before Haig assumed command of the BEF.

Gough continued to enjoy Haig's patronage after the latter became C.-in-C. in December 1915. Haig appointed Gough as commander of the Reserve Corps, later renamed Reserve Army, for the Somme offensive in July 1916. Originally, Gough's command was a mobile formation intended to exploit initial success, but very early in the campaign it became an army along the conventional lines. Haig, having realized that the original Fourth Army front was too wide, handed control of operations north of the Bapaume Road to Gough. Although for most of the campaign Rawlinson's was the primary formation, Reserve Army carried out a series of important operations and was entrusted with the final phase of the Somme campaign, the Battle of the Ancre in November 1916.

Early in the new year, Fifth Army fought a series of minor actions on the Somme front, aimed, in Gough's words, at 'improving our position & hustling the Bosch',[4] and then was involved in following up the German retreat to the Hindenburg Line (March–April). In these operations, Gough generally did well. His role in the BEF's next major offensive, the fighting at Bullecourt in

April–May 1917 that formed part of the wider Arras offensive, did not win many plaudits. The Australians in particular, who already had painful experience of Gough's methods at Pozières in 1916, bitterly resented the way they had been handled. Gough's stock remained high with Douglas Haig, however. Fifth Army was chosen to spearhead the attack around Ypres on 31 July. Results were disappointing and Gough was demoted in September to a supporting role. Disquiet among subordinate commanders over the behaviour of the Fifth Army grew so vocal that even Haig came to hear of it.

Fifth Army bore the brunt of the German spring offensive in March 1918. Haig, faced with a long front to defend and a manpower crisis, had deliberately kept Gough's force weak in relation to the other armies of the BEF, correctly recognizing that he could most afford to give ground in this sector. Fifth Army fought reasonably well in the circumstances, and Gough's performance was generally creditable. However, Gough was sacked, made a scapegoat for problems that were not of his making and over which he had no control. 'Having had to bear the whole brunt of the storm with the few troops at my disposal', Gough wrote on the day that he heard of his dismissal, 'you can imagine my feelings at being removed from my command & handing it over to Rawly. I cannot as yet find out much as to the causes or persons responsible for removing me, but I have been told that it was "political" – & that it was due to a letter from Derby ordering it.'[5] Gough was correct. In spite of Haig's attempts to save Gough, the C.-in-C. on 4 April received a direct order in a telegram from Lord Derby, the Secretary of State for War. Hubert Gough 'became the army's sacrifice to appease the government's critics'.[6] Arguably, while he deserved dismissal for his handling of the Somme, Bullecourt and Third Ypres, Gough was sacked for the one major battle in which he commanded Fifth Army with some competence.

Gough was understandably bitter, referring shortly after the war to Haig's and GHQ's 'stupid obstinacy & pedantry' in delaying reinforcements to Fifth Army.[7] He was consigned to the military wilderness and never again held a major command. A public reconciliation with Haig took place in 1924, and Gough received official rehabilitation in 1937 when he was appointed GCB by King George VI. It is clear that the scars ran deep: in 1951 Gough was still parading his grievances, blaming 'Tavish' Davidson, Haig's director of military operations, and Herbert Lawrence, Haig's chief of staff, for their lack of influence over Haig's decision making, and asserting that:

> the gravest error I made, was not to ask for an interview with Haig, as soon as I saw the storm brewing ... I think our tactics should have been to hold the front line as thinly as possible, & bring back the rest of the army as secretly as possible behind the Somme, several days before the attack. But would Haig have agreed to abandon any ground?[8]

The parameters of the debate on Gough were set while the war was still in progress. The aspersions cast on Fifth Army's performance by Lloyd George in the House of Commons tended to focus attention on March 1918 rather than earlier battles. This tendency was reinforced by a vigorous defence of Gough and Fifth Army by W. Shaw Sparrow, who, according to Gough, was a 'fine old fighter, & much more interested in the 5th Army's fortunes & mine than I am myself!'[9] The British official historian, Sir James Edmonds, also reached generally favourable conclusions about Gough's generalship in 1918. However, his later volume on Third Ypres was less favourable to Gough. Historian Tim Travers has charted the progression of Edmonds's thinking, which became markedly less sympathetic to Gough during the prolonged gestation of the book.[10] Moreover, the official volume on the latter stages of the Somme also contains some guarded criticism of Gough.[11] Charles Bean subjected Gough's generalship to some forthright criticism in the volumes of the Australian official history.[12] Gough himself entered the lists with his book *The Fifth Army* (1931). He was reconciled with Lloyd George, and the latter's complimentary comments about Gough in his *War Memoirs* (1936), part of his campaign of denigrating Haig, also played a role in restoring the Fifth Army commander's reputation.[13]

One should not underestimate the importance of the passage of time in allowing passions to cool. By the late 1930s, the controversies of 1914–18 were, to many people, ancient history. During the Second World War, Gough behaved as an elder statesman, offering comments to the press on military events.[14] Paradoxically, Gough's reputation probably benefited from being scapegoated over March 1918. His battle for rehabilitation, and its eventual success, may have deflected attention away from the controversy over his generalship in 1916 and 1917.

During the resurgence of interest in the First World War that occurred from the late 1950s onwards, Gough was treated fairly mildly by iconoclasts such as Alan Clark and A.J.P. Taylor. That Gough lived until 1963, and was in a position to put forward his own views, may be of relevance. He published his memoirs, *Soldiering On*, in 1954 and was interviewed on television, using one occasion to attack his long-dead rival Henry Wilson. Gough also probably benefited from the fact that the fire of critics of British generals tended to be directed at Douglas Haig. Indeed, to extend Dan Todman's argument that Haig became a 'symbol rather than [an] individual', the British C.-in-C. subsumed the perceived follies of his subordinate commanders.[15] Anthony Farrar-Hockley, a serving soldier who himself went on to high command, wrote a sympathetic biography of Gough in the mid-1970s, placing much of the blame for Gough's unpopularity on his chief of staff, Major General Neill Malcolm.

In the late 1990s Gough was defended by Ian Beckett, who placed his conduct into the context of the evolution of the British army. Building on the work of Tim Travers, he argued that 'there was little real improvement in the understanding of command' in the BEF by 1918 and that, 'lacking a doctrine and common practice for command ... the British Army as a whole was ... its own worst enemy'.[16] However, more recent research has suggested that this concept of a command vacuum has been exaggerated and that the BEF experienced a 'learning curve', albeit not a consistent one, in this field as in those of tactics, logistics and the like. By 1918 the BEF was operating to a significant extent on the principles of devolved 'mission command'. Moreover, since, in spite of the undoubted problems experienced by the BEF, by 1918 a number of, in Haig's words, 'highly capable generals' had emerged. This suggests that Gough himself rather than the system was at fault. His poor performance during Third Ypres can mask the BEF's genuine tactical and operational improvements that began on the Somme and culminated in the 'Hundred Days' of 1918.

Certainly, other recent historians have been critical of aspects of Gough's performance. Lord Anglesey highlights Gough's 'insubordination' in deliberately separating his 3rd Cavalry Brigade from Allenby's Cavalry Division in August 1914.[17] Gary Sheffield's study of Gough's generalship on the Somme in 1916 concludes that the Reserve Army commander's 'military vices outweighed his virtues'.[18] Jonathan Walker likewise builds a case against Gough's performance at Bullecourt in May 1917.[19] Andrew Wiest, and Nigel Steel and Peter Hart, have levelled strong criticism at Gough over his handling of the Third Battle of Ypres.[20] Robin Prior and Trevor Wilson are rather more charitable about Gough's conduct of the attack on 31 July 1917 than has been the case with some other writers, but they balance this with criticism of his 'abysmal' subsequent operations.[21] In the early twenty-first century, Hubert Gough remains a deeply controversial figure among historians.

Gough's experience of command was shaped by a series of structural and personal challenges. In many respects, on taking command of Reserve Army in 1916, Gough's problems were similar to those of all commanders of large formations during the First World War. Few generals had anticipated the peculiar difficulties that would characterize this war. In 1914 evenly matched industrial powers applied their industrial muscle to warfare and created a stalemate on the Western Front. The siege warfare that resulted from powerful, mass-produced weaponry favoured the defender to such an extent that the stalemate took four long years to resolve.[22]

The BEF had undergone wholesale changes in the first years of the war to adapt to the new requirements of continental trench warfare. The pre-war force that had been trained to deal with policing duties in far-flung corners of the Empire expanded from seven to seventy-seven divisions in three years.[23] Army commanders were faced with commanding large, inexperienced formations in large-scale operations over long periods of time.[24] They also had to cope with poor communications between their formations, which hampered

1. Edmund Allenby photographed following the Battle of Megiddo in September 1918.
(IWM)

2. William Birdwood pictured at Grevillers while commanding the Anzac Corps, May 1917. *(IWM)*

3. Julian Byng *(left)* accompanying King George V *(centre)* and an unnamed battalion commander *(right)* through cheering Canadians at Reninghelst on 14 August 1916 while commanding the Canadian Corps. *(IWM)*

4. Hubert Gough as commander of 2nd Cavalry Division, 1914.   (IWM)

5. Charles Monro. (IWM)

6. Herbert Plumer *(left)* with Herbert Lawrence *(centre)* and Douglas Haig *(right)* on the steps of GHQ, 1918. *(IWM)*

7. Henry Horne *(right)* with King George V *(left)* and the commander of the Canadian Corps, Arthur Currie *(centre)*, during the King's visit to First Army. *(IWM)*

8. Henry Rawlinson on the steps of Fourth Army headquarters at Querrieu Chateau, July 1916.   *(IWM)*

9. Horace Smith-Dorrien.

effective and swift decision-making, the rapid evolution and introduction of technology and an overall re-evaluation of tactical thought.[25] The army commanders of 1916 were facing challenges that had never been considered by the British military in pre-war years. Indeed, even after two years of war, commanders, staff officers and the troops in the trenches all had much to learn about the new scale and type of warfare for which few, if any, had adequate experience or training.[26] The ways in which generals dealt with these new challenges and fashioned their style of command depended on a number of factors, including their previous experience of command, their relationship with others in the military hierarchy, their political acumen and their personalities. For Hubert Gough, each of these factors was to have a profound effect on his style and experience of the command of Fifth Army.

Hubert Gough's command philosophy can be seen, in part, as a reaction to the practical challenges of command and control he encountered in the early years of the war. Pre-war *Field Service Regulations*, largely crafted by Douglas Haig, had outlined the duty of the commander when issuing operational orders. They stated that:

> the object to be attained ... should be briefly but clearly stated; while the method of attaining the object should be left to the utmost extent possible to the recipient with due regard to his personal characteristics. Operation orders, especially in the case of large forces should not enter into details except when details are absolutely necessary. It is usually dangerous to prescribe to a subordinate at a distance anything that he should be better able to decide on the spot with a fuller knowledge of local conditions for any attempt to do so may cramp his initiative in dealing with unforeseen developments.[27]

Thus, the regulations *were* clear that it was a commander's responsibility to set objectives and shape a battle, without dictating to and inhibiting the plans of those carrying out his orders. However, as one of Gough's chiefs of staff highlighted, there was an inherent tension in this conception of command. According to Neill Malcolm, in June 1916 Gough and the staff of Reserve Army were grappling with the conundrum that 'Troops must be given a free hand and yet we must not lose control at all costs'. Malcolm believed that, on the Somme, Gough and his staff had been able to strike a happy medium between maintaining overall control of the direction of operations and allowing subordinate commanders to exercise their own initiative on the battlefield.[28] However, Malcolm's confidence was misplaced, and the happy medium proved virtually unattainable during Gough's tenure in command of Fifth Army.

On the one hand, Gough recognized the need for subordinates to have a free rein to exploit tactical opportunities as they arose. Throughout the war, Gough held the firm belief that success in battle was often time-sensitive, and afterwards he wrote to James Edmonds that he believed that too much time and too many opportunities had been lost because commanders had been too slow in preparing to meet new situations and lacked the necessary offensive spirit to capitalize on success.[29] He claimed that 'it is a great mistake to throw away the opportunity to seize points in the enemy's position if the chance offers', adding that many bitter lessons from Gallipoli, Loos and the Somme substantiated his view.[30] Gough's willingness to take risks, and his impatience with those commanders who did not use initial success to their advantage, is well documented.[31]

In contrast to Gough's views on the importance of initiative were his contradictory opinions on the necessity of a commander to provide his subordinates with strict guidelines, particularly in the planning phase of an operation. Indeed, Gough frequently complained that fellow army commanders and several of their own corps commanders did not provide enough direction to those below them.[32] It is with regard to the interventionist aspect of command that Gough appeared to depart from the principles laid down in the *Field Service Regulations*, providing his subordinates with far more detailed guidance on the 'method of attaining the object' than they had been led to expect.

One of the many challenges facing Gough in 1915–16 was the inexperience of many of his commanders. He simply did not trust all his commanders to lead troops effectively in battle. As a result, he felt the need to control the actions and decision making of his corps, divisional and even brigade commanders very closely. In a letter written in September 1916 he acknowledged, 'We have so many very incompetent Divisional Generals and Corps Commanders, and owing to their previous slackness and weakness, no one is accustomed to obey orders … It requires a considerable exercise of firmness to get one's orders carried out sometimes and one has to closely supervise the plans of everyone!'[33] And Gough meant literally 'everyone'. During the Battle of Loos in September 1915, as I Corps commander, Gough interfered with the plan of 9th (Scottish) Division to such an extent that the divisional commander, Major General G.H. Thesiger, 'disassociated himself' from it and made it clear that these orders were not his own, but Gough's.[34]

Major General Thesiger was not the only subordinate commander to interpret *Field Service Regulations* in a different manner from Gough. Other commanders also expected to have the freedom to execute their operations using their own judgement. Not only did this involve being free to choose the disposition of their units and headquarters, but also discussing the nature and implications of the orders themselves. For example, Philip Howell, chief of staff of II Corps, was described by Gough as a 'great thorn' because he spent his time, in Gough's jaundiced view, 'trying to argue', avoiding fighting and disloyally disobeying orders.[35]

Some historians have interpreted Gough's constant interference in the affairs of lower formations as a product of his own inexperience as a commander.[36] His rapid promotion from a brigade commander at the outbreak of war to an army commander by 1916 required Gough to make significant adjustments to his method of command. The hands-on approach of a brigade commander who knows his forces intimately was not practical or advisable for an army commander, who was responsible for much larger and more complex formations which required him to take a broader view of the battle. Gough's reputation for touring trenches to spot dirty rifles and his tendency towards micro-management of decision making suggests that he found the transition to higher command and the adoption of an appropriate command style difficult.[37]

Gough's propensity to exercise detailed control over the planning process may also have been driven by the knowledge that during an attack he would have little opportunity to direct events.[38] It was as commander of I Corps in 1915 that he experienced first-hand the difficulties faced by a senior commander when attempting to communicate with troops on the battlefield.[39] Telephone communications between brigade, division, corps and army were notoriously unreliable, and even at the end of the war wireless communications were still in their infancy, leaving army commanders with little option but to trust the judgement of their subordinates closer to the front.[40]

Not only did Gough interfere in the affairs of his subordinates and require constant detailed explanation of events, he also had a reputation for sacking commanders he considered inefficient, disloyal and negative.[41] He himself acknowledged that there were some in the British army who 'seem to have hated coming into Fifth Army', although he claimed that these constituted a minority of men who were lacking boldness, resolution and energy.[42] While Ian Beckett and Andy Simpson have highlighted that there were many commanders who challenged Gough throughout the war and survived, Gough had still created a command culture based on fear and uncertainty.[43] As Neill Malcolm feared in November 1916, in this kind of atmosphere subordinates were often unwilling to express their own opinions for fear of appearing 'disloyal' and losing their positions.[44]

It has been suggested that Malcolm himself was at least part of the problem, if not the source of the dissatisfaction in Fifth Army as a result of his critical, often tyrannical control of subordinates.[45] In 1936 Gough supported this interpretation in a conversation with Liddell Hart, but during the war Gough appeared to appreciate Malcolm's support.[46] He even suggested in his post-war memoirs that he was to blame for poor communication with lower formations as he took his chief of staff with him on tours of corps and divisional commands which prevented subordinates speaking freely and discussing important difficulties with Malcolm.[47] Thus, while Malcolm may have been disliked by some in Fifth Army and may have failed to rein in some of the unreasonable demands made by his commander,[48] most negative comments were directed at Gough. Indeed, Gough's harsh control of subordinates began before Malcolm became his chief of staff, and continued after he had been moved on.[49]

Gough's tendency to undermine, bypass and even remove subordinate commanders whom he did not wholly trust was a trait that he maintained to the end of his command, but by 1917 he had gathered around him more experienced subordinates. Certainly Gough rated highly his corps commanders at this time, later writing that Ivor Maxse (XVIII Corps) was 'energetic and resourceful', Claud Jacob (II Corps) always gave 'energetic and wholehearted support' to Fifth Army, and Walter Congreve (XIII Corps) had few equals among generals in the British Army.[50] Andy Simpson has suggested that long association and greater experience may explain Gough's willingness to introduce a more genuinely consultative approach to his command for the Third Battle of Ypres, engaging in discussion and seeking advice from corps commanders.[51] However, Gough was still selective in the advice he solicited and there were those who remembered that the 'climate of fear' which had prevented frank discussion between Gough and some of his commanders on the Somme still pervaded the formation in 1917 and 1918. Simon Robbins has built a convincing case to show that, notwithstanding some supportive corps commanders, Gough and his staff were feared and disliked by subordinates throughout his career in charge of Fifth Army.[52] Gough may have wanted in theory to cultivate initiative within his command, but he was not appreciative of challenge and discussion in practice.

While Gough's abrasive personality and his bullying command style may have been at the root of his unpopularity within Fifth Army, professional jealousy and political allegiance also played a part in complicating his command.[53] His rapid rise to become the youngest army commander on the Western Front in 1916 made his contemporaries envious of his good fortune, but, more importantly, the legacy of the Curragh affair meant that a number of his contemporaries counted him as an enemy.[54] Philip Howell's negative comments on Gough's generalship need to be viewed in this context. Although there were serious disagreements over Gough's interference in II Corps during the Somme, part of the antagonism stemmed from the fact that they had been politically opposed over the Curragh.[55] Similarly, relations with Henry Wilson, who commanded IV Corps in 1916, were strained and adversarial.[56] Wilson was to prove one of Gough's most damaging enemies. A consummate politician, Wilson surpassed Gough in terms of rapid promotion, becoming chief of the Imperial General Staff in February 1918, and certainly used his influence to criticize the command of Fifth Army and helped to hasten Gough's demise.[57]

Gough's relationship with General Headquarters was often little better than with those below him in the military hierarchy. In spite of his good relationship with Douglas Haig, his relations with many of Haig's staff and even Haig himself on occasion were difficult, not least because Haig and GHQ were facing similar command difficulties to Gough's own. Haig found it difficult to gauge when to intervene in a subordinate's planning and when to leave him to solve a problem alone. Throughout the war, Haig vacillated between providing Gough with contradictory advice, when advice was not necessary, and refraining from intervention when strong direction was imperative.[58] Haig's shortcomings as a commander were exacerbated by Gough's propensity to ignore orders from above. Ironically, those independent traits that Gough abhorred in his subordinates he embodied in practice.[59] His inability to take direction, and his wholehearted and often unjustified confidence in his own planning, led him to overestimate his army's abilities and contributed to his disastrous operations at Bullecourt and Third Ypres.[60]

Given Gough's adversarial style of command, and some of the difficult relationships between Gough and both his superiors and subordinates, it is unsurprising that he found it difficult to draw important lessons from his military experience. Indeed, in Simon Robbins's estimation, unlike generals Plumer and Allenby, Gough 'does not seem to have learned' anything from his experiences in 1915 and 1916. While this interpretation is a little harsh, the operations Gough's formations mounted between 1915 and 1917, on the whole, followed similar patterns and faced similar problems, despite the overall improvement in technology and low-level tactics that had been steadily achieved within the British army by 1917.[61]

Gough had been initially chosen by Douglas Haig to lead his exploitation force on the Somme because of his decisiveness, his optimism and his ambitious attitude to push forward and exploit opportunity.[62] However, it was precisely these traits that hampered Gough's success as the war progressed. The objectives for his offensives were too ambitious, and he often pushed his subordinates to attack before their preparations were complete, and to exploit enemy weakness when his formations were too exhausted to perform adequately. He was also overconfident in that he felt able to ignore the advice of his superior commander. These were problems that were not tempered by Gough's experience of command.

Gough's unrealistic aims and objectives were all too often evident in his conduct of operations on the Somme in 1916. In his eagerness to push forward, Gough forced subordinate commanders to attack before they were ready with little allowance made for preparation time. Gough was to repeat this behaviour in February 1917 during his pursuit of the Germany army to the Hindenburg Line, and in April 1917 at Bullecourt, where the infantry plan was severely disrupted at a late stage by Gough's ill-fated employment of tanks.[63]

The lessons Gough took from the Somme and applied in later battles were laid out in his October 1916 memorandum written for the guidance of divisional and infantry brigade commanders (issued over the heads of the corps commanders). The memorandum encapsulated Gough's views that attacking troops should seek to advance as far as possible through enemy defences, attacking up to five separate objectives, if this proved feasible, to gain maximum enemy territory. He did not appear to be aware that at this point in the war it was unreasonable to ask tired and relatively inexperienced troops to attempt five consecutive attacks.[64]

Gough's approach diverged significantly from other tacticians in the British army, who had taken different lessons from their wartime experience. Commanders such as Rawlinson and Plumer were developing a methodical approach to operations, known as bite and hold, in which a series of limited objectives were taken with the aid of comprehensive artillery support.[65] However, Gough's optimistic breakthrough methods were precisely why Haig chose Fifth Army to spearhead the main attack around Ypres on 31 July 1917 as it was Gough's views that accorded most closely with those of Haig himself.[66]

As in previous operations, Gough's command style influenced the planning and execution of the Third Battle of Ypres. Convinced that his approach to assaulting the German positions was correct, he ignored advice from Haig and the director of military operations, Davidson, that he should take the high ground on his right flank near the Gheluvelt Plateau first, or that he should consider a form of 'bite and hold' in order to deal with the new type of defence in depth the enemy had instituted in their positions around Ypres.[67] Gough failed to understand that pressing his advance as far as possible in the initial attack would leave his infantry out of range of their own artillery, vulnerable to counter-attack by the enemy and unable to hold their gains. Following Gough's failure, Fifth Army was relegated to a supporting role and Plumer's army took centre stage.

That Gough still did not understand the principles of defence in depth is evident in his handling of Fifth Army during the German spring offensive in March 1918, although he was not alone in his misunderstanding and, given the lack of fortifications on his front, nor would they have been easy to apply.[68] His army retreated over 40 miles and communication between the component formations broke down, but despite little direction from GHQ, few reserves and little support from the French, Gough managed to avert complete disaster, and the enemy did not effect a complete breakthrough.[69] His reward was the sack.

The Ancre, November 1916

The first months of Reserve Army's operations on the Somme illustrated Hubert Gough's command style.[70] He was a practitioner of 'top down' rather than mission command, issuing prescriptive orders using corps, in Andy Simpson's words, as 'postboxes' for relaying orders. By contrast, Rawlinson's Fourth Army devolved authority and responsibility to corps in planning and executing operations. Gough amply lived up to his reputation as an interventionist commander who did not hesitate to give direct orders to subordinates, even missing out intervening levels of command, and as a thruster, impatient for success. He was a hard taskmaster. Demands directed to subordinate

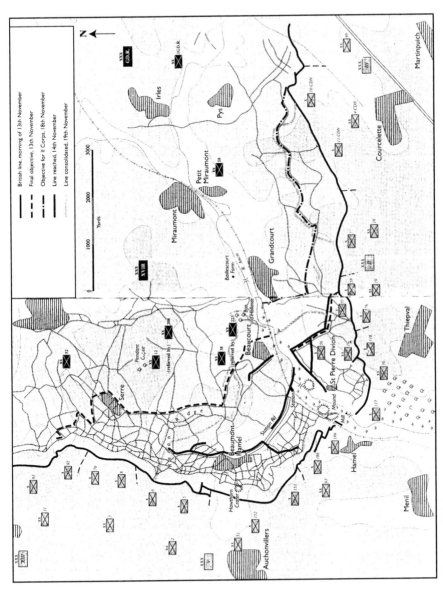

The Ancre, 1916.

commanders for 'An explanation in writing' of why something did or not happen was part of his arsenal.[71] Archie Wavell's comment that battles on the Western Front were too often treated as 'Open Warfare at the Halt' rather than siege operations certainly applied to Gough on the Somme.[72]

The Battle of the Ancre in November 1916 was perhaps Gough's finest hour as an offensive general. It resulted in the capture of Beaumont Hamel and Beaucourt, and ensured that the Somme offensive ended with a victory, albeit a limited one that took ground that was supposed to have fallen on 1 July. Haig and GHQ took a particularly close interest in this attack, for several reasons. Whereas Fourth Army's operations had generally taken precedence earlier in the battle, on this occasion Gough's attack was the BEF's 'main effort'. The offensive had wider ramifications in a European context, to pin down German troops that might otherwise have been sent to the campaign in Rumania, to influence Russian opinion on the efforts of their Anglo–French Entente partners, and to demonstrate to the Germans that the BEF had every intention of continuing to bring pressure on the Somme front. Even more importantly, it represented the last chance for the BEF to achieve a substantial success before Haig went to the inter-allied conference at Chantilly, and Gough's success strengthened Haig's hand. Moreover, as Gough later noted, by November 1916 the first 'murmurs' against Haig were beginning to be heard. Indeed, Gough himself was later to be mentioned as a possible successor to Haig, although on hearing this rumour Brigadier General Home of the Cavalry Corps remarked in his diary that it was 'too comic as I don't think they could ever make him do what they wanted'.[73] It is small wonder that Haig wrote in his diary at the end of the first day of the battle, 'The success has come at a most opportune moment'.[74]

Fifth Army's success was due to a number of factors. Throughout the battle, army and corps had been drawing and disseminating lessons,[75] and many were applied on the Ancre.[76] An attack in this sector had several logistic advantages; the planning and staff work were generally sound; and the assaulting divisions were supported by a respectable weight of artillery, far superior to that employed on 1 July. The operation also benefited from being planned and prepared over a period of weeks, rather than being a hasty attack. The original, ambitious plans devised by GHQ in October had to be reduced in scope as a consequence of bad weather, which turned the battlefield to a muddy morass. The assault had to be postponed on several occasions and the weather was so poor that the entire enterprise remained in doubt almost to the last minute. Haig on 2 November told Gough 'to have patience, and not to launch the main attack until the weather was better and the ground dry. It was better to wait than to start a series of small operations which would not have the same decisive results'.[77] On 6 November, Haig repeated his instruction that the attack should not begin until the ground was sufficiently dry 'for the infantry to advance freely', and when there was the likelihood of two days of 'fair weather'.[78]

There were frequent contacts between GHQ and HQ Fifth Army, and between Gough and his corps commanders, in the preparatory period. Haig dispatched Launcelot Kiggell, his chief of staff, to Fifth Army HQ on 8 November to explain the political background of the attack, although, as a memorandum by Malcolm stressed, Haig did not 'desire to press Sir H. GOUGH into an action where the prospect of success was not sufficiently good to justify the risk'. Gough then consulted with his corps commanders, Jacob (II), Fanshawe (V) and Congreve (XIII), on 10 November, and the attack was settled for the 13th 'unless there was more heavy rain'. According to Malcolm, at the meeting, held at 10 am at Senlis, Fanshawe and Congreve argued to extend the range of the attack, pushing for deeper objectives. 'General JACOB, whose task was lighter, was ready to conform with either decision.' The final decision was to go for deeper objectives.[79]

Still the question of the state of the ground and the weather placed a question mark over the attack. 'Staff officers and patrols' went out every day to check on the ground, and it is clear that there was no consensus among senior commanders. However, Gough decided, on the morning of 11 November, to attack on 13 November as planned. He then consulted several divisional and brigade commanders, to find that there was '[s]till some difference of opinion'; however, 'the ground [was] undoubtedly improving fast'. That afternoon, Fanshawe of V Corps visited army HQ and the time of the attack was debated; the question was whether a night or dawn attack was preferable, given the 'state of the moon'. Eventually, after further consultation with Jacob and the divisional commanders, the decision was made to attack at 5.45 am.[80]

On 12 November, the day before the attack, Kiggell was sent by Haig to ascertain Gough's opinion of the prospects for success. Gough weighed up the impact on the morale of the troops of a further delay, and concluded that:

> the time had come when we must either attack on Monday or make up our minds to withdraw and rest the bulk of the troops. Further postponement would have a very bad effect, and should not be considered. There had been no rain for four days – although there has been heavy fog – and similar conditions are likely to maintain throughout tomorrow. We can hardly hope for anything more favourable during the winter months.[81]

Two decades later, Gough recalled the loneliness of the commander having to make a weighty decision:

> It seemed to me that the responsibility placed on my shoulders was a very heavy one. I can remember our sitting at a small deal table in my poorly furnished room that I used as a bed-sitting room ... in a

farm[,] ... and as Kiggell gravely elaborated the great issues at stake, and my mind turned over the tactical situation of my troops and that of the enemy, I gazed out of the poky little window looking on the dull and dirty courtyard, and considered what my decision should be.[82]

He eventually consulted with subordinate commanders before reporting to Haig. The C.-in-C. visited Gough's HQ at 4 pm that afternoon, and ordered the attack to go ahead on 13 November, if weather conditions remained favourable.

It is interesting that, in spite of the political capital riding on a successful attack, Haig was insistent that it should not go ahead unless it was likely to be successful, and he paid close attention to the preparations. It was by no means certain that the battle would be launched until Haig took the decision on the afternoon of 12 November. It is probable that Haig regarded a failed battle as worse than no battle at all, that while a successful attack would strengthen his hand at the forthcoming conference, another failure would weaken it. This interpretation differs from Robin Prior's and Trevor Wilson's recent argument that Gough read between the lines of Haig's instructions that the C.-in-C. was so desperate for a success – any success – in reality he had no alternative to attack unless the weather made it absolutely impossible.[83] While Haig was undoubtedly an optimist, he also had a strong streak of pragmatism in his make-up. While the capture of Beaumont Hamel – a 1 July objective – was 'nice to have', it was essential to avoid a highly visible failure. Moreover, since at least mid-October Haig had been aware (from Major General F.I. Maxse, who had heard from his brother Leo, editor of the *National Review*) that there was a plot, centred on F.E. Smith, the Attorney General, to sack him from his post as C.-in-C.[84] Significantly, in his diary for 12 November, while Haig noted 'I am ready to run reasonable risks', he also stated, 'the necessity for a success must not blind our eyes to the difficulties of ground and weather. Nothing is as costly as failure!'[85]

This episode also throws some interesting light on command relations. Haig's relationship with Gough seems to have been rather closer than his dealings with the other army commander on the Somme, Rawlinson. However, the degree of supervision of the preparations for this attack suggests that Haig was not blind to his protégé's faults. As for Gough's relations with commanders further down the chain of command, in the words of the official historian, he 'consulted his subordinate commanders freely'.[86] The extent to which corps, divisional and brigade commanders actually felt able to speak their minds is, of course, another matter. Simon Robbins, citing the evidence of post-war letters by G.D. Jeffreys (commander of 57 Brigade, 19th Division, II Corps) and G.M. Lindsay (brigade major, 99 Brigade, 2nd Division, V Corps) to Edmonds, argues that Gough launched the battle over 'the protests of various Corps and divisional commanders and staff who pointed out the appalling conditions and the exhaustion and disorganisation of his troops'. Haig decided in favour of the attack because Gough was 'so keen and confident'.[87]

Gough was only partially satisfied with the results of the attack. A good deal of ground was taken in some sectors, Beaucourt and Beaumont Hamel falling to the 63rd (Royal Naval) and 51st (Highland) Divisions respectively. Edward 'Moses' Beddington, Gough's GSO2, took an officer of the 63rd Division to dinner with Gough, who listened to his account and paid the division a handsome compliment.[88] However, at Serre in the north there was little success. As befitted a 'hands-on', interventionist commander, on hearing of problems in this sector at 2 pm on 13 November, Gough intervened, going 'at once' to the V Corps to order fresh attacks to support 31st Division in the Serre area. By early evening, Gough had decided in the light of further evidence to switch V Corps's effort to seize 'the Yellow Line from Beaucourt to the ridge North of Beaumont Hamel'.[89] Encouraged on the morning of the following day by optimistic reports from Fanshawe at V Corps, Gough approved a scheme to take Munich and Frankfort trenches as a preliminary to attacking Serre.[90] This initiated a vicious localized struggle.

As Peter Simkins has commented, all too often on the Somme 'the set-piece phase' of an assault resulted in culmination, and 'subsequent attacks became piecemeal, hastily-organized affairs which lacked both weight and co-ordination'.[91] This was certainly true of V Corps's operations on the Ancre after 13 November. While there were compelling tactical reasons to seize the remainder of the high ground on V Corps front after the partial success of the first day of the attack, this was always going to be an operation fraught with difficulties. The very factors that had led to much success on 13 November – careful preparation and a heavy artillery bombardment – were largely absent in succeeding days. In Paris on 14 November, Haig was informed of Gough's far-reaching plans and was not at all happy, telephoning GHQ 'to the effect that the Commander-in-Chief did not wish the Fifth Army to undertake any further operations on a large scale until after his return from PARIS'. Haig was, no doubt, worried that a setback would negate, or at least reduce the impact of, the success of 13 November. Gough did not hear of Haig's views until 9 am on 15 November, at the exact time that two divisions of V Corps (2nd and 51st) were crossing the start line. Again, Gough conferred with his corps commanders and obtained consensus that the attack should go ahead. Following consultation with Kiggell, Haig that afternoon retrospectively approved the offensive. At 9 am on 16 November, Gough again met Jacob and Fanshawe. His optimism had declined, and a more limited assault was substituted for the ambitious plan to capture ground as a staging post for an attack on Serre.[92]

The post-13 November operations of Fifth Army indicate that Gough repeated many elements of his earlier command style. He was optimistic and aggressive, to the extent that even Haig became concerned about the ambition of Fifth Army operations. However, Haig remained generally indulgent of his protégé. Fifth Army's attacks bore a distinct resemblance to the narrow-front, penny-pocketed attacks around Pozières and elsewhere in the summer, with the added complication of appalling weather. Moreover, there is clear evidence of Gough's use of what the modern British forces call a 'long screwdriver' to interfere with the actions of subordinate formations.

Gough's frequent intervention in the command of 32nd Division in the fighting for Frankfort Trench from 18 November onwards has been noted by several historians.[93] According to Lieutenant Colonel E.G. Wace, the division's GSO1, Gough's decisions on even minor matters were relayed to Major General W.H. Rycroft, the divisional commander 'who was terrified of Gough', via corps. Gough complained to Haig of Rycroft; it seems that the C.-in-C. also had little time for him, and had already earmarked a successor, and Rycroft was sacked.[94] It should be noted that Wace was also removed shortly after the battle, which probably coloured his views passed on to Edmonds in the 1930s, but clearly there is a good deal of substance to his charges.

Less familiar is Gough's treatment of the commander of V Corps, Lieutenant General E.A. Fanshawe. Fifth Army on 16 November demanded a report from V Corps on recent operations, which was forwarded on 21 November.[95] Some of Gough's comments on Fanshawe's report, issued over Malcolm's signature, fairly scorch the page:

> V Corps Order G.267 of 15th November. This order puts too much on to the divisional commanders and does not exercise sufficient control over the operation. The want of strict Corps control is evident in several respects, e.g.
> a) No mention is made of the capture of MUNICH TRENCH ...
> b) The orders to the artillery are not clear. It appears from divisional orders that the barrage was to be on MUNICH TRENCH until Zero + 6, when the infantry was to take the trench. No mention of this is made in Corps orders. Were there no Corps Artillery orders beyond those in the telegram G.267?

In the copy in V Corps War Diary, there are some marginal notes, presumably by Fanshawe. Against these criticisms he noted, in obvious frustration:

> They do not understand that I am at the end of a telephone in touch with both Divisions and Brigade, who arranged for the MUNICH TRENCH in combination with me, but my order went in before. To arrange the time of [artillery] lift i.e. zero + 6 off MUNICH TRENCH took a long time, but was not put in the order.

To the question of whether further artillery orders were issued by V Corps, Fanshawe scribbled 'No. None were considered necessary. The CRAs worked together'.[96]

There is much more of this sort of thing, of Gough posing questions that Fanshawe was compelled to answer. Some of Gough's points were fair, if harshly expressed, but others were not; some were based on factual inaccuracies. All this suggests a commander who had an incomplete grasp of the realities of the battle. They also offer supporting evidence for the idea that Gough developed a climate of fear among his subordinates, perhaps even employing a policy of divide and rule. This is the obvious interpretation of Gough's deliberate humiliation of Fanshawe in front of the latter's subordinates, an event that could only have undermined the corps commander's authority. Against the information that copies of Gough's remarks had been sent to Fanshawe's subordinates, the commanders of 2nd and 51st Divisions, the V Corps commander scrawled a heartfelt 'I hope not all of them'. Unlike Rycroft, however, Fanshawe retained his post.

The fighting on the Ancre witnessed a clash of command philosophies: Gough desired to exercise direct control over subordinate formations, while they preferred to be given great latitude to plan and execute operations. On 16 November, that is when the battle was still in progress, Gough's frustration was displayed in a 'confidential memorandum' issued by Malcolm to the corps. This stated that 'In certain Corps there is a marked tendency to disregard, or to dispute the advisability of, order [sic] issued from Army Headquarters, and to consult their own convenience rather than the good of the Army as a whole.' Gough acknowledged that command was a collaborative activity and subordinates might be right to raise objections to orders, but he added, 'The justification or condemnation of such objections lies entirely in the spirit in which they are made'.[97] This hints at the extent to which relationships had broken down between corps and army.

Hubert Gough was a distinctly 'hands-on' commander. Abrasive of personality, a 'thruster', he was not a success in the period of trench warfare. Some believe that he might have thrived in the conditions of mobile warfare that pertained during the Hundred Days of 1918, but by that time he had been dismissed from command. Douglas Haig's choice of subordinates was by no means as bad as some would claim. However, in the case of Hubert Gough, Haig promoted and sustained a man beyond his level of competence.

Bibliography

Having enjoyed the greatest longevity of all Haig's army commanders, Gough produced two volumes of memoir. General Sir Hubert Gough, *The Fifth Army* (London: Hodder and Stoughton, 1931), was his defence of his record in the First World War, ghosted by the novelist Bernard Newman. Gough also extracted the chapters on 1918 from *The Fifth Army* and published them separately as *The March Retreat*

(London: Cassell, 1934). *Soldiering On* (London: Barker, 1954), Gough's more general memoir, covering his entire life, was written after his rehabilitation. The book is rather more relaxed in mood than *The Fifth Army*. Anthony Farrar-Hockley, *Goughie: The Life of General Sir Hubert Gough* (London: Hart-Davis, MacGibbon, 1975), is a popular biography that contains some useful insights and information. However, it is showing its age. Farrar-Hockley also contributed an essay, 'Sir Hubert Gough and the German Breakthrough, 1918', in Brian Bond, ed., *Fallen Stars* (London: Brassey's, 1991), pp. 65–83. Ian F.W. Beckett, 'Hubert Gough, Neill Malcolm and Command on the Western Front', in Brian Bond, ed., *'Look to Your Front': Studies in the First World War* (Staplehurst: Spellmount, 1999), pp. 1–12, is a cautiously favourable portrait of Gough. By contrast, Gary Sheffield, 'An Army Commander on the Somme: Hubert Gough', in Gary Sheffield and Dan Todman, eds, *Command and Control on the Western Front: The British Army's Experience, 1914–18* (Staplehurst: Spellmount, 2004), pp. 71–96, presents the case for the prosecution. Specific aspects of Gough's command are examined in Jonathan Walker, *The Blood Tub: General Gough and the Battle of Bullecourt, 1917* (Staplehurst: Spellmount, 1998), and Andrew Wiest, 'Haig, Gough and Passchendaele', in G.D. Sheffield, ed., *Leadership and Command: The Anglo-American Military Experience since 1861* (London: Brassey's, 1997), pp. 77–92. Gough's role at the Curragh is highlighted in Ian F.W. Beckett, *The Army and the Curragh Incident, 1914* (London: Bodley Head for Army Records Society, 1986), and in the same author's biography of Gough's brother, *Johnnie Gough VC* (London: Tom Donovan, 1989).

Notes

1 Gary Sheffield, 'An Army Commander on the Somme: Hubert Gough', in G. Sheffield and D. Todman, eds, *Command and Control on the Western Front: The British Army's Experience, 1914–18* (Staplehurst: Spellmount, 2004) pp. 70–72.

2 Hubert Gough, *Soldiering On* (London: Barker, 1954), pp. 15, 23. Details of Gough's life are drawn from this source, from Anthony Farrar-Hockley, *Goughie* (London: Hart-Davis, MacGibbon, 1975), and Brian Bond, 'Gough, Sir Hubert de la Poer', *Oxford Dictionary of National Biography* (Oxford: Oxford University Press, 2004).

3 Farrar-Hockley, *Goughie*, p. 147.

4 Windsor, Royal Archives (hereafter RA), RA/PS/GV/Q832/294, Gough to Wigram, 7 January 1917.

5 RA, RAS/PS/GV/Q 832/302, Gough to Wigram, 4 April 1918.

6 David French, *The Strategy of the Lloyd George Coalition, 1916–1918* (Oxford: Clarendon, 1995), p. 233.

7 Liddell Hart Centre for Military Archives (hereafter LHCMA), Edmonds MSS, II/1/45a, Gough to Edmonds, 22 May 1923.

8 Ibid., II/2/413, Gough to Edmonds, 5 March 1951.

9 Ibid., II/1/45a, Gough to Edmonds, 22 May 1923. See W. Shaw Sparrow, *The Fifth Army in March 1918* (London: John Lane, Bodley Head, 1921).

10 Tim Travers, *The Killing Ground* (London: Unwin-Hyman, 1987), pp. 203–19.

11 W. Miles, *Military Operations: France and Belgium, 1916* (London: Macmillan, 1932), vol. 2, p. 442.

12 See, for example, C.E.W. Bean, *The A.I.F. in France* (1929), vol. 3, pp. 876–77; vol. 4 (1933), pp. 350–51 (new edn, St Lucia: University of Queensland Press, 1982).

13 See David Lloyd George, *War Memoirs*, abridged edn (London: Odhams, 1938), vol. 2, pp. 1741, 2019.

14 Imperial War Museum (hereafter IWM), 69/21/3, Dawnay MSS, Dawnay to Gough, 1 August 1944.

15 Dan Todman, 'The Grand Lamasery Revisited', in Sheffield and Todman, *Command and Control*, p. 40.

16 Ian F.W. Beckett, 'Hubert Gough, Neill Malcolm and Command on the Western Front', in Brian Bond, ed., *'Look to Your Front': Studies in the First World War* (Staplehurst: Spellmount, 1999), p. 10.

17 The Marquis of Anglesey, *A History of the British Cavalry, 1816–1919* (London: Leo Cooper, 1996), vol. 7, pp. 134–5.

18 Sheffield, 'Army Commander', p. 91.

19 Jonathan Walker, *The Blood Tub: General Gough and the Battle of Bullecourt, 1917* (Staplehurst: Spellmount, 1998).

20 Andrew Wiest, 'Haig, Gough and Passchendaele', in G.D. Sheffield, ed., *Leadership and Command: The Anglo-American Military Experience since 1861* (London: Brassey's, 1997), pp. 77–92; Nigel Steel and Peter Hart, *Passchendaele: The Sacrificial Ground* (London: Cassell, 2000), p. 212.

21 Robin Prior and Trevor Wilson, *Passchendaele: The Untold Story* (New Haven: Yale University Press, 2002), pp. 94–5, 123.

22 Ibid., pp. 9–14.

23 Ian F.W. Beckett, 'The Nation in Arms', in Ian F.W. Beckett and Keith Simpson, eds, *A Nation in Arms* (Manchester: Manchester University Press, 1985), pp. 1–36.

24 Simon Robbins, *British Generalship on the Western Front, 1914–18: Defeat into Victory* (Abingdon: Frank Cass, 2005), p. 135.

25 Andy Simpson, 'British Corps Command on the Western Front, 1914–1918', in Sheffield and Todman, *Command and Control*, p. 107; Paddy Griffith, *Battle Tactics of the Western Front: the British Army's Art of Attack, 1916–1918* (New Haven: Yale University Press, 1994), pp. 192–9.

26 Beckett, 'Gough, Malcolm and Command', p. 6; Robbins, *British Generalship*, p. 52.

27 General Staff, War Office, *Field Service Regulations: Part I* (London: HMSO, 1909), p. 23.

28 Malcolm MSS, Malcolm diary, 29 June 1916, quoted in Beckett, 'Gough, Malcolm and Command', p. 7.

29 The National Archives (hereafter TNA), CAB 45/140, Gough to Edmonds, 18 March 1944.

30 Ibid., Gough to Edmonds, 3 May 1944.

31 Robbins, *British Generalship*, pp. 61–2; Sheffield, 'Army Commander', p. 89.

32 TNA, CAB 45/134, Gough to Edmonds, 16 June 1938.

33 Hubert Gough to Dorothea Gough, 23 September 1916, quoted in Beckett, 'Gough, Malcolm and Command', p. 8.

34 N. Lloyd, 'The British Expeditionary Force and the Battle of Loos', unpublished PhD thesis, Birmingham, 2005. We are grateful to Dr Lloyd for making his thesis available to us.

35 Beckett, 'Gough, Malcolm and Command', p. 8.

36 Sheffield, 'Army Commander', p. 83.

37 Robbins, *British Generalship*, p. 16.

38 Simpson, 'British Corps Command', p. 106.

39 Walker, *Blood Tub*, p. 12.

40 Shelford Bidwell and Dominick Graham, *Firepower: British Army Weapons and Theories of War* (London: Allen and Unwin, 1982), pp. 141–3.

41 Walker, *Blood Tub*, pp. 10–11.

42 General Sir Hubert Gough, *The Fifth Army* (London: Hodder and Stoughton, 1931), p. 133.

43 Beckett, 'Gough, Malcolm and Command', pp. 3–4; Simpson, 'British Corps Command', p. 106.

44 Beckett, 'Gough, Malcolm and Command', p. 3; Robbins, *British Generalship*, p. 33.

45 Farrar-Hockley, *Goughie*, pp. 226–9.

46 Sheffield, 'Army Commander', p. 83.

47 Gough, *Fifth Army*, p. 135.

48 Robbins, *British Generalship*, p. 48.

49 See, for example, General Sir Edward Bulfin's comments to Edmonds on serving under Gough in I Corps, 1915, in TNA, CAB 45/120, Bulfin to Edmonds, 11 December 1927.

50 Gough, *Fifth Army*, pp. 143, 151–2, 228.

51 Robbins, *British Generalship*, p. 32; Simpson, 'British Corps Command', pp. 107–9.

52 Robbins, *British Generalship*, pp. 33–4.

53 Beckett, 'Gough, Malcolm and Command', p. 3.

54 Walker, *Blood Tub*, p. 2.

55 Sheffield, 'Army Commander', pp. 74, 85.

56 Keith Jeffery, *The Military Correspondence of Field Marshal Sir Henry Wilson, 1918–1922* (London: Bodley Head for Army Records Society, 1985), pp. 9–10.

57 Sheffield, 'Army Commander', pp. 74–5.

58 Beckett, 'Gough, Malcolm and Command', p. 7.

59 Walker, *Blood Tub*, p. 10.

60 Wiest, 'Haig, Gough and Passchendaele', p. 77.

61 Robbins, *British Generalship*, p. 33.

62 Walker, *Blood Tub*, p. 6.

63 Sheffield, 'Army Commander', p. 88; Griffith, *Battle Tactics*, p. 110.

64 TNA, PRO, WO 95/1293, Reserve Army S.G.43/0/5, 5 October 1916.

65 Robin Prior and Trevor Wilson, *Command on the Western Front* (Oxford: Blackwell, 1992), p. 78.

66 Tim Travers, *How the War Was Won: Command and Technology in the British Army on the Western Front, 1917–1918* (London: Routledge, 1992), p. 15.

67 Wiest, 'Haig, Gough and Passchendaele', pp. 88–9.

68 Travers, *How the War Was Won*, p. 90.

69 J.M. Bourne, *Britain and the Great War, 1914–1918* (London: Edward Arnold, 1989), p. 91.

70 For what follows, see Gary Sheffield, 'The Australians at Pozières: Command and Control on the Somme, 1916', in David French and Brian Holden Reid, eds, *The British General Staff: Reform and Innovation, 1890–1939* (London: Frank Cass, 2002), pp. 112–26; Sheffield, 'Army Commander', pp. 71–95.

71 e.g., TNA, WO 95/851, G.S. 406/49, Reserve Army to X Corps, 3 July 1916.

72 LHCMA, Edmonds MSS, II/1/129, Wavell to Edmonds, 28 December 1949.

73 Gough, *Fifth Army*, p. 155; A. Home, *The Diary of a World War I Cavalry Officer*, ed. D. Briscoe (Tunbridge Wells: Costello, 1985), p. 126.

74 Haig diary, 13 November 1916, in Gary Sheffield and John Bourne, eds, *Douglas Haig: War Diaries and Letters, 1914–1918* (London: Weidenfeld and Nicolson, 2005), p. 255.

75 See e.g. IWM, Loch MSS, II Corps G. 1266, 'Notes on the Attack', 12 September 1916; TNA, Reserve Army S.G. 66/56, 12 October 1916 (points on infantry and tank tactics for forthcoming operations).

76 For instance, a mine was blown near Beaumont Hamel simultaneously with the commencement of the artillery barrage. This produced a greater effect than the blowing of a mine in the same area 10 minutes before the attack commenced on 1 July 1916. Canberra, Australian War Memorial, AWM 41/1–41/7, O.A. 247, Butler to Armies, 5 December 1916.

77 Haig diary, 2 November 1916, in Sheffield and Bourne, *Douglas Haig*, p. 250.

78 Miles, *Military Operations, 1916*, vol. 2, p. 462.

79 TNA, WO 95/518, 'Memorandum on Operations', 13 November 1916, Fifth Army S.G. 72/81.

80 Ibid.

81 Ibid.

82 Gough, *Fifth Army*, p. 156.

83 Robin Prior and Trevor Wilson, *The Somme* (New Haven: Yale University Press, 2005), p. 293.

84 Haig diary, 16 October 1916, in Sheffield and Bourne, *Douglas Haig*, p. 241.

85 Ibid., 12 November 1916, p. 254.

86 Miles, *Military Operations*, p. 476.

87 Robbins, *British Generalship*, pp. 20–21.

88 Southsea, Hampshire, Royal Marines Museum, ARCH 7/17/5 (1), Major J. Montagu to a friend, 20 November 1916; Beddington memoir (in author's possession), pp. 102–3.

89 TNA, WO 95/518, Fifth Army S.G. 72/84, 13 November 1916.

90 Ibid., Fifth Army S.G. 72/90, 16 November 1916.

91 Peter Simkins, 'Somme Footnote: The Battle of the Ancre and the Struggle for Frankfort Trench, November 1916', *Imperial War Museum Review*, 9 (1994), p. 94.

92 TNA, WO 95/518, Fifth Army S.G. 72/90, 16 November 1916.

93 Travers, *Killing Ground*, p. 189; Simkins, 'Somme Footnote', pp. 96–7; Robbins, *British Generalship*, pp. 32–3.

94 TNA, CAB 45/138, Wace to Edmonds, 30 October 1936; National Library of Scotland, Haig MSS, Acc. 3155, Haig diary, 21 November 1916.

95 TNA, WO 95/747, V Corps GX 8325, 21 November 1916.

96 Ibid., Fifth Army S.G. 72/86, 25 November 1916.

97 Ibid., WO 95/518, Fifth Army to Corps, 16 November 1916.

Chapter Five

Henry Horne

First Army, 1916–1918

Simon Robbins

General Lord Horne remains relatively unknown. There is no full-length study, modern or contemporary, of Horne's career, whereas ironically General Sir Arthur Currie, his Canadian subordinate, has three biographies. Remaining 'a rather shadowy figure for historians',[1] 'Horne is the "unknown" general of the Great War. He kept no diary, wrote no autobiography, had no biographer, and is referred to only in passing in the numerous accounts of the time. His wife destroyed his letters, and his entry in the *Dictionary of National Biography* is extremely brief.'[2] Moreover, Horne is eclipsed by the prominence given to Currie, who gets the credit for the successes of 1917–18 in the same way that Alexander has been overshadowed by his subordinate, Montgomery, in 1942–3. Eschewing publicity, Horne was self-effacing, preferring 'not to worry the Corps Commanders while they are busy'.[3]

Henry Sinclair Horne was born in Stirling on 19 February 1861, the second son of Major James Horne of the Highland Light Infantry, whose family had a long association with Stirkoke and had been for several generations one of the best known in Caithness. Both a Scot (like Haig) and a Highlander, Horne was educated at Harrow and attended the Royal Military Academy, Woolwich, receiving his commission on 19 May 1880. He served with the Garrison Artillery from June 1880 at Woolwich and Portsmouth until December 1883, when he transferred to the Royal Horse Artillery.

Promoted captain in 1888, Horne went to India and gained experience of all branches of the regiment (the Garrison, Mountain, Horse and Field Artillery). After an appointment as Staff Captain RA at Meerut, Horne became Adjutant RHA, Kirkee, in 1892. Nearby at the RA practice camp at Hinjaori, where he was camp staff officer, Horne contributed to the development of the 'gun-arc', which was adopted by the Field Artillery in 1895. These appointments marked him as a rising star in the regiment.[4] Having returned home in 1896, Horne married Kate, and purchased Priestwell in East Haddon. His very happy marriage provided much motivation for Horne, who wrote that 'the thought of you urges me on'.[5] On the last day of the war, Horne thanked his

Chronology

19 February 1861	Henry Sinclair Horne born at Stirkoke, Stirling, Caithness
	Educated at Harrow and Royal Military Academy, Woolwich
19 May 1880	Commissioned 2nd Lieutenant in Royal Artillery
December 1883	Transferred to Royal Horse Artillery
17 August 1888	Promoted captain
1892	Adjutant of RHA at Kirkee, India
1 July 1897	Married Kate Blacklock (née McCorquodale)
23 February 1898	Promoted major
May 1900	Appointed to command R Battery, RHA
29 November 1900	Promoted brevet lieutenant colonel
16 April 1902	Appointed to Remount Department, South Africa
14 November 1905	Promoted substantive lieutenant colonel
27 May 1906	Promoted brevet colonel
September 1906	Appointed staff officer, artillery, to Aldershot command
24 September 1910	Promoted substantive colonel
1 May 1912	Appointed inspector of artillery
5 August 1914	Appointed Brigadier General Royal Artillery, I Corps
26 October 1914	Promoted major general
1 January 1915	Appointed GOC 2nd Division
November 1915	Accompanied Lord Kitchener to Gallipoli
12 January 1916	Appointed GOC XV Corps in Egypt and temporary lieutenant general
22 April 1916	XV Corps reconstituted in France
30 September 1916	Appointed GOC First Army and temporary general
1 January 1917	Promoted substantive lieutenant general
1 January 1919	Promoted substantive general
1919	Created Baron Horne of Stirkoke
1 June 1919	Appointed GOC Eastern Command
1923	Went on half pay
May 1926	Retired
14 August 1929	Died at Stirkoke

Appointed KCB 1916, KCMG 1918, KBE 1918, GCB 1919, GBE 1920

wife for being 'a great support & encouragement to me during the past hard four years'.[6]

Having commanded a battery until promoted major in 1898, Horne then commanded an ammunition column in South Africa. He took part in the relief of Mafeking and the subsequent advance into the Transvaal with the Cavalry Division under Sir John French, whose staff included Haig (chief staff officer), Herbert Lawrence (intelligence officer) and Aylmer Hunter-Weston (head of administration). He then commanded a battery at Johannesburg, Diamond Hill and Wittebergen in 1900, prior to operating with mounted columns in the Orange River Valley and Cape Colonies until January 1902, when he took over the remount depots. Mentioned in dispatches, he returned home as a brevet lieutenant colonel in October 1902 to take command of No. 3 Depot at

Weedon. He went to the 31 Brigade RFA at Fermoy in November 1905 (when he was promoted lieutenant colonel), and the 8 Brigade RHA at Newbridge in May 1906 (when he became brevet colonel). He was appointed staff officer for horse and field artillery in the Aldershot command under Haig in September 1906, and inspector of RHA and RFA (as brigadier general) under the inspector general of the Horne Forces in May 1912.

Having left for France on the outbreak of war in August 1914 as Haig's chief gunner (BGRA, I Corps), Horne established a reputation as a skilful and experienced commander of artillery during the battles of Mons, Aisne and Ypres. During the retreat from Mons he was given command of the Corps rearguard by Haig and performed with great success. At Ypres he had a narrow escape when a shell struck the corps report centre in an inn at a crossroads. While Horne and Charteris left by one door, getting 'away scot-free', two staff officers, who left by a different door, 'walked straight into another shell'. One was killed outright, while the other was badly wounded in the leg and died later from gas gangrene.[7]

Promoted in October 1914 to major general 'for Distinguished Service in the Field', Horne was appointed in December that year MGRA to Haig, who now commanded the newly formed First Army. On 1 January 1915 he was given command of the 2nd Division, and took part in the battles of Givenchy (March 1915), Festubert (May 1915) and Loos (September 1915). At his suggestion the system of artillery command was changed after Festubert.[8] Horne accompanied Lord Kitchener in November 1915 to supervise the evacuation of the Dardanelles. He then planned the Suez Canal defences and was given command of the XV Corps in the Canal Zone until April 1916, when his corps headquarters was transferred to France to form part of the Fourth Army under Henry Rawlinson.

As his protégé and one of his principal lieutenants, Horne would claim 'the personal friendship of Earl Haig',[9] whose patronage was a factor in his rapid advance. Haig's 'recommendations' got him command of the 2nd Division, first temporarily and then permanently.[10] In July 1915 Haig informed the prime minister (Asquith) of the 'necessity for promoting young officers to high command', and that 'to make room, some of the old ones must be removed'. Looking through the lists of major generals in the *Army List* for 'young, capable officers', Haig recommended 'in order of seniority' Thomas Morland, Horne, Hubert Gough and Richard Haking for command of corps, believing that 'they should eventually be given command of armies'.[11] Of the four generals mentioned all were commanding corps by the end of 1915, but only Gough and Horne were promoted to command armies (in 1916). Haig himself 'recommended Haking and Horne to be given Corps' in August 1915.[12] Horne's return to France from Egypt and his subsequent elevation to an army command again owed a great deal to Haig's influence.[13]

Both Haig and Sir William Robertson (CIGS) looked to Horne, as the only gunner to command an army, to provide expertise on artillery matters. In 1914 he was used by Haig 'to arrange for close co-operation of the artillery of the divisions' of I Corps. At his request, Horne 'undertook the organization of the artillery fire and the co-operation between artillery and aeroplanes'.[14] In 1915 Haig continued to consult Horne on 'the effect of guns and siege howitzers in battering trenches' and 'the nature of the bombardment required to demolish the enemy's defences in our front', even though he was no longer his MGRA.[15] As late as June 1918 Birch (Haig's MGRA) came 'to stay the night and discuss artillery matters'.[16] In May 1916 Robertson informed Haig that he had 'heard from many different sources' that 'Birch is *not* the best selection to replace Headlam' as MGRA at GHQ, but backed down having seen Horne, who declared that Birch was 'the best selection'.[17] Later in 1917, when looking for someone to succeed Sir Archibald Murray in Palestine, Robertson thought that 'the best man seems to be Cavan', but also mentioned Horne as a possibility.[18]

Horne commanded XV Corps during all stages of the Battle of the Somme until promoted on 30 September 1916 to command First Army. During the assault on 1 July his corps achieved with XIII Corps the deepest penetration of the German front by Rawlinson's Fourth Army, capturing the important Montauban–Mametz spur. The next day, Haig visited XV Corps headquarters to compliment Horne 'on the success of his operations' which had posed 'a most difficult problem'.[19] During subsequent operations, notably on 14 July and 15 September when tanks were first employed, Horne 'gained some notable successes by the skilful handling of his artillery, in particular the development of the creeping barrage',[20] which 'was used by the 15th Divn. at the Battle of Loos' and developed by XV Corps 'during the Somme Battle from 1st July on'.[21] Horne could lay 'some claims to the invention and development of the creeping barrage'.[22] This was in co-operation with Major General E.W. Alexander VC (his CRA), who 'devised a new method of employing his artillery to assist forward the Infantry attack' which 'was quickly improved upon & turned into the "Creeping Barrage" & taken up by all the armies for supporting Infantry attacks with artillery fire'.[23] However, 'it was not until the 15 Sept. attack that an Army Order was issued for a Creeping Barrage'.[24] XV Corps first issued a barrage map to the infantry for the attack on 14 July.[25]

On the Somme, Horne was much involved in the process of weeding out the older or less professional senior officers and replacing them with more experienced and professional officers, earning a reputation in some quarters as Haig's 'enforcer'. For example, Horne was 'dissatisfied' and 'very disappointed with the work' of Brigadier General R.S. Oxley (24 Brigade), Major General T.D. Pilcher (17th Division) and Major General Sir Ivor Phillips (38th Division) in July 1916, and Haig, trusting in Horne's judgement, approved of their removal.[26] Oxley had been adversely reported on by Lieutenant General Sir James Babington (23rd Division) as being only 'fairly satisfactory as a

Brigadier' and 'certainly not fit for promotion to command a division'.[27] Similarly, 17th Division 'got into trouble with General Horne for allowing the enemy to get the upper hand so much & for not knowing where the enemy front line ran'.[28]

Phillips, originally a regular soldier who had retired before the war from the Indian Army and was serving with the Pembrokeshire Yeomanry, was 'ignorant' and lacked the skills required.[29] But, as an MP and a friend of Lloyd George, he had been promoted to command the 38th Division in early 1915 'over the heads of many more senior and meritorious officers'. Phillips 'lacked experience and failed to inspire confidence' and was replaced by men with experience of commanding a battalion and then a brigade on the Western Front, Major General C.G. Blackader and subsequently Sir Thomas Cubitt, who eliminated the political atmosphere and ensured that the division 'did extremely well'.[30]

When General Sir Charles Monro was appointed as commander-in-chief in India, Haking, despite his poor performance as a corps commander at Loos in September 1915 and again at Fromelles in July 1916,[31] was appointed to command the First Army in August 1916 by Haig. Haig claimed that he had been appointed 'to "act temporarily" in Monro's absence' because no other corps commander, such as Byng, Birdwood or Cavan, was available.[32] The War Council, which had to ratify army commands, indicated that Haking would not be acceptable, and Robertson 'was very angry with Haig for appointing Haking'[33] when it was unlikely to be approved by the government. It insisted that Haig choose between Birdwood, Cavan, Horne and Henry Wilson instead, declaring a preference for Cavan, of whom he had 'the highest opinion', or Horne.[34] Haig's critics believed that he chose Horne, who was 'the least brilliant', instead of Cavan, who had 'a great reputation', because 'some people talk of him as the most likely successor to Haig'.[35] In fact Horne was rated by at least one observer as one of the 'two best Corps Commanders in France'.[36] Haig then had to explain to Haking that he was merely a caretaker until Horne could be spared on the Somme. With the approval of his appointment to First Army,[37] Horne had climbed from the rank of colonel with the temporary rank of brigadier general to that of full general in less than two years. It was a meteoric rise equalled only by Gough (Fifth Army) among the army commanders in France – grasping the opportunity provided by the outbreak of the war.

The process of removing incompetent commanders was continuous, and in October 1916 Sir Henry Wilson (IV Corps) was asked by Horne, his army commander, if Major General Count (later Lord) Gleichen 'was fit to command a Divn. on the Somme', and consulted other officers for their opinions. General Sir Charles Fergusson (XVII Corps) was somewhat evasive, but Major General Sir Reginald Barnes (116 Brigade) and Colonel Berkeley Vincent (GSO1, 37th Division) indicated that 'they had no confidence in Gleichen, because he was stupid, pig-headed, & blind'. As a result Horne wrote to GHQ requesting the replacement of Gleichen,[38] who was sent home 'having been found unfit to command a division in the battle' by Haig, who reported that the staff of the division were 'all pleased to have got rid of the Count'.[39] In October 1918 Fergusson (XVII Corps) reported to Horne that Major General H.L. Reed VC was unfit to command 15th Division, while praising the 63rd Division under Major General C.A. Blacklock as the finest he had ever seen.[40] Reed was able to survive as his previous corps commander assessed him to be an 'above average Divisional Commander'.[41]

But Horne was much more than a mere martinet, visiting divisional HQ every day and cheering his subordinates up by creating an atmosphere of confidence.[42] Horne was often 'out all day, inspecting in the morning – conferences ... in the afternoon'.[43] As army commander, Horne favoured a consultative command style, encouraging discussion, explaining the overall plan of operations and asking at conferences 'for the opinion of corps commanders as to whether the enemy intends to withdraw' and 'as to the roads which should be allotted to Corps'.[44] On the basis of his experiences on the Somme in 1916 Horne also arranged administrative details such as reminding the corps commanders that they, as well as the army, could give priorities to corps road officers.[45] They should investigate 'the question of battalion arrangements for resting the men at every opportunity, and of feeding the men before the battle' so that food 'reached ... troops in the line'. Horne also employed conferences 'to obtain the views of Corps Commanders as to the earliest date on which they could launch the attacks for which they were to be responsible'.[46]

Horne was also keen to consult his corps commanders personally when problems arose. For example, rather than delegating Hastings Anderson (his MGGS) to reply as was usually the case, when Haking (XI Corps) wrote to First Army on 18 March to warn of the negative effects of the employment within his corps of only two divisions to hold a four-division front on the troops, who were demoralized by the amount of work required and by anxiety at the width of their frontage, Horne spoke to Haking face-to-face to allay his fears.[47]

The brilliant capture of Vimy Ridge, 'a formidable undertaking' by the I Corps (Lieutenant General Sir Arthur Holland) and Canadian Corps (Julian Byng) on 9 April 1917, which was 'vital to the success of the Third Army' at Arras, owed its success to 'the unprecedented completeness of the preparations' and the destructive power of the artillery.[48] It was one of the most successful Allied operations of the war and Horne's first major operation as an army commander, demonstrating that his rapid promotion was fully deserved. Byng noted that 'Horne has been more than helpful and backed me up in everything'.[49]

An attempt by Allenby (Third Army) prior to the Battle of Arras to achieve a surprise, by employing a shorter intense preliminary bombardment of forty-eight hours rather than the week's bombardment that had preceded the Somme attack, met much resistance. GHQ and the other army commanders 'all stated that they preferred a longer bombardment' to deal with the German defences, notably the wire. By contrast Horne, who seems on the Somme to have favoured a slow and deliberate bombardment 'which was generally more accurate',[50] planned a long preliminary bombardment of six days' duration for his limited attack on Vimy Ridge. This was to ensure that 'the lanes through the backward lines of enemy wire have actually been cut, and that tactical points have been adequately dealt with by batteries of destruction'.[51]

Yet in the final analysis Allenby was correct about the difficulties of wire cutting, because the wire on the Wancourt–Feuchy line could not be cut in ten days, let alone two or four. After the capture of Vimy Ridge in April 1917, Horne reported to Haig that he 'thought he had used too many shells' which 'had broken up the soil so frightfully that all movement was now made most difficult'. He believed that 'owing to the amount of artillery and ammunition available the frontal attack on a position had become … the easiest', but that 'the difficult matter was to advance later on when the enemy had organized a defence with machine guns'.[52] The emphasis on a limited objective and the rigid timetable to co-ordinate the advance of the artillery and infantry had also precluded exploitation of the initial success.[53]

After fruitless operations in April and May to exploit the success at Arras and Vimy, Horne then commenced operations around Lens during the summer and autumn of 1917 to attract German attention and reserves away from Flanders. To threaten Lens, Horne launched successful attacks on 28 June by the XIII Corps (Lieutenant General Sir Frederick McCracken) between Gavrelle and Oppy, and by the I Corps and Canadian Corps astride the Souchez River to assault Hill 65 and the German salient between Avion and Lens, thus gaining observation for further advances. Horne intended to continue these attacks for the encirclement of Lens during July, including the capture of Hill 70, but was forced to postpone operations until August, owing to shortages of artillery.[54] After a personal reconnaissance, Currie believed that the First Army plan to break the German line south of Lens and then take the city by stages, issued on 10 July, ignored the tactical features of the ground, which was dominated by Hill 70 and Sallaumines Hill.

Currie persuaded Horne to alter his plan and make Hill 70 the 'immediate main objective', employing a 'bite and hold' operation to force the Germans to retake this key tactical position and thus commit their reserves. Horne referred the matter to Haig, who came to see Currie at Camblain L'Abbé a few days later, and declared that he liked Currie's plan 'much better than previous suggestions and fully agreed with the desirability of attacking Hill 70 first'.[55] When the Canadians attacked on 15 August, Hill 70 was quickly taken and consolidated, and over the next week numerous German counter-attacks were repulsed with heavy casualties, keeping German reserves from being diverted to Ypres. By September 1917, having concluded that 'the work of destruction has, in the past been carried too far' and that 'complete destruction on the scale carried out prior to the attack on Hill 70 cannot go hand in hand with surprise', Horne proposed to revert to shorter, intense preliminary bombardments in order to restore the 'factor of surprise'.[56]

Meanwhile the Flanders offensive was still continuing, and Horne's plans in early September for the capture of Lens with converging advances, hampered by limited resources, were abandoned when the Canadian Corps departed to capture the Passchendaele Ridge, the final phase of the Third Battle of Ypres. On 3 October 1917 Horne visited Canadian Corps Headquarters to give Currie the bad news that two divisions of the Canadian Corps were to go to Flanders and that they would fight as part of the Fifth Army. In a heated interview Currie insisted that his corps should go to Passchendaele as a collective unit, and refused to serve under the Fifth Army, bluntly telling Horne that 'the Canadian Corps would not fight under General Gough'.

Horne was shocked, crying, 'My God, Currie, that is a terrible thing to say.' Currie 'had talked to many Divisional Commanders who had fought in the Ypres battle', learning that 'they were greatly dissatisfied with the way in which the battle had been conducted'. His own 'lack of confidence in Gough arose from our experience with him on the Somme in 1916', which he did not wish to repeat. Horne left with the promise that he would refer Currie's protests to Haig, whom he saw that afternoon. Summoned to First Army after dinner that evening, Currie was informed that the Canadians were to go into battle as a corps but under the Second Army, whose frontage was to be extended to include the Fifth Army sector where the Canadian Corps was going to attack.[57] Haig had ordered that 'the Canadian Corps should be sent to Plumer of Second Army and not to Gough because the Canadians do not work well with the latter'.[58]

On 28 March 1918 a major German offensive, extending the assault against the Fifth and Third Armies, was launched against Vimy Ridge but was repulsed by First Army after very heavy fighting. The attachment to the First Army of the Portuguese Corps, which first took over the line between Neuve Chapelle and Festubert in May 1917, added to the anxieties of Horne. He believed 'the methods and training of our Allies differed materially from those of the British Army, and their national pride made their assimilation in the British front a matter of anxious thought and difficulty'.[59] In December 1917 'the Portuguese front was a source of anxiety' to Horne, who sought to secure it by reducing the front held by the Portuguese.[60] However, his request to withdraw them from the line because 'they would prove unable to withstand a German attack' was refused, owing to the lack of spare troops to replace them.[61] On 9 April 1918 the Germans broke through the Portuguese Corps on the Lys, just before plans for their relief could be completed, and the situation on the First Army's left flank around Armentières became critical. Horne reported bluntly that 'the Portuguese troops failed to offer any serious resistance'.[62] Currie noted that Horne 'looked very pale and worried',[63] but the front was eventually stabilized. The First Army headquarters, at Ranchicourt since early 1917, was shelled and its withdrawal planned, but Horne refused to leave and later was proud of the fact that he was the only British army commander who was not forced by the German offensive to withdraw his headquarters.[64]

During the German spring offensive of 1918, following their return to First Army, the four Canadian divisions were removed from Currie's command and placed in two different armies and under three different corps. While recognizing that such piecemeal measures had to be made in a desperate crisis, Currie was soon agitating that his corps should be reunited as quickly as possible, lobbying Horne, his army commander, and Haig's chief of staff. By 1 July the Canadian Corps was back together, but this was not the result of Currie's pressure on his superiors but rather pressure through political channels. Embroiled in a titanic struggle with Ludendorff, both Haig and Horne disliked the political pressure from the British and Canadian governments to reunite the Canadian Corps. Horne also resented the implied criticism of the quality of British forces, and on 14 April visited Currie to admonish him for 'any reflections on fighting ability of British Divisions'.[65] Visiting First Army, Haig noted that a 'very confident' Horne believed that Currie 'is suffering from a swollen head'. Horne also compared the efforts of the Canadians – who held 'a wide front near Arras' but *'have not yet been in the battle'* – unfavourably with the Australians, who 'on the other hand have been used by divisions and are now spread out from Albert to Amiens'.[66]

In the second half of 1918 Horne again led the First Army in a series of successful operations against the Germans in the final offensive of the war, notably taking the Drocourt–Quéant line and crossing the Canal du Nord. From August 1918 attacks were 'as far as possible to be a surprise', employing tanks but 'no preliminary registration'.[67] For example, no preliminary artillery preparation was used prior to the Canadian attack on 26 August[68] or during the forcing of the Canal du Nord, although there was some wire cutting,[69] when some 1,347 guns were employed in support of the Canadian and XXII Corps.[70] The First Army had prepared and kept ready plans from April 1918 to regain the high ground of Observation Ridge and Orange Hill, east of Arras, to secure the British line north of the Scarpe. A series of small operations by XVII Corps captured the enemy outpost zone, allowing First Army to engage the German main line of resistance.[71]

As early as June and July 1918 Haig was studying the problem of retaking Orange Hill and Monchy-le-Preux, but abandoned the idea because both Byng and Horne 'were opposed to making the attack'.[72] Instead, 'in order that both the enemy and our own troops may be misled as to the real intentions' of the operation at Amiens, Haig instructed the First and Third Armies 'to prepare offensive operations with a view to advancing their line to a more satisfactory

position south of the Scarpe towards Monchy-le-Preux'.[73] This would mislead
and confuse the enemy by detracting his attention away from the main operation, while undertaking preparations for the next moves (attacks by the Third
and First Armies on 21 and 24 August respectively) if the Fourth Army attack
at Amiens was successful.[74]

By 10 August momentum was lost from Fourth Army's offensive at Amiens.
That morning Haig, needing more effort in other sectors, instructed Horne to
complete his plans for the capture of La Bassée and the Aubers Ridge, an
operation to be mounted in conjunction with assaults on Kemmel Hill by
Second Army and towards Bapaume by Third Army.[75] On 14 August, Haig
postponed the attack on the Roye–Chaulnes front because Currie (Canadian
Corps) and Rawlinson (Fourth Army) said that it 'would be *a very costly
matter*'.[76] Haig informed Horne that Third Army was expected to attack in
about six days' time and that he was to prepare a supporting offensive on its left
flank.[77] On 15 August, Horne was told by Haig 'to be ready to profit by the
advance of our Third Army, to attack and capture Orange Hill and Monchy-le-
Preux', important heights tactically, and that some 100 tanks would be sent to
him.[78] On 14 and 16 August GHQ confirmed that Horne should be prepared to
mount an attack at short notice on Orange Hill and Monchy-le-Preux.[79]
Though Horne submitted a scheme for such an operation to GHQ on
17 August,[80] only minor operations were actually mounted on the First Army
front over the next few days.

Following the offensive by Byng's Third Army on 21 August, Haig notified
his army commanders on 22 August about 'the changed conditions under which
operations are now being carried out' which made it 'no longer necessary to
advance step by step in regular lines as in 1916–17 battles'. On 24 August,
Horne was ordered 'to attack *by surprise* and advance as rapidly as possible
astride the Cambrai road' to take first Monchy-le-Preux. The main object was
'to break through the Drocourt–Quéant line and take the Hindenburg Line
from the rear, pressing on as fast as possible against Marquion'. On 25 August,
the eve of the operation, Haig learnt from Horne, who was 'quite satisfied', that
Currie was 'a little "sticky"'. Haig had already briefed Lieutenant General Sir
Henry Burstall (2nd Canadian Division) and was confident that he would 'do
what was right, whatever Currie might feel on the subject'.[81] The Canadian
attack on 26 August was to cover the left flank of Third Army and gain a position from which the Drocourt–Quéant line could subsequently be assaulted.[82]

On 26 August the First Army began its victorious advance with the Battle
of the Scarpe, when the Canadian and XVII Corps attacked south of the
Scarpe, taking Monchy-le-Preux, Wancourt and Guemappe, bypassing the
Hindenburg Line.[83] Horne was 'pleased' at this 'most successful' advance[84] as
the operation was a complete surprise to the enemy. The Germans had
expected the attack to be north of the Scarpe towards Douai as a result of the
constant raids and artillery bombardments by the VIII Corps for some time

prior to the assault, which diverted their attention.[85] Next day Haig 'directed Horne not to attack the Drocourt–Quéant line until he had all the means at hand to follow up the success, in the hope of passing the Canal du Nord line and pushing forward the Cavalry Corps at once'.[86]

Resistance stiffened considerably during the next few days, and there was much hard fighting before a jump-off position for an assault on the Drocourt–Quéant line, and dominating ground, such as Greenland Hill, was captured, allowing the artillery to support this operation.[87] By 28 August the First Army had 'made good progress' and Horne was 'satisfied with the rate of progress and very pleased'.[88] At a conference on 29 August, Horne 'impressed' on Currie 'the necessity for the economy of tanks, with a view to having the greatest possible number available for the attack of the wired defensive system of the Drocourt–Quéant line'.[89] At a meeting with his five army commanders and his CGS on 30 August, Haig felt 'justified in taking very great risks in our forthcoming operations' which aimed 'to reach the front Cambrai-St Quentin'. Haig then saw Byng and Horne alone and 'arranged for the attack on the Drocourt–Quéant line to take place'.[90]

Haig sent Lawrence, his CGS, to see Horne and Currie, 'to tell them that I have no wish to attack the Drocourt–Quéant line, if they have any doubts about taking it',[91] since he 'was opposed to doing more attacking than was absolutely necessary'.[92] As the main attack was being made by the Third and Fourth Armies, it was made clear to Horne by Haig that 'the number of divisions and the amount of artillery available for the First Army were limited; that he could expect no increase; and that he must carry out his task as best he could with what he had at his disposal'.[93] The First Army took the Drocourt–Quéant line on 2 September, and Horne's troops burst through the elaborate hostile defences of this section of the Hindenburg Line, creating a large gap in a key section of the enemy's front. Horne reported that the battle had been 'a great success', 'one of the biggest things of the war' and a 'very great victory', with over 5,000 prisoners taken and the inflicting of 'very heavy casualties on the Germans'.[94]

By 3 September the enemy was retreating on the front of the Third and First Armies between Lens and Péronne, and continued to withdraw until the Hindenburg Line was reached.[95] Despite orders that emphasized the seizure of the crossings over the Canal du Nord, resistance stiffened considerably and it became evident that the enemy would not give up these crossings except to a strong set-piece attack.[96] Tiredness of the troops and their inexperience in open warfare had meant that the three divisions that broke through the Drocourt–Quéant line had failed to follow up the retreating enemy and to reach and cross the Canal du Nord on their heels.[97] Nevertheless, Horne's advance to the Canal du Nord was 'a bad knock for the Boche'.[98] Inspecting the ground afterwards, Horne was 'very pleased with the success & the splendid way in which the troops must have fought', believing that 'an advance of about

12 miles in 8 days through a succession of strong positions is really a very fine performance & all may be proud of it'.[99] Yet, although Germany had 'suffered very heavy defeats', Horne did not believe that 'she will be *defeated* till next year'.[100]

On 11 September, Horne submitted a report to GHQ advocating an attack across the Canal du Nord by the Canadian Corps, an operation whose results 'are likely to be far reaching'.[101] This was approved on 13 September by Haig, who held a conference on 15 September with Byng, Horne and Rawlinson to discuss breaking through the Hindenburg Line.[102] As the Germans had 'a strong, well sited series of defences', Haig did not propose to attack until the American–French attack had been launched on 26 September. This would 'draw off some of the enemy's reserves from our front' and set a timetable for the First and Third Armies to attack on 27 September, the Second Army with the Belgians to attack in Flanders on 28 September, and the Third and Fourth Armies on 29 September.[103]

The Canal du Nord

The 'primary role' of the First Army was 'to cover the left flank of the Third Army' while the flank of the Canadian Corps was guarded by Vimy Ridge, which was 'garrisoned lightly enough by the Eighth Corps, none too strong in numbers and strung out on a long front'.[104] The planning for assault across the Canal du Nord in September 1918 shows the partnership of Currie and Horne in action. Currie's proposal to cross the Canal caused Horne much disquiet when submitted on 18 September during a conference at First Army head-quarters. Horne was full of misgivings and worried about the efficacy of Currie's daring plan for the Canal crossings, to which there were grave objec-tions, and his initial reaction was to discard it because 'the possibilities of failure with heavy loss' were obvious,[105] noting later: 'It was necessary to get the attacking troops across on a narrow front and then to deploy outwards like a fan. It was this that constituted the difficulty & some risk if the Boche recognized that we were advancing & put a heavy artillery fire on the position of the Canal when we were crossing.'[106]

Currie was prepared to run these risks and understood that such a failure endangered not only his own career and the prestige of the Canadian Corps but also the attacks of all three British armies against the Hindenburg Line. On the other hand a successful attack would retain the element of surprise, offering the hope of minimizing losses and gaining the objectives, whereas a more frontal assault on a wider frontage would inevitably result in heavy casualties without any assurance of success.

On 21 September, Horne went with Haig to Currie's headquarters to discuss the operation. After a progress report Haig agreed to Currie's plan, and Horne also tentatively approved but had second thoughts, telling Anderson three times on the way back to his own headquarters, 'I don't believe I ought to let

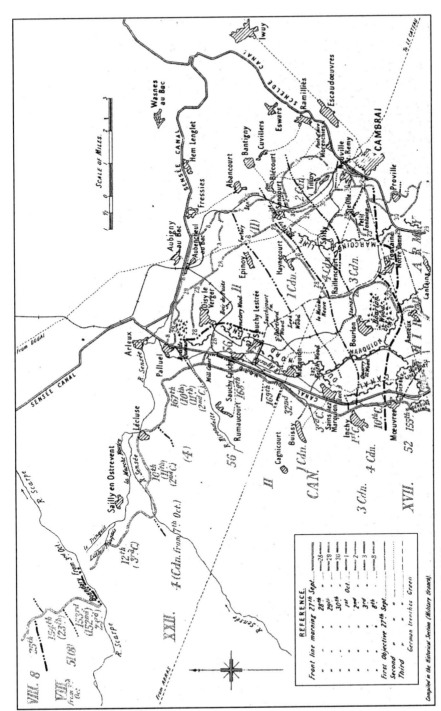

Crossing the Canal du Nord, 1918.

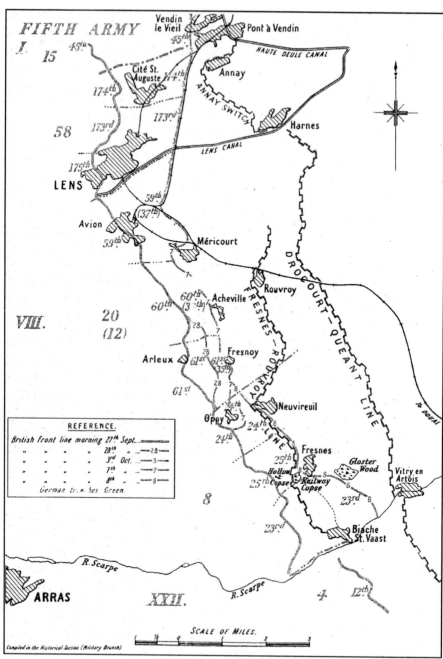

Crossing the Canal du Nord, 1918.

them do it'. Anderson tried to reassure Horne that 'If Currie says they can do it, they will'.[107] But for Anderson's urging, Horne would have gone back to Canadian Corps headquarters to alter his decision. Instead Horne asked Byng (Third Army), who was a close friend of Currie as a result of his command of the Canadian Corps, to dissuade the well-built Canadian from his reckless course. Byng saw Currie to inspect his plan, and to warn him that he was 'attempting one of the most difficult operations of the war' and 'if you fail, it means home for you'.[108]

This was the last hint of doubt from Horne. He not only allowed Currie to complete his preparations for the assault, which was a brilliant triumph,[109] but also helped to guarantee that success by ensuring that the Canadian Corps assault was preceded by a minor operation carried out by VIII Corps near Arleux in front of the Vimy Ridge. This diverted the enemy's attention from the real attack and delayed the movement of reserves,[110] pinning down the bulk of the enemy's forces north of the Scarpe until the Canadian Corps could secure its foothold across the Canal.[111] The Canadian Corps 'owed much' to 'the unselfish co-operation of the VIII and XXII Corps', whose 'elaborate preparations for attack on the north of the Scarpe' included 'feints, raids, bombardments, Chinese attacks and small operations' which misled the enemy 'as to the point of attack'.[112]

By the end of 27 September the First Army had forced Canal du Nord and captured two powerful defensive systems and the important tactical positions of Bourlon Wood and Oisy-le-Verger and the commanding ridge between. It had advanced 5 miles on a front of 9 miles, securing a favourable position for launching future operations towards Cambrai and the Escaut.[113] Horne noted that 'this very satisfactory result', which was 'a heavy defeat for the Boche', was achieved 'by good artillery work' which made the enemy 'think we were going to try and cross further north', and by 'some minor operations' which attracted his attention to the Douai front further north, so that 'we were able to surprise him and the crossing took place, whilst the Boche shelled the Canal elsewhere'.[114] 'The co-operation of artillery, engineers, machine guns, infantry, tanks, aeroplanes, smoke and gas' made the crossing of the Canal du Nord 'a typical example of a modern battle at the end of 1918, on the Western Front'.[115] Haig 'personally corrected [the] communiqué and put General Horne's name in with the doings of his corps in detail'.[116] This brilliant success was a vital prelude to the main attack of the Fourth Army two days later. In the subsequent advance the towns of Lens (3 October), Douai (17 October), Denain (20 October) and Valenciennes (2 November) were liberated and Mons, the town from which Horne retreated in 1914, was captured on the morning of the armistice (11 November).

The war ended with the First Army on the French border. Horne summed it up 'as a red letter day', the anniversary of the defeat of 'the great attack of the

Prussian Guard' in 1914, exultant that: 'Now the mighty German nation is completely humbled and the great German Army, which regarded itself as the most powerful fighting machine in the world, is in retreat to its own frontiers, broken and defeated!'[117] Characteristically, Horne also wrote to thank Currie, calling the capture of Mons 'a splendid crowning effort on the part of the Canadian Corps' and stating that: 'Personally I am simply delighted. I commanded the rearguard of the I Corps when we left Mons on Aug. 24, 1914, and I am glad to have had the good fortune to command the army that took Mons back. I do congratulate you and your fine troops with all my heart.'[118] Horne's trust of and admiration for Currie were expressed in his confidential report of February 1919:

> Many great qualities as a leader, commander and organizer. He has inspired and created an *esprit* and morale throughout all ranks which is second to none. His perseverance and tact has smoothed away many difficulties ... I have felt confident that any task I called upon General Currie to perform would be carried through to my satisfaction.[119]

Currie, who was sensitive to any perceived slights, becoming incensed when XXII Corps (Godley) was included by Horne in a parade to celebrate the liberation of Valenciennes,[120] complained in March 1919 that a pamphlet issued by First Army outlining its operations during 1918 undervalued the achievements of the Canadian Corps. Horne ignored the rather acid remark by a staff officer that the Canadian Corps was 'apt to take all the credit it can for everything, and to consider that the BEF consists of the Canadian Corps and some other troops'.[121] He took instead the opportunity to assure Currie diplomatically that the author, a publicity officer attached to First Army from GHQ, 'had no intention in his mind of deprecating the great work done by the Canadian Corps'. He thanked 'you and all ranks of the Canadian Corps for the loyal support I have invariably received and for the splendid work so gallantly carried through'.[122] Horne and his MGGS (Anderson) both supported Currie's case by writing to deny the charges and offering their assistance when he instituted a libel suit in 1928 against accusations of sacrificing the lives of his men needlessly. Horne wrote that 'I am in a position to state that such an accusation is grossly unfair and as false as it is unfair.'[123]

Not required for the Army of the Rhine, Horne returned home at the end of March 1919. He took part in the great victory marches through London on 19 December 1918 and Paris on 14 July 1919. For his services he received the thanks of both Houses of Parliament, was raised to the peerage as Baron Horne of Stirkoke with a grant of £30,000, and appointed GCB. On 1 June he took up the Eastern Command, although he 'was very angry at not getting Southern Command',[124] which was given to Lieutenant General Sir George Harper, his junior. At the end of his tenure in 1923 he refused several offers of colonial governorships, notably Malta, as he did not wish to leave the United Kingdom, and was on half pay until May 1926, when he retired having been unemployed for three years. But that same month he became head of his regiment, as master gunner.

Interested in the welfare of former soldiers, Horne worked for many charities, notably those of the Royal Artillery; the British Legion; the National Association for Employment of Regular Sailors, Soldiers and Airmen; the Navy, Army and Air Force Institutes; and veterans' associations. He was also deputy lieutenant for Caithness, and governor and commandant of the Church Lads Brigade. In May 1929 he was appointed colonel of the Highland Light Infantry, his father's regiment, but died suddenly while shooting on his estate at Stirkoke on 14 August 1929, the fifteenth anniversary of his embarkation with the BEF. He was buried at Wick.

'A man of marked nervous sensibility, and deeply conscious of his responsibility for the casualties caused by the operations under his orders',[125] Horne's forte was 'strength of character rather than the intellectual attainments'. His success was based on the 'intimate knowledge of men, determination, tireless effort, and steadiness of purpose, undeterred by the weariness of long waiting, and by reverses of fortune', and was 'strengthened by a steadfast faith in God, and complete devotion to duty'.[126] Horne 'had the stern unbending sense of duty',[127] and admitted that 'I am always forgetting about things other than the war, that occupies all my time & thought'.[128] Horne had a simple and economic lifestyle. Whereas Currie, a corps commander, had three ADCs, Horne, an army commander, had only one.[129] Of 'deep religious sentiment',[130] having read 'the Bible from cover to cover including the dull bits',[131] Horne, like Haig, closely identified his God with the Allied cause. He believed not only that 'every blow at the Germans is a blow for the Kingdom of Christ',[132] but also that 'no men fight better than those who fight for their religion and the more we foster the spirit of the Covenanters the better will our men fight & the more rapid will be our success'.[133] A staff officer remarked that: 'He was perhaps the most completely upright man I have known. I can think of no better description of him – completely without fear morally and physically (or appeared to be which is the same thing), courteous always but firm, and with great charm.'[134]

As a personality, Horne combined an 'inflexible insistence on efficiency with the greatest kindness and courtesy to all ranks' and ran 'essentially a "happy" unit'.[135] But he 'was impatient of indiscipline, of slackness, of eyewash, and especially of a lack of care in Commanders for the lives and the comfort of their men'. He disliked seeing 'a slack trace, men lounging on their horses at a halt, or horses across the road, when he passed a battery on the march', and such sights 'would bring him bounding from his car, with quick sharp words to the officers'.[136] However, 'his naturally strong and impulsive temper was always kept under iron control'.[137]

Like Haig, Horne was a fine sportsman,[138] with 'the graceful easy seat of the hunting soldier', whose interest in hunting, polo, pig sticking, and sport formed 'his character as a soldier'.[139] Having begun his long association with the Pytchley Hunt in the early 1880s, Horne hunted with this pack, apart from interruptions caused by the South African War, the First World War and a period of service in Ireland, until 1926. In Ireland, Horne so enjoyed riding with the Duhallow that he was nearly persuaded to leave the army to become master of the fox hounds.[140] As a commander:

> He was not robust, and the exertions and strain of command told upon his constitution; but he was fully alive to the importance of his own physical fitness, and he kept himself keen and hard, he ate little and drank nothing; once a heavy smoker, he had reduced himself to one cigarette a day after dinner, and one on going to bed. Whenever possible he rode, and his great delight was to send horses some ten miles from home to meet his car on return from some official visit, and to ride home hard across country.[141]

This enthusiasm for riding had its own dangers. He broke a bone in his foot in April 1917 and sustained a black eye in October 1918, when his horse came down on him.[142]

Like other senior officers who had not attended Staff College, Horne's success rested upon strong partnerships with his senior staff officers, notably Norman Macmullen (XV Corps), John Vaughan (2nd Division and XV Corps) and Hastings Anderson (First Army). 'One of the outstanding features of XV Corps 'was the "very happy family" of the Corps Staff.'[143] Horne 'was splendid to serve with', as he 'always knew which staff officer to send for when he had a job to do'. As a result 'the staff work went like clockwork' and he 'could get his orders carried out'.[144] In praising the 'first rate' and 'splendid' Macmullen, Horne emphasized what he believed a staff officer should be: 'clever, energetic, hard working & loyal'.[145] Horne noted that 'Father' Vaughan 'bears the burden & heat of the operations like a hero', and 'is a splendid staff officer'. He admitted that 'his services are very valuable to me'[146] and that 'I miss him very much as he has been my right hand man during all these operations', because 'Vaughan & I understand each other's ways so well that it is not easy to replace him'. Between September 1916 and March 1917 Horne's concern with Vaughan's appendicitis on the eve of the Battle of Guedecourt, his treatment and his eventual recovery[147] reflects the close bond between the two men.

The strengths of the regimental officer, such as attention to detail and knowledge of the troops, in the person of Horne were combined with the more intellectual and cerebral gifts of Anderson, 'supreme as a Staff Officer'. Their partnership formed 'a strong combination',[148] which was to survive until the end of the war and is beaten for longevity only by that of Rawlinson and Archie

Montgomery (later Field Marshal Sir Archibald Montgomery-Massingberd) at Fourth Army. Horne noted in June 1918 that Anderson 'has earned promotion if anyone in the army has'.[149] Anderson was moved at an hour's notice to Horne's XV Corps on the Somme as the result of the illness of Vaughan.[150] At their first meeting Anderson 'found a stern, reticent, soldierly-looking General, distressed by the sudden loss of a trusted senior Staff Officer, and anxious about the details of the impending attack, but calm, confident, and in no way fussing'. A week later Horne left to assume command of the First Army.[151]

At the beginning of February 1917 Anderson, 'said to be a particularly good man' and 'well known as a very good staff officer',[152] was ordered to join the First Army as Horne's MGGS. The Vimy Ridge offensive was imminent and preparations were already well in progress. His first interview with Horne was characteristic:

> He told me frankly that he had been anxious to get his old Brigadier-General, General Staff, on the Somme, as his senior Army Staff Officer, but on being told that other officers senior to him could not be passed over, he had asked for me, having known me for a short time on the Somme. He appeared to me typically a Highlander, suspicious of strangers, slow to give his confidence to those he had not thoroughly proved, reticent, and somewhat lonely in his high position, and very conscious of the great duties and responsibility which it imposed on him.[153]

Following the success of operations on Vimy Ridge, Horne 'seemed satisfied that his staff had proved themselves' and 'from that time until the end of the War' he gave to Anderson and 'to his other principal staff officers, his absolute and complete confidence'.[154] Horne's 'ignorance of staff work' had the advantage that: 'He knew what he wanted, his decisions were sound, crisp and reasoned, and once given they were adhered to; the detailed execution was left to his staff, and that staff, once proved in his estimation, were given the fullest trust and confidence, and knew that whether results were favourable or unfavourable, honest endeavour would receive full backing.'[155] The arrival of Sir Frederic Mercer (MGRA) and Sir Gerald Heath (chief engineer), both old and tried friends, who joined Horne's mess, and Sir Geoffrey Twining (senior administrative staff officer) to replace Major General P.E.F. Hobbs, who had resigned because he could not get on with Horne,[156] 'completed the immediate family entourage of senior Staff Officers who served the Army Commander in complete amity during the strenuous days of 1917'.[157] Horne later replaced Mercer as his MGRA in April 1918 with Ernest Alexander, who had been his BGRA at XV Corps on the Somme in 1916. But, apart from a number of promotions, no further changes were made by Horne to his First Army staff. Horne relied on this close-knit team and on Anderson, who undertook the basic administrative and bureaucratic tasks, in particular to ensure that his decisions were put into effect. Although 'a light sleeper, ever fully alive to the implications of the booming of the German guns, and the dawn bombardments of the British attacks', Horne never once sent for Anderson 'between 11 o'clock at night and 7 o'clock in the morning from the dawn of Vimy in April 1917 until the Armistice of the 11th November 1918'.[158]

It has been suggested that Horne 'never suffered a disaster but did not really behave like an Army commander'. It is said that 'from the attack on Vimy Ridge on 9 April 1917 he seems to have acquired the habit of giving all substantial offensive tasks to the Canadian Corps and leaving both planning and execution very largely to that corps commander and his staff'.[159] At first glance it would appear that Haig was prepared, when the need arose, to accept the tactical advice of Horne's subordinates – especially Currie – rather than that of Horne himself. Moreover, 'Haig's refusal to overrule Currie on Horne's behalf supports the position that Haig trusted Currie's judgement in operational matters more than some of his own Army commanders'. Indeed, Horne's 'unwilling acquiescence' in Currie's plan undoubtedly 'underlined Currie's primacy in operations where his Corps formed the "spearhead"'.[160]

But there were a number of other factors involved. More than any other army commander Horne had to deal diplomatically with troops of sovereign nations, Canada and Portugal, under his command. In dealing with Currie, Horne was hamstrung by the fact that he was more of an ally than a subordinate and the growing realization that the Canadian Corps, and by extension Canada, was now an ally, although still a junior one. Horne was under pressure both from Haig and the politicians at home to ensure that casualties were at a minimum. Far from showing that even at this stage of the war there were officers who still preferred a costly frontal assault, Horne's actions show how conscientious he was and the consultative process at all levels by which the successful campaign of 1918 was arrived at. His relationship with Currie was at times prickly but reflected a trust in each other and Horne, after expressing his misgivings, was bound to respect the advice of the man on the spot or to sack him. This is indicative of how well he had learnt the main lesson of 1916–17, namely the supremacy of the man on the spot. By mid-1918 effective army commanders, such as Byng, Horne, Plumer and Rawlinson, and corps commanders, such as Currie, Haldane and Monash, were given greater participation in planning.

Certainly Horne was not the type of man to let subordinates take liberties with him or to shirk telling his superiors unpalatable truths. For example, Horne told Haig in May 1917 that 'the divisions in the First Army are not equal to much offensive action at the present moment'.[161] In July 1918, with Byng, Horne opposed a plan to retake Orange Hill and Monchy-le-Preux suggested by Haig, who 'at once decided to give up the idea of an immediate attack'.[162] Horne was seen as a safe pair of hands by his contemporaries, notably Haig, and one staff officer noted how much he was trusted in making essential decisions.[163] When Sir Ivor Maxse (XVIII Corps) 'made difficulties' about holding his front, Horne told him that 'if his dispositions were not satisfactory, it was his (Maxse's) fault, and if he felt that he could not hold his front, let him say so, and another corps commander would be put in to relieve him at once'.[164] Horne only allowed Currie to proceed when he was fully satisfied, providing the framework for offensives by his corps and a link at the operational level between Haig at the strategic level and his corps commanders, notably Currie, at the tactical level.

It says much for Horne that he was trusted by both Haig and Currie, despite some tensions yet, as Anderson noted:

> The just fame of the Canadians who were throughout his command the backbone of the First Army, and the prominence rightly given by the Canadian press to their prowess, tended to obscure the part played by Lord Horne as an Army Commander in directing, guiding, and combining with the work of other Corps, the operations in which they participated.[165]

Horne was a member of the cadre of the 'surprisingly large number of very capable Generals' on whom 'are our successes to be chiefly attributed',[166] which had slowly been built up during the war and whose accomplishments were behind the British victories which resulted in the triumph of November 1918. Horne's prestige rests on 'the successful command of an Army during two years of arduous campaigning against the picked divisions of the great German Nation in Arms – of an Army which amounted often to no less than 500,000 men, with some 1,300 guns', winning impressive victories at Vimy Ridge, Hill 70, the Scarpe, Drocourt-Quéant and Canal du Nord. The conclusion that 'Horne was a competent officer' and 'handled his army with skill and was respected, if not greatly loved, by all who served with him'[167] is a fair one. Although not a great general, Horne was nevertheless seen by his contemporaries as being 'a first rate soldier',[168] who, although best known for capturing Vimy Ridge, should be better known for his achievements during the last hundred days of the war.

Bibliography

As indicated earlier, there is no biography of Horne, but Lieutenant General Sir Hastings Anderson wrote an appreciation, 'Lord Horne as Army Commander', *Journal of the Royal Artillery*, 56 (January 1930), pp. 407–18, a copy of which is retained among the Horne papers at the Imperial War Museum. Similarly, there is also an appreciation, 'General the Lord Horne of Stirkoke' by General Sir Herbert Uniacke, in the same collection. In addition, Anderson wrote three articles on operations by First Army, 'The Crossing of the Canal du Nord', *Canadian Defence Quarterly*, 2/1 (October 1924); 'The Operations Round Valenciennes by the First Army, October–November 1918', *Canadian Defence Quarterly*, 2/3 (April 1925); and 'The Breaking of the Quéant–Drocourt Line by the Canadian Corps, First Army', *Canadian Defence Quarterly*, 3/2 (January 1926). Currie is covered by Lieutenant Colonel Wilfred Bovey, 'General Sir Arthur Currie: An Appreciation', *Canadian Defence Quarterly*, 3/4 (July 1926); Daniel G. Dancocks, *Sir Arthur Currie: A Biography* (Ontario: Methuen, 1985); A.M.J. Hyatt, *General Sir Arthur Currie* (Toronto: University of

Toronto Press, 1987); and Hugh M. Urquhart, *Arthur Currie: The Biography of a Great Canadian* (Toronto: J.M. Dent, 1950). The contribution of the Canadian Corps is covered by many works, including Daniel Dancocks, *Spearhead to Victory: Canada and the Great War* (Edmonton: Hurtig, 1987); D.J. Goodspeed, *The Road Past Vimy: The Canadian Corps, 1914–1918* (Toronto: Macmillan of Canada, 1969); Shane B. Schreiber, *Shock Army of the British Empire: The Canadian Corps in the Last 100 Days of the Great War* (Westport: Praeger, 1997); Jeffrey Williams, *Byng of Vimy: General and Governor-General* (London: Leo Cooper, 1983); and Larry Worthington, *Amid the Guns Below: The Story of the Canadian Corps, 1914–1919* (Toronto: McClelland and Stewart, 1965). The Hundred Days generally is dealt with by J.P. Harris and Niall Barr, *Amiens to the Armistice: The BEF in the Hundred Days' campaign, 8 August – 11 November 1918* (London: Brassey's, 1998).

Notes

1 J.P. Harris and Niall Barr, *Amiens to the Armistice* (London: Brassey's, 1998), p. 153.
2 Robin Neillands, *The Great War Generals on the Western Front, 1914–18* (London: Robinson, 1999), p. 327. The same applies to the updated entry in the new *DNB*. Horne's copious papers are now held in the Imperial War Museum (hereafter IWM).
3 IWM, Horne MSS, Horne to his wife, 23 April 1917.
4 IWM, Horne MSS, General Sir Herbert Uniacke, 'General the Lord Horne of Stirkoke', p. 3.
5 IWM, Horne MSS, Horne to his wife, 1 January 1915.
6 Ibid., Horne to his wife, 11 November 1918.
7 Brigadier General J. Charteris, *At GHQ* (London: Cassell, 1931), pp. 56–7.
8 Major General Sir Frederick Maurice, 'General Lord Horne', *Dictionary of National Biography, 1922–1930* (Oxford: Oxford University Press, 1937), p. 430.
9 Lieutenant General Sir Hastings Anderson, 'Lord Horne as an Army Commander', *Journal of the Royal Artillery*, 56 (January 1930), p. 407.
10 IWM, Horne MSS, Horne to his wife, 1 and 2 January 1915; The National Archives, Public Record Office (hereafter PRO), Haig MSS, WO 256/3, Haig diary, 31 December 1914.
11 Ibid., WO 256/4, Haig diary, 8 July 1915.
12 Ibid., WO 256/5, Haig diary, 16 August 1915.
13 Ibid., WO 256/12, Haig diary, 11, 13 and 20 August 1916; IWM, Horne MSS, Horne to his wife, 26 March, 11 April, 28, 29 and 30 August, and 26, 29 and 30 September 1916.
14 PRO, WO 256/1, Haig diary, 23 August and 18 September 1914.
15 Ibid., WO 256/3–4, Haig diary, 1 March and 11 May 1915.
16 IWM, Horne MSS, Horne to his wife, 17 June 1918.
17 PRO, WO 256/10, Haig diary, 10 and 15 May 1916, and Robertson to Haig, 15 May 1916.
18 National Library of Scotland (hereafter NLS), Haig MSS, Robertson to Haig, 15 April 1917.
19 PRO, WO 256/11, Haig diary, 2 July 1916.
20 Gregory Blaxland, *Amiens: 1918* (London: Muller, 1968), p. 14.
21 PRO, CAB 45/137, Major General E.W. Alexander to Brigadier General Sir James Edmonds, 21 February 1930.
22 Anderson, 'Horne as Army Commander', p. 407.
23 PRO, CAB 45/134, Lieutenant Colonel R.S. Hardman to Edmonds, 30 March 1930.
24 Ibid., CAB 45/137, Alexander to Edmonds, 21 February 1930.
25 Ibid.
26 Ibid., WO 256/11, Haig diary, 4, 8, 9 and 10 July 1916.
27 Ibid., WO 256/6 and 9, Haig diary, 16 November 1915 and 18 March 1916.
28 Ibid., CAB 45/135, Major G.H. King to Edmonds, 27 March 1930.
29 Churchill Archives Centre, Churchill College, Cambridge (hereafter CAC), Bonham-Carter MSS, 9/2, General Sir Charles Bonham-Carter, 'Autobiography', ch. 8, pp. 13–14.
30 PRO, CAB 45/132, Major G.P.L. Drake-Brockman to Edmonds, 7 February 1930.
31 IWM, Wilson MSS, Field-Marshal Sir Henry Wilson diary, 19 July 1916.
32 PRO, WO 256/12, Haig diary, 11 August 1916.
33 IWM, Wilson MSS, Wilson diary, 21 August 1916.
34 PRO, WO 256/12, Robertson to Haig, 10 August 1916.

35 Brian Bond and Simon Robbins, eds, *Staff Officer: The Diaries of Walter Guinness (First Lord Moyne)*, *1914–1918* (London: Leo Cooper, 1987), pp. 129–30.

36 King's College, London, Liddell Hart Centre for Military Archives (hereafter LHCMA), Brigadier Sir Edward Beddington MSS, 'Memoir', p. 92.

37 PRO, WO 256/12, Haig diary, 13 and 20 August 1916.

38 IWM, Wilson MSS, Wilson diary, 11, 12 and 14 October 1916.

39 PRO, WO 256/13, Haig diary, 24 October 1916.

40 IWM, Horne MSS, 73/60/2, Fergusson to Horne, 10 October 1918.

41 Ibid., Holland to Horne, 12 October 1918.

42 PRO, CAB 45/123, General Lord Jeffreys to Edmonds, 31 July 1931.

43 IWM, Horne MSS, Horne to his wife, 13 June 1918.

44 PRO, WO 95/168, Minutes of Conference of Corps Commanders held by GOC, First Army, at Château Philomel, 29 March 1917.

45 Ibid.

46 Ibid., WO 95/169, Minutes of Conference of Corps Commanders held at Headquarters, Canadian Corps, Camblain L'Abbé, 5 p.m., 15/4/17.

47 Ibid., WO 95/168, XI Corps SS.1226/16, 18 March 1917.

48 Captain Cyril Falls, *Military Operations: France and Belgium, 1917*, vol. 1 (London: Macmillan, 1940), pp. 300, 302, 312 and 316.

49 Byng to his wife, 15 April 1917, quoted by Jeffrey Williams, *Byng of Vimy: General and Governor-General* (London: Leo Cooper, 1983), p. 165.

50 IWM, Fourth Army MSS, vol. 6, Conferences and Various Somme Papers, 5 February to 16 November 1916, 'Notes of Conference held at Fourth Army Headqrs, 8th July 1916'.

51 PRO, WO 95/168, Major General W.H. Anderson to Canadian Corps, First Army No GS 529/12(G), 8 March 1917.

52 Ibid., WO 256/17, Haig diary, 12 April 1917.

53 Colonel G.W.L. Nicholson, *Official History of the Canadian Army in the First World War: Canadian Expeditionary Force, 1914–1919* (Ottawa: Queen's Printer, 1964), p. 258.

54 Brigadier General Sir James Edmonds, *Military Operations: France and Belgium, 1917*, vol. 2 (London: HMSO, 1948), pp. 112–15.

55 Nicholson, *Canadian Expeditionary Force*, p. 285; Hugh M. Urquhart, *Arthur Currie* (Toronto: J.M. Dent, 1950), p. 169; Daniel G. Dancocks, *Sir Arthur Currie* (Ontario: Methuen, 1985), pp. 105–7; A.M.J. Hyatt, *General Sir Arthur Currie* (Toronto: University of Toronto Press, 1987), pp. 76–7.

56 PRO, WO 158/189, Horne, 'General Artillery Plan', 2 September 1917.

57 Dancocks, *Currie*, pp. 110–11; Urquhart, *Currie*, pp. 171–2.

58 PRO, WO 2456/23, Haig diary, 5 October 1917.

59 Anderson, 'Horne as Army Commander', p. 410.

60 PRO, WO 256/25, Haig diary, 16 December 1917.

61 Ibid., WO 158/90, Horne to Lieutenant General Sir Launcelot Kiggell, 27 December 1917 and Kiggell to Horne, 29 December 1917.

62 Ibid., Horne to GHQ, First Army No GS 1167, 6 May 1918.

63 Urquhart, *Currie*, p. 212.

64 Anderson, 'Horne as Army Commander', pp. 412–13.

65 Dancocks, *Currie*, pp. 110–11.

66 PRO, WO 256/30, Haig diary, 18 April 1918.

67 Ibid., WO 95/178, Horne to GHQ, First Army No GS 1376/8, 17 August 1918.

68 IWM, First Army General Staff (First Army, March 1919), 'Report on First Army Operations, 26th August – 11th November, 1918', p. 3.

69 Brigadier General Sir James Edmonds and Lieutenant Colonel R. Maxwell-Hyslop, *Military Operations: France and Belgium, 1918*, vol. 5 (London: HMSO, 1947), p. 20.

70 Major General W.H. Anderson, 'The Crossing of the Canal du Nord', *Canadian Defence Quarterly*, 2/1 (October 1924), p. 67.

71 IWM, First Army, 'Report on First Army Operations', p. 1.

72 PRO, WO 256/32–3, Haig diary, 23 June, 5 and 16 July 1918.

73 Ibid., WO 256/33, Haig to Foch, OAD 895, 17 July 1918.

74 Ibid., Haig diary, 16 July 1918.
75 Edmonds and Maxwell-Hyslop, *Military Operations: France and Belgium, 1918*, pp. 119 and 139.
76 PRO, WO 256/34, Haig diary, 14 August 1918.
77 Ibid., WO 158/191, GHQ to Horne, 14 August 1918, OAD 907/1.
78 Ibid., WO 256/34, Haig diary, 15 August 1918.
79 Ibid., WO 158/191, GHQ to Horne, 14 August 1918, OAD 907/1, and 16 August 1918, OAD 907/2.
80 Ibid., First Army to Advanced GHQ, 17 August 1918.
81 Ibid., WO 256/35, Haig diary, 22, 24 and 25 August 1918.
82 First Army, *Report on First Army Operations*, p. 2.
83 PRO, WO 256/35, Haig diary, 26 August 1918.
84 IWM, Horne MSS, Horne to his wife, 27 August 1918.
85 First Army, *Report on First Army Operations*, pp. 3–4.
86 PRO, WO 256/35, Haig diary, 27 August 1918.
87 First Army, *Report on First Army Operations*, pp. 5 and 9.
88 IWM, Horne MSS, Horne to his wife, 28 August 1918.
89 PRO, WO 95/178, Lieutenant Colonel O.H.L. Nicholson, 'Notes on Conference held at Canadian Corps headquarters, 29th August, 1919', First Army No GS 1376/30, 30 August 1918.
90 PRO, WO 256/35, Haig diary, 30 August 1918.
91 Ibid., 31 August 1918.
92 Ibid., WO 256/36, Haig diary, 1 September 1918.
93 Major General W.H. Anderson, 'The Breaking of the Quéant–Drocourt Line by the Canadian Corps, First Army', *Canadian Defence Quarterly*, 3/2 (January 1926), pp. 121–2.
94 IWM, Horne MSS, Horne to his wife, 2 and 3 September 1918.
95 Anderson, 'Breaking of Quéant-Drocourt Line', p. 127.
96 First Army, *Report on First Army Operations*, p. 13.
97 Anderson, 'Breaking of Quéant-Drocourt Line', p. 126.
98 IWM, Wilson MSS, file 40, Lawrence to Wilson, 2 September 1918.
99 Ibid., Horne MSS, Horne to his wife, 6 September 1918.
100 Ibid., Horne to his wife, 12 September 1918.
101 PRO, WO 158/91, Horne to GHQ, First Army No GS 1409/2, 11 September 1918.
102 Ibid., WO 256/36, Haig diary, 15 September 1918.
103 Ibid., 21 and 29 September 1918.
104 'Remarks by General Lord Horne', in Anderson, 'Crossing of Canal du Nord', p. 75.
105 Ibid., p. 76.
106 IWM, Horne MSS, Horne to his wife, 27 September 1918.
107 Lieutenant Colonel Wilfred Bovey, 'General Sir Arthur Currie: An Appreciation', *Canadian Defence Quarterly*, 3/4 (July 1926), p. 378; see also Larry Worthington, *Amid the Guns Below* (Toronto: McClelland and Stewart, 1965), p. 146.
108 Dancocks, *Currie*, pp. 2–3.
109 Urquhart, *Currie*, pp. 251–3, and Daniel Dancocks, *Spearhead to Victory* (Edmonton: Hurtig, 1987), pp. 132–4.
110 Anderson, 'Crossing of Canal du Nord', p. 68.
111 PRO, WO 95/179, First Army Instructions for Operations, First Army GS 1427/1, 18 September 1918.
112 Anderson, 'Crossing of Canal du Nord', p. 74.
113 Ibid., p. 73; First Army, *Report on First Army Operations, 26th August – 11th November, 1918*, p. 31.
114 IWM, Horne MSS, Horne to his wife, 27 September 1918.
115 Anderson, 'Crossing of Canal du Nord', p. 63.
116 PRO, WO 256/36, Haig diary, 27 September 1918.
117 IWM, Horne MSS, Horne to his wife, 11 November 1918.
118 Dancocks, *Spearhead to Victory*, p. 208.
119 Urquhart, *Currie*, p. 182.
120 Dancocks, *Currie*, p. 171.
121 IWM, Horne MSS, 73/60/2, Note by H.M.M.C. [Brevet Lieutenant Colonel H.C. Maitland-Makgill-Crichton, GSO1, First Army], [March 1919].
122 Ibid., Horne to Currie, 27 March 1919.

123 Dancocks, *Currie*, p. 238; Urquhart, *Currie*, p. 319.

124 IWM, Wilson MSS, 2/46A/4, Major General Sir C.H. Harington to Wilson, 6 April 1919.

125 Anderson, 'Horne as Army Commander', p. 409.

126 Ibid., p. 407.

127 Ibid., p. 418.

128 IWM, Horne MSS, Horne to his wife, 19 October 1918.

129 Dancocks, *Currie*, p. 244.

130 Anderson, 'Horne as Army Commander', pp. 417–18.

131 CAC, Bonham-Carter MSS, 'Autobiography', ch. 9, pp. 27–8.

132 Reverend George S. Duncan, Diary, 28 September 1917, quoted in Gerard DeGroot, ed., 'The Reverend George S Duncan at GHQ, 1916–18', in *Military Miscellany I* (Stroud: Sutton for Army Records Society, 1996), pp. 391–2.

133 IWM, Horne MSS, Horne to his wife, 25 December 1916.

134 CAC, Bonham-Carter MSS, 'Autobiography', ch. 9, pp. 27–8.

135 Uniacke, 'Horne of Stirkoke', p. 4.

136 Anderson, 'Horne as Army Commander', p. 418.

137 Ibid., p. 409.

138 CAC, Bonham-Carter MSS, 'Autobiography', ch. 9, pp. 27–8.

139 Anderson, 'Horne as Army Commander', pp. 408 and 417.

140 Uniacke, 'Horne of Stirkoke', pp. 4–5.

141 Anderson, 'Horne as Army Commander', p. 417.

142 IWM, Horne MSS, Horne to his wife, 23 April 1917 and 24 October 1918.

143 PRO, CAB 45/132, Major P.J.R. Currie to Edmonds, 23 April 1930.

144 Ibid., CAB 45/136, C.M. Page to Edmonds, 25 August 1934.

145 IWM, Horne MSS, Horne to his wife, 11 April 1916.

146 Ibid., Horne to his wife, 22 September 1916.

147 Ibid., Horne to his wife, 18, 22, 23, 24 and 25 September 1916.

148 CAC, Bonham-Carter MSS, 'Autobiography', ch. 9, pp. 27–8.

149 IWM, Horne MSS, Horne to his wife, 3 June 1918.

150 Anderson, 'Horne as Army Commander', p. 408.

151 Ibid.

152 IWM, Horne MSS, Horne to his wife, 23 and 24 September 1916.

153 Anderson, 'Horne as Army Commander', pp. 408–9.

154 Ibid., p. 409.

155 Ibid., p. 417.

156 PRO, WO 256/16, Haig diary, 3 March 1917.

157 Anderson, 'Horne as Army Commander', pp. 408–9.

158 Ibid., p. 409.

159 Harris and Barr, *Amiens to the Armistice*, pp. 153–4.

160 Shane B. Schreiber, *Shock Army of the British Empire* (Westport: Praeger, 1997), pp. 98–9.

161 PRO, WO 256/18, Lieutenant General Sir Launcelot Kiggell, 'Note of Proceedings at Army Commander's Conference, held at Doullens on Monday, the 7th May, 1917, at 11 a.m'.

162 Ibid., WO 256/33, Haig diary, 16 July 1918.

163 Brigadier General Sir Archibald Home, Diary, 30 August 1918, quoted in Diana Briscoe, ed., *The Diary of a World War I Cavalry Officer* (London, 1985), pp. 181–2.

164 PRO, WO 256/31, Haig diary, 14 May 1918.

165 Anderson, 'Horne as Army Commander', p. 417.

166 PRO, WO 256/36, Haig diary, 20 September 1918.

167 Neillands, *Great War Generals*, p. 327.

168 CAC, Bonham-Carter MSS, 'Autobiography', ch. 9, pp. 27–8.

Chapter Six

Charles Monro

Third Army, 1915; First Army, 1916

John Bourne

Sir Charles Monro is probably the least known of the men who commanded British armies on the Western Front during the Great War. He is also – arguably – the least important. Third Army in 1915 was charged only with holding the line while under his command. First Army in 1916 saw more action, suffering a series of minor reverses and launching one botched and unnecessary attack, at Fromelles, but engaging in no operations on the scale of those of Fourth and Fifth armies on the Somme. Monro's name is therefore associated in the public mind neither with disaster nor with triumph. He seems doomed to be remembered only for the part he played in bringing the Gallipoli campaign to a conclusion, and as the butt of Churchill's magisterial gibe 'he came, he saw, he capitulated'.[1] But this disguises an interesting and significant career as a military administrator and trainer of troops, both before the war, during it on the Western Front, and finally as commander-in-chief, India.

Monro was descended from an old Scottish family, most prominent in the field of medicine. His mother, however, was Irish and it was said of him that he was 'Scotch on duty and Irish off duty'.[2] Although Monro seems to have been destined for the army from an early age, his apparent personal preference for the military life was not reflected in an early commitment to high professional seriousness, quite the contrary in fact. He passed out 120th from the Royal Military College, Sandhurst, where he was described as 'below average, unpunctual and a bad rider'.[3] Regimental soldiering with the 1st Battalion, Queen's (Royal West Surrey Regiment), also did little to dispel the impression that Monro regarded the officer corps as an exclusive travel, sports and social club, though he did become adjutant of his battalion, usually a sign of administrative ability and ambition. The next step on the professional ladder was entry into the Staff College, Camberley, which Monro achieved in 1889, but he made little impression there, except as captain of cricket, even among a dull group of contemporaries, of whom only one – R.G. Broadwood – later held high command on the Western Front (as GOC IV Corps). What changed Monro and brought him to the fore was the serious business of a real war in South

Chronology

15 June 1860	Charles Carmichael Monro born at sea on *Maid of Judah*
	Educated at Sherborne School and Royal Military College, Sandhurst
13 August 1879	Gazetted to 2nd Foot (later 1st Battalion, Queen's [Royal West Surrey Regiment])
24 July 1889	Promoted captain
1889–90	Attended Staff College, Camberley
1890	Appointed ADC to governor of Malta
23 February 1898	Promoted major and appointed brigade major, Gibraltar
	Appointed DAAG Guernsey
	Appointed DAAG Aldershot
1899	Appointed DAAG 6th Division
29 November 1900	Promoted lieutenant colonel
19 February 1901	Appointed chief instructor, School of Musketry, Hythe
28 March 1903	Appointed commandant, School of Musketry
29 November 1903	Promoted colonel
12 May 1907	Appointed GOC 13th Infantry Brigade
31 October 1910	Promoted major general and appointed GOC 2nd London Division
1 October 1912	Married Mary Caroline Towneley-O'Hagan
5 August 1914	Appointed GOC 2nd Division
26 December 1914	Appointed GOC I Corps
13 July 1915	Appointed GOC Third Army
27 October 1915	Appointed C.-in-C. Mediterranean Expeditionary Force
28 October 1915	Promoted lieutenant general
23 November 1915	Appointed C.-in-C. Eastern Mediterranean Forces
4 February 1916	Appointed GOC First Army
1 October 1916	Promoted general and appointed C.-in-C. India
August 1920	Retired as C.-in-C. India
1921	Created baronet and appointed Bath king of arms
1923	Appointed governor of Gibraltar
August 1928	Retired as governor
7 December 1929	Died at London

Appointed CB 1906, KCB 1915, GCMG 1916, GCSI 1919, GCB 1919

Africa, where he served as deputy assistant adjutant general, 6th Division, and was mentioned in dispatches.

The South African War, of course, had an impact beyond one British officer. It galvanized the British state, the British army and what would now be called the 'defence establishment'. A series of important social reforms were designed to improve the health and potential military effectiveness of the urban working class. British diplomacy abandoned 'splendid isolation'. An important alliance was concluded with Japan (1902). Improved relations with France and Russia were sought and achieved (1904, 1907). The Elgin Commission and the Esher Committee began the top-to-bottom reform of the British army, establishing an Army Council and a General Staff, reforming the Committee of Imperial Defence, abolishing the post of commander-in-chief and introducing promotion by selection board above the rank of captain. The army's weaponry and equipment were modernized. 'Doctrine', something the British army was deemed to lack, was encapsulated in *Field Service Regulations, Parts 1 and II*. Three outstanding commandants, Henry Wilson, Henry Rawlinson and William Robertson, gave the Staff College a renewed sense of purpose. The lawyer–philosopher R.B. Haldane created the Territorial Force and the British Expeditionary Force. In this heady atmosphere of military reform, Charles Monro finally emerged from the professional pack.

The South African War was a double affront to Monro, first as a 'Briton' and second as a soldier. The South African War represented a crisis of British imperialism. Monro was an ardent and sincere imperialist. He saw the empire not only as a source of British power and influence in the world, but also as a moral influence and a moral challenge, at the heart of which lay the need for discipline and the demands of duty. 'Discipline' and 'duty' were ever Monro's guiding principles. Like most of his contemporaries, he could not envisage a satisfactory world in which the British Empire did not endure. The South African War was a timely reminder of how important were efficient military forces to the empire's security. The war had exposed the army's limitations before the world in a most embarrassing way. Monro was destined to play a leading part in remedying some key deficiencies.

Even before the South African War ended, Monro was appointed chief instructor (CI) at the School of Musketry, Hythe. He held this position from 19 February 1901 until 28 March 1903, when he became the school's commandant, a post he retained until 28 March 1907. Monro's appointment as CI and then commandant is indicative of the army's conviction that the shooting skills, tactical awareness and field craft of ordinary soldiers had to be greatly improved. Monro was not the only talented officer to be appointed to Hythe during this important period of reform. He was succeeded as CI by W.D. Bird (1903–5),[4] N.R. McMahon (1905–9)[5] and John Campbell (1909–13),[6] and as commandant by G.G.A. Egerton (1907–9),[7] Walter Congreve VC (1909–11)[8] and the guardsman Harold Ruggles-Brise (1911–14).[9] Theirs was a collective effort and a collective success, but none served at Hythe longer than Monro (six years) and he should be given a lion's share of the credit for what was achieved.

What was achieved? No less than a revolution in the shooting prowess of the ordinary British soldier, armed from 1907 with an excellent new weapon, the Short Magazine Lee Enfield Mark III with its extreme accuracy, smooth, ergonomic bolt action and ten-round detachable magazine. New battlefield tactics, based on 'fire and manoeuvre', replaced the old advance in extended line. This system was based on a company skirmishing with alternate platoons dashing forward, covered by the suppressive fire of the other platoons. The reality of these achievements has recently been doubted.[10] But soldiers themselves seemed convinced of the improvement, taking pride and confidence from the excellence of their training, as Corporal W. Holbrook later recalled to Lyn Macdonald.[11] Infantrymen fired 500 rounds each a year. A qualified marksman while prone could fire 15 rounds a minute at moving khaki-coloured targets at ranges of up to 500 yards. These skills were to prove themselves and to confirm their reality during the epic battles of 1914.

Having established a reputation as a progressive modernizer, it is no surprise that Monro was given command of one of the new Territorial Force divisions, the 2nd London, in October 1910. Had the European War not broken out it is difficult to know where Monro's career would have gone. In August 1914 he was coming to the end of a standard four-year tour with the Territorials. Sir Archibald Murray was slated to command the Regular 2nd Division, but his selection as chief of the General Staff to Sir John French (commander-in-chief of the BEF) – an appointment made necessary by the Liberal government's refusal to accept French's choice, Sir Henry Wilson – created a vacancy that Monro filled. 2nd Division was in Douglas Haig's I Corps. The tone of Haig's diary in noticing Monro's appointment does not suggest that Haig was consulted about the change. 'The 2nd Division has just been given a new commander,' Haig wrote on 13 August. 'Monro proved himself to be a good regimental officer and an excellent Commandant of the Hythe School of Musketry, but some years with Territorials has resulted in his becoming rather fat. There is, however, no doubt about his military ability, although he lacks the practical experience in commanding a Division.'[12] In fact, Monro had no 'practical experience' of commanding anything very much, only an infantry brigade and a Territorial division in peacetime and not so much as a battalion in war. He took over a division with which he was entirely unfamiliar and which did not know him, and found himself commanding it in battle within eighteen days of his appointment.

It is difficult to detect Monro in the act of generalship in 1914. Indeed, it is difficult to detect any of the BEF's leaders in the act of generalship in 1914, except perhaps Sir Horace Smith-Dorrien. Even Haig was reduced at times to behaving like a battalion commander. The battles of 1914 were pre-eminently soldiers' battles. At the small unit, tactical level, the BEF confirmed the value of the lessons taught by Monro and his colleagues at Hythe. But in other respects the fighting revealed the BEF's severe weaknesses: in weaponry (especially heavy artillery); in ammunition supply (especially of high explosive); in all-arms' co-operation; and in command and control.[13]

I Corps was less engaged than II Corps during the retreat from Mons, but Monro seems to have done little to endear himself to Haig. When Haig discovered that 2nd Division was retiring south of the Marne, he commented in his diary on 9 September that Monro's withdrawal showed 'what might happen with nervous commanders who are ready to make use of any excuse to avoid coming to conclusions with the enemy'.[14] This was unfair. It also displayed for the first time Monro's willingness to make sensible tactical decisions – in his view 2nd Division's position was dangerously exposed north of the river – even at the cost of being seen to yield ground without a fight. This theme was to be repeated in 1916.

After the Marne, 2nd Division's war became more severe. Monro had already lost one of his three original brigade commanders during the retreat. Robert Scott-Kerr, 4 (Guards) Brigade, was seriously wounded on 1 September at Villers-Cotterets and never returned to a combat command. Richard Haking (5 Brigade) was wounded on 16 September, though he was able to return before the end of the year. Monro also requested the removal of the New Zealander, R.H. Davies, from command of 6 Brigade on 23 September. Davies had insisted on marching to the front at the head of his men. This contributed significantly to his mental and physical collapse. Monro acted swiftly once he realized Davies's state of health. Monro himself was also nearly a casualty when a German shell hit Hooge Château, in which the staffs of 1st and 2nd Divisions were meeting, on 31 October. The explosion mortally wounded Major General Lomax (GOC 1st Division) and killed six staff officers. Monro was stunned for some hours, before making a complete recovery. During the desperate fighting that followed the Marne, Monro displayed physical courage and understanding of the situation. His orders were clear, to the point and personally delivered. 'Your brigade is on that hill,' he told the Earl of Cavan when he arrived to replace Scott-Kerr: 'see they stick to it.'[15] It was Monro who loaned 2nd Battalion Worcestershire Regiment to Lomax, making possible the vital counter-attack at Gheluvelt. Monro remained self-possessed and confident amid the supreme confusion and violence of modern war. His presence uplifted others. Henry Page Croft, a razor-keen Territorial officer and another ardent imperialist, recalled a meeting with Monro early in 1915. 'The General is a typical Great-Briton,' he wrote, 'with bright eyes, a rugged countenance, middle height, with big shoulders and a cheery way which endears him to all he meets.'[16] Monro had passed the test of battle. He could command.

At the end of 1914 the BEF was reorganized into armies. Sir Douglas Haig became GOC First Army and Sir Horace Smith-Dorrien GOC Second Army. Monro succeeded Haig in command of I Corps. There was a certain inevitability about this. Of the six infantry division commanders of the original BEF, one (Hamilton) was dead, another (Lomax) was mortally wounded, a third (Snow) was incapacitated by a fall from his horse and a fourth (Fergusson) had rather harshly been sent home. Monro, who had begun the war with no battlefield command experience, was now one of the most experienced commanders in the BEF.

Monro's command of I Corps was short-lived and generally subservient to the battles fought by IV Corps, whose commander, Sir Henry Rawlinson, was already emerging as the preferred executioner of Haig's plans. In July 1915 Monro became the first commander of Third Army. His tenure was again destined to be short-lived, a mere 97 days. During that period Third Army engaged only in line holding, but Monro nevertheless left an important mark not only on Third Army but also on the future development of the BEF.

Monro's promotion had been swift. In less than a year he had risen from a superannuable general of Territorials to commander of a formation without precedence in pre-war planning and organization. There was no training offered for new army commanders. They brought to the task their accumulated experience and learned as they went along. Monro's accumulated experience was biased towards training and military education. It is perhaps, therefore, no surprise that Third Army became the first to introduce army schools, which eventually spread throughout the BEF (and down to corps and division), energizing its professional performance and disseminating 'good practice' across a wide range of military activities and skills. Monro was among the first to recognize that the army in the field needed training, as well as the volunteers at home. According to the ineffable R.J. 'Reggie' Kentish, the development of army schools was due to the 'individual effort' of Monro.[17] Monro was particularly concerned with what he saw as the declining quality of regimental officers and NCOs. The Third Army School of Instruction was concerned originally with matters such as 'leadership'. Kentish designed the syllabus, which was later taken up and developed by J.F.C. Fuller, most didactic of soldiers, who began to find an effective outlet for his restless intelligence and imagination. By 1917 the initiative begun by Monro could truly be called a system which embraced every aspect of the BEF.[18]

The other thing that Monro truly understood was shooting. It is equally unsurprising that he should have sponsored the BEF's self-proclaimed sniping expert, Major Hesketh Prichard, traveller, big-game hunter, novelist and cricketer. Monro was not a man to miss out on a good idea because it came from an unusual and completely unofficial source. The BEF was not doing well in the sniping war at this time and the loss of men to snipers was particularly demoralizing. Prichard recalled Monro's words when they met: 'It is not only that a good shot strengthens his unit, but he adds to its *morale* – he raises the *morale* of his comrades – it raises the *morale* of the whole unit to know that it contains several first class shots.'[19] Third Army was accordingly the first to have a sniper school. Similarly, when Monro took over First Army in January 1916, Prichard was one of the first people he summoned to his headquarters to dine, reiterating the importance he attached to sniping and snipers.[20]

In a few short months Monro had shown himself to be a perceptive and innovative army commander. A 'Confidential Report' on him might have read 'has started well, has the confidence of his staff and subordinates, very promising'.[21] But, in October 1915, all was to change in Monro's career. Kitchener chose him to succeed Sir Ian Hamilton as commander-in-chief of the Mediterranean Expeditionary Force (MEF). The failure of the August offensives to break Turkish resistance on the Gallipoli peninsula and the return of a frustrating and costly stalemate had forced the government's hand and

Hamilton was recalled. Kitchener made it clear to Monro that his first task as C.-in-C. was to recommend whether the campaign should be maintained or the peninsula evacuated. Monro's appointment and subsequent actions have always been controversial. Winston Churchill, principal architect of the Dardanelles/Gallipoli strategy, argued that Monro came to his task with the closed mind of a convinced 'Westerner', whose examination of the situation on the peninsula was perfunctory and whose recommendation – evacuation – was a foregone conclusion. It is difficult to agree with this argument.

Monro met Kitchener four times before he set out for the eastern Mediter-ranean. He spent days reading relevant documentation at the War Office and familiarizing himself with the situation. Kitchener made it clear that he wanted an honest assessment, honestly arrived at. He also made it clear that evacuation was the least acceptable alternative, fearful as ever of how a British defeat by a Muslim power would affect the empire's many Muslim subjects. As a convinced imperialist himself, Monro would have understood the force of this concern. C.F. Aspinall-Oglander, the British official historian of Gallipoli, summarized the instructions Monro received and the spirit in which he received them:

> The special instructions which he [Monro] carried from Lord Kitchener were definite and precise: his first duty was to report fully and frankly on the military situation in Gallipoli; he was to consider the best means of removing the existing deadlock, and to report as soon as possible whether, from a purely military point of view, it would be better to evacuate the peninsula or to try again to capture it. He was to estimate the probable loss that would be incurred in evacua-tion and, alternatively, the number of troops that would be required to ensure the opening of the Straits. He was further to state if this number would suffice to keep the Straits open, and how many more would be needed to capture Constantinople. All these estimates were to be made on the alternative assumptions that the Germans did not reopen the through line to the Turkish capital.[22]

If Monro was given a 'steer', it was not towards the decision he eventually took.

Monro's first call was at the headquarters of the MEF on the island of Imbros, where he immediately impressed the staff with his professionalism, his grasp of the situation and his decisiveness (not always a characteristic associated with Sir Ian Hamilton). Monro landed on the Gallipoli peninsula on 27 October. He spoke to all the corps commanders and their staffs and visited the three beachheads, at Suvla, Anzac and Helles. He was shocked by what he saw. At Anzac his comment was 'It's just like Alice in Wonderland, "curiouser and curiouser".[23] Monro's views were often shared by other officers sent to the peninsula from the Western Front, where the fighting had taught one vital lesson, the need to achieve artillery superiority before an infantry attack could proceed at 'acceptable cost'. Artillery was one of the many things that the MEF lacked, but even had it been more adequately endowed with guns there was nowhere effective to deploy them. It was virtually impossible to ensure the success of an infantry assault. This view was certainly shared by H.L. Reed VC, a gunner, who was sent from the Western Front to be chief of staff to IX Corps at Suvla. Reed, far from 'gingering up' the cautious corps commander, Sir Frederick Stopford, made him even more cautious.

The speed of Monro's decision was not the result of a perfunctory investigation but of pressure from Kitchener. The Secretary of State for War pressed Monro, as early as 29 October, for an answer to the fundamental question 'leaving or staying?' On 31 October, Monro replied. His answer was 'leaving'. His reasons were clear and compelling. The situation on the peninsula and in the eastern Mediterranean meant that there was no prospect of strategic or operational surprise. The British positions had no depth. There was no room for concealment of reinforcements. Artillery support was very difficult, making expensive frontal infantry assaults the only tactical option. The troops on the peninsula were in poor health and badly needed rest and reorganization. The strength of these views was reinforced by faulty British intelligence that suggested the Germans were reinforcing the peninsula.

Was this the report of a man who was telling his superiors what they wanted to hear? Clearly not in the case of Kitchener, who was shocked by what he read. He telegraphed his protégé Sir William Birdwood (GOC Anzac Corps) on 4 November, saying, 'I regard evacuation as a frightful disaster that should be avoided at all costs'. It was only after he himself went out to Gallipoli that Kitchener accepted the logic and force of Monro's report. In the end, on 7 December, it was the Cabinet not Monro that decided to terminate the campaign.

Monro's report and the subsequent confirmation of its recommendation by the British government did not let him off the hook, however. Having recommended evacuation, he had now to carry it out. The Duke of Wellington had famously described a retreat while in contact with the enemy as one of the most difficult operations of war. Monro agreed. He was far from sanguine about the chances of getting off the peninsula unscathed, believing that he might lose as much as a third of his force. In the event, of course, the troops were evacuated without the loss of a man, the one element of triumph in a campaign bedevilled by wishful thinking, poor preparation, inadequate resources and indecisive leadership. Although the Churchillian view, that Gallipoli was one of the few examples during the Great War of 'strategic genius', a magnificent opportunity to bring the war to a speedier, cheaper and more satisfactory conclusion fumbled by lesser men, continues to influence posterity, the balance of scholarly opinion favours Monro. The judgement of history might more fairly read 'he came, he saw, he evacuated' and was right to do so.

Monro's immediate reward, on 23 November 1915, was to be given command (jointly with Gallipoli) also of another 'failing campaign', Salonika, but in February 1916 he was recalled to France, where he found many changes. Sir John French had been replaced as commander-in-chief of the BEF on 19 December 1915 and replaced by Haig. This left a vacancy at First Army. Haig made it clear that he wanted Rawlinson to succeed him, and Rawlinson did so briefly, but Kitchener refused to confirm the appointment and Monro took command on 4 February 1916. Monro thus became the only man to be appointed to army commands under both French and Haig.

Haig inherited three army commanders, none of whom he had personally chosen. He had unsuccessfully opposed the appointment of Monro at First Army. He harboured at this time grave doubts about 'the old man', Plumer, at Second Army, doubts that were soon confirmed by Second Army's loss of a position known as 'The Bluff' on 14 February. Four days later Haig gave Plumer a clear and unambiguous warning that he must 'shape up or ship out'.[24] Haig's relationship with Allenby at Third Army has often been portrayed as one animated by professional jealousy on Haig's part (rather tendentiously in the view of this author). Although their relationship was invariably 'professional', it was certainly not a close or friendly one.

Haig's concerns about his army commanders were sharpened by his awareness that the BEF was to contribute to a joint Franco-British attack on the Somme later in the year. This was to be part of an Allied grand strategy, adopted during a meeting at Chantilly in December 1915, to press the Central Powers on every front. Haig soon resolved his dilemma by creating a new army, the Fourth, command of which was given to Rawlinson, and later a Reserve (then Fifth) Army, command of which was given to Hubert Gough. There was a real sense in which these were not only 'Haig appointments' but also 'Haig men'. Haig immediately gave responsibility for planning the 'big push' to Rawlinson. Monro was left to contemplate his own inheritance.

This was a dismal one. First Army occupied some of the least desirable real estate in the world. Monro's forward troops were suffering vile weather in inadequate defences often overlooked by the enemy. Trench lines had not been chosen for reasons of tactical advantage or habitability but because that is where the combatants had 'ended up' after the fighting round Loos in September and October 1915. Monro was not a man for committing any inner thoughts he might have to paper. But we may speculate. Gallipoli had made him for the first time a public figure, but his claim to fame was that he had organized a successful evacuation. He knew well enough that wars were not won by evacuations. If he needed a reminder (after his experience with 2nd Division on the Marne) that even minor 'evacuations' were frowned on by high authority on the Western Front it was provided by Plumer's loss of 'The Bluff'. Monro took over a line that might well have been improved by judicious withdrawal, to which he was professionally and temperamentally suited, but he operated in a professional environment in which such advocacy was high risk. Monro's actions as GOC First Army must been seen in this context.

Monro's time at First Army was again short-lived, 185 days. During that time First Army initiated no major attacks. Monro was, however, often forced to respond to German actions: the fight for the Hohenzollern craters (2–18 March); the gas attacks at Hulluch (27–29 April); the loss of 'The Kink' (11 May); and the attack on Vimy Ridge (21 May). The only time First Army took the fight to the enemy in any significant way was the attack by XI Corps at Fromelles (19 July). These events provide thin evidence for assessing Monro's 'operational method' or for judging his ability and potential as an army commander. The loss of 'The Kink' and the attack at Fromelles are perhaps the most revealing, but what they reveal is contradictory and ambiguous, not least in relation to Monro's character.

'The Kink' was an especially insalubrious salient in First Army's line, located south-east of the Hohenzollern Redoubt on the old Loos battlefield. The British position was overlooked by the redoubt itself, by the German position on the Fosse 8 spoil heap and by the lips of numerous mine craters that littered no man's land, which was only about 100 yards wide. 'The Kink' suffered daily shelling from artillery and trench mortars. The area was also the scene of intense mining activity by both sides. In war vital positions are not always convenient ones. But it is difficult to regard this inconvenient position as a vital one. By the time 'The Kink' was lost Monro had been in command of First Army for over three months. During that period he showed no sign of wishing to straighten his line in this area. In the end the Germans straightened it for him.

It was apparently the gradual gaining of the upper hand by the British in the mining war that forced the Germans to do something about 'The Kink'. The salient became the subject of even more intense and abnormal German shelling, reinforced by machine-guns at night, from 27 April, the day of the gas attack at Hulluch. Something of an artillery duel developed with I Corps, but the area soon returned to 'normal'. This was a misleading sign. On 11 May, after a day of periodic but intense German shelling, the German artillery began a bombardment that the British official historian, Sir James Edmonds, described as 'one of the heaviest concentrations of artillery in a small area in the war'.[25] The bombardment fell upon men of the 15th (Scottish) Division, a New Army formation that had created a good reputation in the early fighting at Loos. One shell exploded in the headquarters dug-out of 13th Battalion Royal Scots, killing all the battalion staff and inflicting a fatal paralysis on the chain of command and communications. The German infantry, skilfully using the shelter afforded by numerous mine craters, simply occupied the ground that their artillery had conquered. Immediate counter-attacks were ordered by the GOC 45 Brigade (Brigadier General W.H.L. Allgood), but they were weak and unavailing. Under pressure from I Corps, 15th Division made a renewed effort on 14 May, but this was shattered by German machine-guns at great cost to the attackers. It was at this point that the GOC 15th Division, Major General

F.W.N. McCracken, decided enough was enough and called off any further attempts to recapture the ground lost. During the first two years on the Western Front decisions like this were often followed by recriminations and sackings. The favoured technique was for 'superior' commanders to blame 'inferior' commanders before blame fell upon them, but this did not happen at any level. McCracken sent a message of congratulation to the CO 8th Battalion King's Own Scottish Borderers, who had carried out the attack on 14 May.[26]

All three brigade commanders survived, as did the divisional commander, who went on to command a corps. Sir James Edmonds summed up this bloody, violent and forgotten affair. 'Although possession of them [the former British trenches] decidedly improved the enemy's position, the line taken up in Sackville Street, with a new support line with extra traverses, was a better and stronger one than that near the exposed Kink. [General McCracken's] decision was approved by the commander of the First Army, General Sir C.C. Monro.'[27]

So, there were no recriminations from Monro either. This confirms the impression of him as a prudent, sensible commander, who did not expect his men or their commanders to do the impossible, a view that was not always in fashion in the BEF, especially in 1915 and 1916. But in other respects Monro does not come out of the narrative well. A more decisive and interventionist commander, confident in his position and the support of *his* superiors, might well have done by choice what the enemy forced upon him and at great cost to the defenders, who fought hard in difficult circumstances to retain ground that senior officers rapidly decided was not worth the retention. Interestingly, there were also no recriminations from Haig. Monro did not experience his 'Plumer moment' after the loss of 'The Kink'. Perhaps Haig was too focused on preparations for the Somme.

By the end of May, Monro had also acquiesced in another potentially embarrassing forced withdrawal, carried out by Henry Wilson's IV Corps on Vimy Ridge.[28] The decision was as sensible as the one in which he had acquiesced at 'The Kink', though if he wanted to protect himself by scapegoating someone, Wilson looks like a very tempting goat. That he did not scapegoat Wilson reflects some credit on Monro, but he was in danger of developing a reputation for losing ground. Fromelles needs to be seen in this context.

Fromelles

Fromelles was the only significant attack conducted by First Army under Monro's command. The attack's origins were haphazard. Haig's energies were focused on the great battle that had been launched by Fourth Army on the Somme on 1 July, but he was looking for a contribution from his other armies. He was especially anxious to remind the Germans that they could not afford to thin out their line on 'quiet sectors' in order to reinforce their Somme

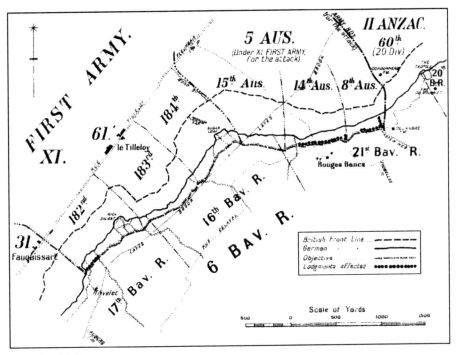

Fromelles, 1916.

positions. He favoured an attack towards Lille that would pin down German divisions and prevent their deployment further south. That this might be achieved by an attack at Fromelles, a village south of Armentières, was suggested by one of Monro's corps commanders, Richard Haking (GOC XI Corps). Initially, it looked as though Second and First armies might co-operate, but Plumer blew hot and cold, distracted by his own plans for an offensive at Messines. Monro showed no real enthusiasm for the attack at any stage. That it took place at all owed most to the ambition and willingness of Haking to carry it out, and his unshakeable confidence that it would work.

Fromelles is difficult to justify as the point for an attack, even a feint attack. The one advantage seems to be that it was on the front of the corps that wished to make an attack. The ground held by First Army in this area was appallingly flat, intersected by tactically difficult water features, and dominated by the Aubers Ridge, which repeated British attempts to capture in the spring and early summer of 1915 had met without success and with sanguinary losses. Haking had already begun to achieve a reputation as something of a loose cannon. Seemingly frustrated by the dull routine of line holding in First Army, he was ever at the forefront in advocating an aggressive policy. He did more than anyone in the BEF to encourage trench raids and the 'spirit of the bayonet'. Monro was typically cautious about raids, believing that they must have a real purpose to be justified. How many of Haking's raids met this criterion is a moot point. Shortly before Fromelles, Haking had also organized (if that is the right word) an unnecessary and unsuccessful attack against a German position known as the 'Boar's Head' (29–30 June 1916), in which the 39th Division received a severe mauling.[29] Monro's attitude to his subordinate appears to have been remarkably indulgent.

Fromelles might now have been forgotten had it not been the baptism of fire on the Western Front of the Australian Imperial Force. One Australian commander, the British officer H.B. 'Hooky' Walker (GOC 1st Australian Division), made his views apparent from the outset and reinforced them by point-blank refusing to allow his division to take part in the attack. Whether he would have got away with such a piece of rank insubordination had he been commanding a British division may be doubted. Walker's refusal reflects well on his professional judgement and force of character, but it did not prevent the attack taking place or Australian involvement in it. Instead, the task was handed to the least experienced of the Australian divisions, the 5th (commanded by an Australian, the Hon. J.W. McCay), which had been in France only a short time.

Walker's concerns are easy to understand. Haking advocated a 'surprise' attack to follow an eleven-hour preliminary bombardment on a narrow two-division front in broad daylight over a wide, flat, machine-gun-swept no man's land, dominated by a virtually impregnable German strong point, protected by thick concrete, known as the 'Sugar Loaf'. The attacking infantry were to 'rush' the German front line and press on to the German second line, some 400 yards to the rear, without artillery support. It was as though the battles of 1915 had not taken place.

The infantry assault began at 6.00 pm on 19 July. Surprisingly, perhaps, given the very inadequate nature of the bombardment fired by inexperienced gunners and old, worn guns, 8th and 14th Australian Brigades quickly gained their objectives. After pressing on to the second line, however, they confronted a problem familiar to anyone who had bothered to follow the Somme fighting. They found no trenches and no means of consolidating or defending their position. Isolated and denied reinforcement, they were expelled from their gains the following day, incurring worse casualties from enfilade German machine-gun fire in the retreat than they had in the advance. An even less happy time was had by 15th Australian Brigade and 184th British Brigade (61st Division), scythed down by machine-guns as they attempted to cross no man's land. The 61st Division sensibly cancelled a renewal of the attack, scheduled for 9.00 pm, but forgot to inform 15th Australian Brigade (under the redoubtable 'Pompey' Elliott). The 58th Australian Battalion attacked alone, suffering huge losses for no effect.

The battle as a whole had no effect, other than to sour British–Australian relations. German units had been detached from their line on this front and sent south to the Somme before the attack was launched. Even if they had not been, it is doubtful whether an attack on such a narrow front with such limited forces could have been seen as anything other than a feint.

The unhappy involvement of the Australians at Fromelles has had important consequences for Monro's reputation. It was inevitable that Australian historians would take a greater interest in Fromelles than any others, not least the Australian official historian, C.E.W. Bean, whose account remains the most detailed and influential.[30] Bean blamed Haking for the debacle, as did 'Pompey' Elliott, for whom Haking became a lifelong object of hate.[31] Monro gets off lightly in Bean's account. He does not deserve to.

GHQ itself had also expressed reservations about an attack at Fromelles. Richard Butler, Haig's deputy chief of staff, had twice visited Monro's GHQ and raised uncomfortable questions about the resources available for the attack (especially artillery) and the wisdom of attacking over such open ground in daylight. At his second visit, on 16 July, Butler raised further concerns about the weather and stressed that First Army had the complete authority to cancel the operation if, for whatever reason, they thought it inadvisable. Significantly, perhaps, Monro was not present at this meeting. He heard Butler's views second-hand from his staff later. Following further concerns about the weather, Haking asked Monro for a 24-hour delay in launching the attack, from 17 to 18 July. Monro refused and decided to call off the operation. He informed GHQ of this and asked permission to inform Plumer. Haig sent him the following reply: 'The Commander-in-Chief wishes the special operations mentioned in the above letter [Monro's dispatch] to be carried out as soon as possible, weather permitting, provided always that General Sir Charles Monro is satisfied that the conditions are favourable, and that the resources at his disposal, including ammunition are adequate both for preparation and execution of the enterprise.' This left the ball firmly in Monro's court. He fumbled it.

There is considerable evidence for regarding Monro as a capable, sensible, prudent soldier, not afraid to take difficult or unwelcome decisions. How is it that he allowed such a pointless and ill-prepared attack to take place, especially when he had the power and authority to stop it? There is no simple answer. Haig's reply had put him in an unenviable position and was a classic example of Haig's tendency at this time to send mixed messages to his subordinates. The commander-in-chief had signalled that he wished the attack to take place and that there were compelling strategic reasons why it should. Monro seems to have taken this message more to heart than the 'freedom' he was given to cancel it if the criteria for success were not met. He had once before stressed that the resources for an attack were adequate. It would look odd if he suddenly changed his mind. Amid these doubts and uncertainties there was the constant determination of Haking that the attack should take place and his invincible optimism that it would succeed. Monro simply abandoned his responsibilities in the face of these difficulties and his men paid the price. There is much evidence here to support Peter Simkins's severe description of Monro's attitude as 'compliant'.[32] Monro said of himself, 'I was brought up never to question the decisions of my superiors and never to refuse any appointment offered me however much I dislike it.'[33] Monro had a strong sense of duty, generally an admirable quality, but like most qualities not foolproof. At Fromelles it overrode his better judgement.

The last word on Fromelles should lie with the British official historian, Captain Wilfrid Miles, whose magisterial analysis must remain Monro's epitaph as an Army commander:

> The pity of it was that the action need not have been fought, since the First Army had perfect liberty to cancel it. To have delivered battle at all, after hurried preparation, with troops of all arms handicapped by their lack of experience and training in offensive trench-warfare betrayed a grave underestimate of the enemy's powers of resistance. The utmost endeavours of the artillery were unable either to subdue the German batteries or to 'reduce the defenders to a state of collapse before the assault', so the infantry, advancing in broad daylight, paid the price. Even if the German defences had been completely shattered by the British bombardment, and the infantry assault had succeeded, it would probably have proved impossible to hold the objective under the concentrated fire of the enemy's artillery directed by excellent observation. Such a situation had arisen only too often during the minor engagements fought earlier in the year.[34]

In October 1916 Monro left the Western Front for the final time to become commander-in-chief, India. It seemed a surprising choice. Monro had not been to India for twenty years. He was in no sense an 'old India hand', but this is what probably clinched his appointment. The British government had had enough of 'old India hands'. The surrender of General Townshend's force to the Ottomans at Kut in April 1916 had been a major defeat that showed up the inadequacies of the traditional way of doing things. India needed to be 'sorted out'. Monro's position was strengthened by the appointment of a new viceroy, Lord Chelmsford, who was also without India connections. Even so, his task was a mammoth one.

The most important year of the Great War was 1916, the year that finally punctured what Holger Herwig has called 'the short war illusion'. The full implications of what states needed to do to achieve victory became increasingly apparent and increasingly concerning to political elites. The British had begun the full-scale mobilization of their industry in 1915. They had introduced conscription and 'manpower planning' in 1916. The British Empire had never been properly exploited, in the sense of developing its full economic and military potential. In part, this was deliberate. Economic development meant 'modernization' and modernization threatened the social and political authority of traditional elites, through whom the British often governed. These concerns were apparent with regard to the Indian Army. Although there were many who waxed sentimental about the mystical bond between the sepoy and his sahib, the shadow cast by the Indian Mutiny was a long one. The Indian Army was essential in maintaining British control of India, but it was also – potentially – the greatest threat to that control. The Indian Army needed to be a relatively efficient internal security force with a capacity for fighting 'brush fire' wars against the tribesmen of the North-West Frontier and Afghanistan, but not a modern army with an educated Indian officer corps capable of threatening British rule. The British preferred to recruit from among India's 'martial races', but these were found among the illiterate peasant farmers of rural society. Official suspicion of educated, urban Indians was very great. So was objection to giving educated Indians commissions.

The limitations of the Indian Army were cruelly exposed on the battlefields of 1914 and 1915. Indian troops lacked initiative once their British officers were killed, as they often were. They suffered badly in the cold, sodden, miasmic winter of 1914–15. The outbreak of war with the Muslim Ottoman Empire, in November 1915, raised concern about the loyalty of the Indian Army's many Muslim soldiers. Haig's diary for 1915 has many references to these concerns.[35] The impact of the high casualties suffered by Indian troops in the battles of 1915 were magnified, as with the British 'Pals' battalions' in 1916, by the often localized nature of their recruitment. There had been much enthusiasm for the war in India in 1914, but by the end of 1915 this had considerably diminished, eroded by casualties and by the damaging blow to British imperial mystique inflicted by the defeat at Gallipoli.

India's principal resource was manpower (a word first used in this sense in 1915). Monro's principal task was to augment the strength of the Indian Army. He did this very effectively and without destroying traditional arrangements. Some of his reforms were simple. He encouraged new recruitment by abolishing the requirement that soldiers paid for their own rations. A signing-on bonus of 3 rupees was introduced. Pay and pensions were improved. He also sought recruits from 'non-martial races' (seventy-five new classes were declared 'martially eligible') and appointed recruiting officers to specific districts rather than to specific races. The Indian Defence Force Act of 1917 made all British European subjects in India between the ages of eighteen and forty-one liable to military service. Recruiting was eventually centralized and proper planning procedures introduced, designed to adjust military resources to military need. The training of new recruits became much more systematic and intensive, and was designed to equip soldiers to fight modern wars against enemies with modern armies. What Monro did not do was equally important. He did not change the ethnic and social structure of new units, nor did he threaten the Indian Army's traditional values and loyalties. Educated Indians

were used in 'tail' formations not in the combat arms. By the time of the
armistice in Europe the Indian Army stood at 573,000 men. These men were
much better trained and equipped than their predecessors. This was a remarkable achievement.

The first theatre of war to benefit from Monro's reforms was the one in
which an embarrassing imperial defeat had brought about his appointment,
Mesopotamia. The new C.-in-C. in Mesopotamia, Sir Stanley Maude, was
nicknamed 'Systematic Joe'. He understood the profound importance of what
Lord Wavell called the 'back arrangements' and what we would now call
logistics. Maude's ability to be systematic was greatly augmented by the supply
of labour sent to him by Monro. This labour allowed Maude to rest, refit and
retrain his battered and – in many cases – sick troops. He also received a stream
of skilled railwaymen and riverboat men, who transformed his logistical
infrastructure and allowed him to resume effective offensive operations in
1917. Maude was initially less enthusiastic about the new soldiers sent to him
by Monro, considering them raw and untrained, but he gradually recognized
their potential. Confidence in the military reliability of Indian units returned
and Maude's plans were able to rely less on the small number of overstretched
British troops under his command. The full military impact of Monro's
reforms were not felt, however, until near the end of the war, in October 1918,
when his new Indian armies defeated numerically superior Ottoman forces at
Mosul. Monro's augmentation of the Indian Army also allowed the eventual
'Indianization' of Allenby's infantry in the Egyptian Expeditionary Force,
allowing the release of British divisions to join the war on the Western Front in
1918.

The end of the war in Europe brought no release for Monro. Within less
than a year he found himself conducting another war on a familiar imperial
battlefield, Afghanistan, and later in 1919 a more prolonged campaign against
the tribesmen of Waziristan. By 1920 Monro had had enough. He had been in
almost constant employment, most of it mentally and physically – even morally
– demanding, for six years. He went on half pay and returned to London. In
1923 he became governor of Gibraltar, serving for five years. He died of cancer
in December 1929.

There is an important sense in which Monro was never one of 'Haig's
generals'. Haig hardly greeted Monro's appointment as GOC 2nd Division
with a ringing endorsement. He opposed Monro's appointment as GOC First
Army and did nothing to try to retain his services when Monro was sent to
India. He never trusted Monro's First Army with any significant military task.
Monro's principal achievement as an army commander, the innovation of army
schools, came when he commanded Third Army, under Sir John French.
Monro has rarely received the credit he deserves for this, not least perhaps
because of the lack of surviving archival documentation, nor for the correct
and courageous recommendation that he made as C.-in-C. Mediterranean

Expeditionary Force. His reviews as GOC First Army must necessarily be mixed. As ever, he appeared to be a man of sound ideas and a realistic appreciation of what was and was not possible in the conditions of the Western Front. But he showed few signs of possessing true self-confidence in his own judgement and the willingness to challenge the views of his superiors, in short the moral courage required by a great field commander. Monro's transfer to India gave him a final opportunity to display his considerable administrative and diplomatic skills. That his achievements as C.-in-C. India did not have a greater impact was the result of his tardy appointment.

Monro was a well-read and cultivated man. He hated war and enjoyed the arts of peace. He was a faithful servant of the British Empire in its late Edwardian afternoon. He brought impressive qualities of mind and knowledge to the task of soldiering in a war that few Britons had anticipated and none welcomed. His achievements stemmed from his personal sense of duty and belief in discipline. He was loyal not only to his superiors, but also to his subordinates. He could spot talent and was willing to advance it. He would now be described as an excellent 'facilitator'. These were fine qualities, but they were also limiting ones. He was a decent, modest man, a good soldier, but – on the evidence of 1916 in particular – a very limited general.

Bibliography

Monro has not been well served in secondary literature. Sir George Barrow, his chief of staff at First Army, wrote Monro's biography, *The Life of Sir Charles Carmichael Monro* (London: Hutchinson, 1931), but beyond this there is very little. On Fromelles, see Mike Senior, *No Finer Courage: A Village in the Great War* (Stroud: Sutton, 2004), pp. 120–77; Peter Pederson, *Fromelles* (Barnsley: Pen & Sword, 2003); and Robin Corfield, *Don't Forget Me, Cobber: The Battle of Fromelles* (Rosanna: Corfield, 2000).

Notes

1 Winston S. Churchill, *The World Crisis* (London: Thornton Butterworth, 1923), vol. 2, p. 516.

2 Monro's wife, whom he married at the age of 52, was also Irish.

3 Quoted in George H. Cassar, 'Sir Charles Carmichael Monro, Baronet (1860–1929)', *Oxford Dictionary of National Biography* (Oxford: Oxford University Press, 2004).

4 Major General Sir Wilkinson Dent Bird (1869–1943), professor Staff College India (1905–9), author; severely wounded on 14 September 1914 while commanding 2nd Battalion Royal Irish Rifles. Leg amputated. Later director of staff duties, War Office.

5 Norman Reginald McMahon (1866–1914), killed in action while OC 4th Royal Fusiliers, 11 November 1914, just before he could take up an infantry brigade command.

6 John Campbell (1871–1941), OC 2nd Cameron Highlanders, 1914–15; GOC 121 Brigade, 1915–18, 31st Division, 1918–19.

7 Granville George Algernon Egerton (1859–1951), an able, if temperamental, officer, who had an unhappy time at Gallipoli as GOC 52nd (Lowland) Division.

8 Walter Norris Congreve VC (1862–1927), GOC 18 brigade, 1911–15; 6th Division, 1915, XIII Corps, 1915–17, VII Corps, 1918.

9 Harold Ruggles-Brise (1864–1927), GOC 20 Brigade, 1914, 40th Division, 1915–17; military secretary GHQ, 1918–19.

10 Martin Samuels, *Doctrine and Dogma: German and British Infantry Tactics in the First World War* (London: Greenwood, 1992), pp. 162–8.

11 Lyn Macdonald, *1914* (London: Penguin, 1989), p. 98.

12 Gary Sheffield and John Bourne, eds, *Douglas Haig: War Diaries and Letters, 1914–1918* (London: Weidenfeld & Nicolson), p. 57. Haig was considerably more complimentary about the other divisional commander in I Corps, S.H. Lomax.

13 For recent accounts that stress the BEF's limitations, see Nikolas Gardner, *Trial by Fire: Command and the British Expeditionary Force in 1914* (Westport, CT: Praeger, 2004), and Ian F.W. Beckett, *Ypres: The First Battle, 1914* (Harlow: Pearson, 2004).

14 Quoted in Gardner, *Trial by Fire*, p. 81.

15 Quoted in John G.E. Cox, 'Lambart, (Frederic) Rudolph, Tenth Earl of Cavan (1865–1946), Army Officer', *Oxford Dictionary of National Biography* (Oxford: Oxford University Press, 2004).

16 Brigadier General H. Page Croft, *Twenty Two Months Under Fire* (London: John Murray, 1917), p. 22.

17 Imperial War Museum, Maxse Papers, 69/57/7, Brigadier General R.J. Kentish to Lieutenant General Sir Ivor Maxse, 21/22 February 1917. I owe this reference to Dr Simon Robbins.

18 See Simon Robbins, *British Generalship on the Western Front, 1914–1918* (London: Frank Cass, 2005), pp. 83–97. The role of army and other schools in the development of the BEF is under-written, partly because few, if any, archival sources seem to have survived.

19 Major H. Hesketh-Prichard, *Sniping in France, 1914–1918* (1920; Solihull: Helion, 2004), p. 9.

20 Hesketh-Prichard, *Sniping in France*, p. 36.

21 The British Army introduced a system of Annual Confidential Reports in the mid-1890s. They were used by the post-Esher Committee selection boards in deciding promotions and appointments. The system appears to have lapsed on the outbreak of war.

22 Brigadier General C.F. Aspinall-Oglander, *Military Operations: Gallipoli*, vol. 2, *May 1915 to the Evacuation* (London: William Heinemann, 1932), pp. 399–400. Kitchener's instructions to Monro are reprinted in Appendix 17.

23 These visits are well described in Alan Moorehead, *Gallipoli* (London: Four Square, 1956), p. 293.

24 Sheffield and Bourne, *Haig*, p. 180. 'The Bluff' was duly recaptured on 2 March.

25 Sir James E. Edmonds, *Military Operations: France and Belgium, 1916*, [vol. 1] (London: Macmillan, 1932), p. 207.

26 The message is reprinted in Lieutenant Colonel J. Stewart DSO and John Buchan, *The Fifteenth (Scottish) Division 1914–1919* (Edinburgh and London: William Blackwood, 1926), p. 72.

27 Edmonds, *Military Operations, 1916*, pp. 208–9.

28 For an account of this, see ibid., pp. 210–26.

29 The GOC 39th Division, Major General Robert Dawson, was sacked after the failure of the 'Boar's Head' attack.

30 C.E.W. Bean, *The Official History of Australia in the War of 1914–1918*, vol. 3, *The A.I.F. in France, 1916* (1929; St Lucia: University of Queensland Press, 1982), chapters 12 and 13.

31 See Ross McMullin, *Pompey Elliott* (Carlton: Scribe, 2002), ch. 9 and pp. 228, 232.

32 Peter Simkins, 'Haig and the Army Commanders', in Brian Bond and Nigel Cave, eds, *Haig: A Reappraisal 70 Years On* (Barnsley: Leo Cooper, 1999), p. 91.

33 Sir G. de S. Barrow, *The Life of Sir Charles Carmichael Monro* (London: Hutchinson, 1931), p. 114.

34 Captain Wilfrid Miles, *Military Operations: France and Belgium, 1916*, [vol. 2] (London: Macmillan, 1938), p. 134.

35 See, for example, Haig's diary entry for 4 March 1915 in Sheffield and Bourne, *Haig*, pp. 106–7.

Chapter Seven

Herbert Plumer

Second Army, 1915–1917, 1918

Peter Simkins

Even the harshest critics of British generals in the Great War are normally prepared to acknowledge that Herbert Plumer at least was not a 'donkey' or a 'butcher and bungler'. Liddell Hart, for instance, paid tribute to 'the impartial common-sense of his judgement'. On Plumer's death, Liddell Hart went so far as to write that 'he was perhaps the nearest approach to military genius in a war singularly devoid of that inspired quality'. Many of those who served under Plumer in Second Army similarly sang his praises. To take just one example, Arthur Behrend – adjutant of a siege battery in Flanders in 1917 – wrote nearly fifty years later that Plumer remained in his mind's eye as 'a father, even grandfather figure' whose attack at Messines 'was so much a model of what a battle for limited objectives should be that it was almost a pleasure to take part in it'.[1] In more recent years, aspects of Plumer's command have been questioned, thereby throwing a shadow of doubt upon his widely accepted reputation as a 'soldier's general' who had a remarkable grasp of the unique demands of the Western Front. Evidence exists to support both points of view, although, in the final analysis, Plumer's standing as a sound, methodical and sometimes outstanding army commander emerges here largely, if not wholly, unshaken.

Plumer was born on 13 March 1857 into an upper middle-class family with strong Yorkshire links. Much of his childhood was spent in Torquay until, in 1870, he went to Eton. Eton's influence on Plumer remained strong, though he was remembered for taking bets on the Derby of 1875 and for playing truant the same year to attend Hunt Cup Day at Ascot, two early indications of a lifelong interest in horse racing. On leaving Eton in 1876 he was commissioned direct into the 65th Foot (York and Lancaster Regiment). By 1879 he was adjutant of his battalion. After service in Aden, he underwent his baptism of fire in the Sudan in 1884. Between 1886 and 1888 he attended Staff College, passing out nineteenth of twenty-six officers. His first staff appointment was as DAAG in Jersey from 1890 to 1893. He then joined his regiment's 2nd Battalion in Natal before being ordered, in April 1896, to raise some 750 irregulars to help quell the Matabele rebellion. In the ensuing months, by

Chronology

13 March 1857	Herbert Charles Onslow Plumer born at Sussex Place, London Educated at Eton
11 September 1876	Gazetted to 65th Foot (later 1st Battalion, York and Lancaster Regiment)
29 April 1879	Appointed adjutant
29 May 1882	Promoted captain
22 July 1884	Married Annie Constance Goss
1884	Served at Suakin
1886–88	Attended Staff College, Camberley
7 May 1890	Appointed DAAG Jersey
22 January 1893	Promoted major
2 December 1895	Appointed acting military secretary to GOC Cape Colony
1 April 1896	Appointed commander of Matabeleland Relief Force
5 March 1897	Appointed DAAG Aldershot
8 May 1897	Promoted brevet lieutenant colonel
15 July 1899	Appointed CO Rhodesia Regiment
17 October 1900	Promoted substantive lieutenant colonel
29 November 1900	Promoted brevet colonel
22 August 1902	Promoted major general
1 October 1902	Appointed GOC 4 Brigade at Aldershot
8 December 1903	Appointed GOC Eastern District
14 February 1904	Appointed quartermaster general
17 December 1905	Dismissed as quartermaster general
30 April 1906	Appointed GOC 5th Division
4 November 1908	Promoted lieutenant general
10 November 1911	Appointed GOC Northern Command
8 January 1915	Appointed GOC V Corps and temporary general
7 May 1915	Appointed GOC Second Army
11 June 1915	Promoted substantive general
13 November 1917	Appointed C.-in-C. British Forces, Italy
18 March 1918	Reappointed GOC Second Army
2 April 1919	Appointed GOC British Army of the Rhine
April 1919	Created Baron Plumer of Messines and Bilton
4 June 1919	Appointed governor of Malta
31 July 1919	Promoted field marshal
16 May 1924	Retired as governor of Malta
14 August 1925	Appointed high commissioner for Palestine
July 1928	Retired as high commissioner
1929	Appointed President MCC and elevated to viscount
16 July 1932	Died at London

Appointed CB 1900, KCB 1906, GCMG 1916, GCVO 1917, GCB 1918, GBE 1924

careful planning and administration, he successfully trained the Matabeleland Relief Force and led it through a series of sharp engagements. After an interlude as DAAG at Aldershot Plumer was sent, shortly before the outbreak of the South African war to raise another irregular mounted infantry unit, the Rhodesia Regiment, at Bulawayo. As well as South Africans and Rhodesians, the force contained volunteers from Australia, Canada and New Zealand, and Plumer's tactful but firm handling enabled him to form the same kind of close relationship with Dominion troops that he enjoyed in the Great War.

Having taken part in the relief of Mafeking, Plumer won more laurels as a resourceful and energetic column commander. Now nationally known, he returned home in May 1902, soon to be promoted to major general and given command of the 4th Infantry Brigade at Aldershot. At the end of 1903 he was transferred to command a district at Colchester but had been there for barely two months when he was appointed quartermaster general and third military member of the newly created Army Council. However, his loyalty to the Secretary of State for War, H.O. Arnold-Forster, and his support for the latter's short service scheme, cost Plumer this post when the Liberals took office in December 1905. He was compensated by being appointed KCB and, in April 1906, he was offered the command of 5th Division at the Curragh. His novel training methods included sending small columns out into the Wicklow Mountains, with orders to practise guerrilla-type operations and fend for themselves. In November 1908 he was promoted to lieutenant general but spent over two years on half pay until appointed GOC Northern Command.[2]

Shortly after the outbreak of war in August 1914, Sir John French wanted Plumer to take over II Corps, Sir James Grierson having died on his way to the front. However, Kitchener, the Secretary of State for War, opted for Horace Smith-Dorrien.[3] Plumer finally reached the Western Front in January 1915 and was given command of V Corps at Ypres – a sector with which Plumer would henceforth forever be associated. Praised by French for the 'confidence and *order*' which prevailed in V Corps during Second Ypres, Plumer was chosen to command Second Army in May 1915 following the removal of Smith-Dorrien, even though he shared the latter's desire to withdraw to a shorter, more defensible line closer to Ypres and was indeed subsequently permitted to carry out just such a move.[4]

In June 1917, after lengthy preparations, Second Army captured the Messines–Wytschaete Ridge in a limited-objective attack regarded at the time, and since, as providing a model of operational planning. Similar successes were achieved at Menin Road Ridge, Polygon Wood and Broodseinde during Third Ypres, but Second Army's next operations at Poelcappelle and Passchendaele proved more controversial. In the aftermath of Caporetto, Plumer left the Western Front to become GOC of British Forces in Italy for a four-month period, resuming command of Second Army on 18 March 1918. His acceptance of tactical realities was again evident on 13–14 April 1918 when, albeit reluctantly, he abandoned the hard-won Passchendaele position in the face of the German Flanders offensive.[5] As part of the Groupe d'Armées des Flandres (GAF) under the overall command of the King of the Belgians, Second Army had the satisfaction of leading the final breakout from the old Ypres Salient on 28–29 September 1918. Promoted to field marshal and created a baron in 1919,

Plumer briefly commanded the British Army of the Rhine before serving as governor of Malta and high commissioner in Palestine. Elevated to viscount in 1929, Plumer died in London on 16 July 1932, aged seventy-five, and was buried in Westminster Abbey.

With his ruddy cheeks, drooping white moustache, portly frame and thin legs, Plumer seemed to be the personification of David Low's later caricature 'Colonel Blimp'. The fact that he often wore a monocle in his right eye only added to the image.[6] Indeed, for a general widely credited as having a considerable understanding of modern warfare, Plumer was, in some ways, curiously old-fashioned. 'Tim' Harington, his chief of staff from 1916 to 1918, related how Plumer disliked telephones, refusing to have one in his own room. He also had distaste for typewritten personal letters, feeling that typewriters destroyed personality.[7] Yet this bluff exterior was more than counterbalanced by the intrinsic kindness, courtesy and sensitivity which he regularly displayed in his dealings with all ranks. He occasionally found it difficult to hide his emotions, breaking down into tearful incoherence, for example, when bidding farewell to his staff on his departure for Italy.

His nicknames – 'Daddy', 'Plum' and 'Old Plum and Apple' – signified the affectionate esteem in which most held him. He was a devout Christian who, before major attacks, was sometimes seen, by his batman, on his knees and praying beside his bed. He was also a leading supporter of Toc H, a movement that originated at Poperinghe in the Second Army area. At least twice, in 1895 and 1911, he had seriously contemplated leaving the army, suggesting that, deep down, he lacked the single-minded professional ambition of contemporaries such as Haig. On the lighter side, Plumer's interest in racing was matched by his enthusiasm for hunting and by his passion for cricket. An appointment which gave him as much delight as any came in 1929, when he was elected President of the MCC.[8]

It was Plumer's wife who was probably most instrumental in dissuading him from giving up his military career. He had married his second cousin, Annie Goss, in 1884 and they remained a devoted couple for nearly forty-eight years. By all accounts, Lady Plumer was a gracious, shrewd and efficient hostess, but, unlike her husband, she was also apparently a remote and somewhat forbidding figure to her children and grandchildren. Plumer and his wife seem to have become disillusioned by the lifestyle of their son Thomas, who had emigrated to Canada and served in the Canadian Corps during the First World War. Plumer never saw his son again after the summer of 1919 and Lady Plumer appears to have met Thomas only once after her husband's funeral.[9]

In November 1918 Plumer was the BEF's longest-serving army commander and the only one who had been in post when Haig became C.-in-C. Despite the fact that Haig was barely four years junior to Plumer, he often referred to the latter as 'the old man'.[10] Relations between the two were sometimes distinctly edgy. Harington once told Edmonds that the 'only real enemy' that Plumer had 'was Douglas who was jealous of him'.[11] There are suggestions that Haig harboured a lasting resentment after being given low marks by Plumer in a Staff College examination in the 1890s, even if one must remain just a little wary of the waspish gossip exchanged between Edmonds and Liddell Hart during the inter-war years.[12] Given Haig's close association with Haldane's army reforms, there may also have been some residual antipathy resulting from Plumer's unswerving support for Arnold-Forster, Haldane's predecessor.[13] Tom Bridges, who commanded 19th Division in Second Army in 1917, subsequently commented that Plumer, not Haig, would have been the army's choice to succeed French.[14] What is certain is that Plumer was skating on extremely thin ice for at least the first six months after Haig became C.-in-C.

Haig considered 'degumming' Plumer following the loss of The Bluff, 2 miles south of Ypres, by 17th Division on 14–15 February 1916. As early as 17 February Haig asked the CIGS, Sir William Robertson, to try to find some other job for Plumer 'so as to let him down lightly'.[15] Having visited Second Army the next day, Haig recorded that Plumer had been prepared to go 'if I thought it desirable' but then added that Plumer 'behaved in such a straight-forward way and is such a thorough gentleman that I said I would think over the matter and let him know tomorrow'. Later on 18 February Haig wrote to Plumer, informing him that he wanted him to stay so long as he ensured that his defences were strengthened as swiftly as possible. However, Plumer was warned that if Second Army's 'general arrangements and conditions' did not improve, Haig would ask him to resign. Haig feared that Plumer was too kind to some of his subordinates and instructed Plumer 'to take hold of his Corps Commanders more, and to make them in their turn grip their Generals of Division and so on down the scale'. Robertson agreed that Plumer 'never has been quite hard enough on his Corps Commanders' who were 'not too good', singling out Charles Fergusson (II Corps).[16]

More problems arose in April 1916 when 2nd Canadian Division lost the craters at St Eloi. With Haig's admonishments no doubt still fresh in his mind, Plumer attempted to display 'grip' by recommending the removal of Major General Richard Turner VC, the divisional commander, and Brigadier General H.D.B. Ketchen of 6th Canadian Brigade. While conceding that these two officers were 'not very efficient', Haig was obliged to take a broader view, asserting that:

> the main point is whether the danger of a serious feud between the Canadians and British is greater than the retention of a couple of incompetent commanders. After careful thought I have decided not to concur with Plumer as regards Turner but to keep him on. My reasons are that the conditions were abnormally difficult, under such conditions mistakes are to be expected, but that all did their best and made a gallant fight.

On 23 April, Sir Max Aitken, representing the Canadian government, informed Haig that the Canadian prime minister, Sir Robert Borden, was making a personal request that Turner should remain in post, although he declared that, should Haig decide otherwise, the Canadian government would 'loyally accept' it. Haig was able to reassure Aitken that Turner and Ketchen would remain, but their discussion on 23 April did hasten the departure of Lieutenant General Sir Edwin Alderson from the command of the Canadian Corps. Before the end of May, Alderson had been succeeded by Julian Byng.[17]

In the command shake-up which followed Alderson's removal, Brigadier General C.H. 'Tim' Harington – who had previously been serving under Alderson and (briefly) Byng as BGGS of the Canadian Corps – was elevated on 13 June 1916 to become Plumer's new chief of staff at Second Army.[18] Harington had first caught Plumer's eye as GSO1 of 49th (West Riding) Division. Having recommended Harington for brigade command in 14th (Light) Division, Plumer clearly played a major part in his selection as Second Army's MGGS in June 1916. Harington later emphasized that Plumer 'kept all patronage in his own hands. Every appointment was approved by him personally'. However, it has been suggested that Haig also had a hand in the process.[19] Whoever was responsible, Harington's arrival was to transform Second Army, and the nature of their subsequent partnership was probably the biggest single factor in creating its particular ethos and widespread reputation for operational efficiency.

Even so, Haig was not immediately convinced of Second Army's improvement. In the preliminary planning stages for Third Ypres, the proposals submitted by Plumer and Harington were – though endorsed in some respects by Rawlinson – ultimately rejected by Haig as being too cautious and limited in scope.[20] Haig's dissatisfaction plainly helped to shape his decision to hand the main role in the forthcoming offensive to Gough. Gough later admitted that it was a serious mistake not to entrust the offensive to Plumer and Harington, who knew the sector well. Even John Terraine, Haig's principal apologist, sees this as his 'greatest and most fatal error'.[21]

As the preparations for the great set-piece assault on Messines Ridge gathered pace, Haig was undoubtedly beginning to recognize Second Army's virtues. He noted on 22 May 1917 that he found Plumer 'a most pleasant fellow to work with and Harington . . . and all his staff work very kindly with GHQ. All are most ready to take advice'. Haig's praise was not totally unqualified for he felt that some senior officers in Second Army had been on the defensive in the Salient so long that '*the real offensive spirit*' still needed developing.[22] After subjecting Plumer's corps and divisional commanders to rigorous cross-examination about their plans, Haig insisted on the immediate 'degumming' of Major General A.R. Montagu-Stuart-Wortley from 19th Division. Liddell Hart claimed that Haig similarly tried to get rid of Second Army's MGRA, Major General G. McK. Franks, but that Plumer resisted. It seems relevant to observe that Franks nevertheless left Second Army shortly after Messines and was succeeded by C.R. Buckle on 7 July.[23]

Haig had already persuaded Plumer to extend his first-day objectives, a change which doubled the distance to be traversed to around 3,000 yards and which also, in the event, led to a marked increase in casualties. Plumer does not appear to have raised serious objections even if he did have reservations concerning Haig's plea to consider a subsequent advance of 20–30 miles to the line Courtrai–Roulers.[24] When, on 24 May, Haig concluded his three-day visit to Second Army, he noted with satisfaction that all his 'criticisms and suggestions were most cordially received'. He was also happy to tell Plumer that 'of all the attacks which had been made under my orders, I considered the present one was the most carefully "mounted", and that all commanders and troops were better prepared for their work than on any previous occasion'. As soon as it was realized that the initial assault at Messines had been a brilliant success, Haig admitted that 'the old man deserves the highest praise' and confided to Charteris that Plumer was now 'his most reliable Army Commander'.[25]

Gough's failure to achieve the desired progress, and Haig's growing respect for Second Army, made it easier for him, in the last week of August, to decide belatedly to entrust to Plumer the main operational burden.[26] Prior to Plumer's next big assault – on the Menin Road Ridge on 20 September – Haig again interrogated corps and divisions about their plans. He was not only reassured but was also glowing in this praise for Second Army's methods: 'Every detail had been gone into most thoroughly and the troops most carefully trained ... Altogether I felt it was most exhilarating to go round such a very knowledgeable and confident body of leaders.'[27]

Such a tribute, coupled with Second Army's successes at Menin Road Ridge and Polygon Wood in late September, may have caused Plumer and Harington to become a trifle overconfident. Having expressed minor misgivings with regard to the scope and timing of the possible exploitation phase to follow the Broodseinde attack in early October, they even forgot their own tried and trusted principles and allowed themselves – in spite of deteriorating conditions – to be seduced into rushing preparations for the Battle of Poelcappelle.[28]

As will be discussed later, there seems, however, to have been no fundamental disagreement between Haig and Plumer as to the need to continue the offensive. For all Lloyd George's assertions to the contrary, Plumer was as shocked and 'sick' to be sent to Italy in November 1917 as Haig was reluctant to see him depart.[29] Plumer's loyalty to Haig and Robertson was reaffirmed in February 1918 by his rejection of an opportunity to become CIGS.[30] On returning from Italy to Second Army in March, he soon received a welcoming letter from Haig, who told Plumer that it was 'a great satisfaction to me to have you again at the head of an Army here'.[31] Plumer was quick to respond by helpfully releasing formations to buttress other threatened sectors during the

German offensives, a doubly appreciative Haig remarking that: 'It is most satisfactory to have a Commander of Plumer's temperament at a time of crisis like the present.'[32]

Haig's gratitude did not extend to giving Plumer a leading part in the final Allied offensive and, for most of the 'Hundred Days', Plumer and Second Army were attached to GAF, under the Belgian king and a French staff. Its main role in the Allied attack on 28 September 1918 was to act as right-flank guard to the Belgians further north and to secure a bridgehead south of the Lys. Plumer and his staff were not particularly impressed by, or at ease with, their allies. As one recent study has put it, they viewed Degoutte, King Albert's French chief of staff, as an 'officious and inefficient' officer who 'did little to co-ordinate planning between themselves and the Belgians'.[33]

As the campaign progressed, Plumer became aware of the possibilities to do more than act as flank guard and he displayed an uncharacteristic tendency to ignore orders, pushing on to occupy Courtrai on 19 October. Haig initially felt compelled to remind Plumer that his task was primarily to cover the Belgian right and enable his allies to advance eastwards. Haig, however, was increasingly suspicious of the French and grew simultaneously more tolerant of Plumer's desire to break free from the constraints imposed upon him. By mid-October Second Army was, in effect, the 'strike force' of the GAF, and Haig began to fight vigorously for its return to British control. At first Foch, the Allied supreme commander, flatly refused. Haig concluded that the real object was to use Second Army to open the way for 'dud' French divisions, and ensure they reached Brussels to claim the credit for 'putting the King back into his capital'. In the end, after Lord Milner, the Secretary of State for War, had applied pressure to the French government, Foch relented, but it was not until 4 November that Second Army reverted to Haig's command. Just a week later the armistice was signed and Haig was able to relax with his army commanders at Cambrai, even posing for a cinematographer. A fleeting glimpse of an almost affectionate regard for Plumer may perhaps be detected in Haig's diary entry for that day: '[Plumer] went off most obediently and stood before the camera, trying to look his best while Byng and others near them were chaffing the old man and trying to make him laugh.'[34]

Haig's respect for, and trust in, Plumer had been slow to develop. Plumer experienced far fewer problems in his relations with his own staff. Most appear to have been intensely loyal and to have felt a genuine affection for him, none more than Harington, whose special bond with his chief was an indispensable ingredient in Second Army's success in 1917. The war correspondent Philip Gibbs wrote of Harington's 'extreme simplicity of manner and clarity of intelligence'. Gibbs described Harington's memory for detail as being like a card-index system, though his mind did not become clogged with such minutiae. When working on complex plans, Harington was 'highly wrought, with every nerve in his body and brain at full tension, but he was never flurried, never irritable, never depressed or elated by false pessimism or false optimism'. Often acerbic in his comments on staff officers, Gibbs was only too willing to praise Harington as an officer who dealt with war 'as a scientific business, according to the methods of science'.[35] Another severe critic of British commanders, staff and troops – Brigadier General H.E. 'Pompey' Elliott of 15th Australian Brigade – was also willing to make an exception in Harington's case. Thus, Harington 'was the only one of the British Staff officers who ever impressed me that he had a proper conception of his job – to save the infantry casualties by the measures which they took'.[36]

Harington himself stated at the end of the Ypres offensive in 1917 that it had been his ambition to foster cordial relations 'between battalion officers and the Staff'. Gibbs judged that, under Plumer and Harington, there was in general 'a thoroughness of method, a minute attention to detail, a care for the comfort and spirit of the men, throughout the Second Army staff which did at least inspire the troops that whatever they did in the fighting . . . would be supported with every possible help that organization could provide'.[37] Charteris, Haig's head of intelligence, saw Plumer and Harington as 'a wonderful combination . . . nobody knows where Plumer ends and Harington begins'.[38]

This was not strictly true, as Harington himself was keen to point out. 'No detail escaped' Plumer, recalled Harington, 'and he spared no effort to see that everything possible was done for those under his Command'.[39] There was absolutely no question, in Harington's view, as to who was the 'supreme head' of Second Army. Plumer 'listened to all and then made his decision, which was final. He liked to know exactly what was going on. He wished all matters of importance referred to him'. Plumer, added Harington, would not tolerate decisions, except on minor details, which had been reached without his knowledge, and he 'kept his fingers on the pulse of everything'. Lieutenant Colonel C.H. Mitchell, Second Army's talented Canadian head of Intelligence during this period, also affirmed that Plumer retained 'a rigid control' once battle plans and other arrangements had been agreed. Harington was often able to draft memoranda that Plumer would approve without comment. Nevertheless, while apparently writing very little himself, Plumer demonstrated 'an extraordinary faculty of putting his finger on where any draft submitted to him failed'.[40]

Every morning at 8.30 am (or at 5.30 pm in winter), Plumer held a conference attended by his principal staff officers. In addition to these daily meetings, he took pains to talk individually to all the heads of branches. He was invariably considerate when dealing with subordinates and would frequently call in at the office of his head of intelligence or those of the GSO2 and GSO3 if he thought that Harington might be busy and should not be distracted.[41] On the other hand, Plumer could be a strict disciplinarian when required. He abhorred unpunctuality, expecting his staff to be present when he walked into breakfast at 7.30 am. Although he enjoyed a joke, he was quick to show his displeasure at any story in bad taste and he came down hard on any junior officers who referred to seniors in an over-familiar way.[42]

On 10 June 1916 Neill Malcolm, Gough's chief of staff, declared somewhat loftily that Plumer's 'system of command merely appears to be to tell the corps to carry on'.[43] There may have been a germ of truth in this at the time, since it echoed Haig's earlier complaints, but it pre-dated Harington's arrival. Under the Plumer–Harington partnership, the watchwords of Second Army were 'Trust, Training and Thoroughness'. These guiding principles were embodied in a set of notes compiled by Harington after conferring with battalion commanders, and then circulated to corps and divisions on 6 February 1917. Harington had found that too many battalion officers did not really regard commanders and staffs as 'friends', knew 'little of what is going on' and were 'inundated with writing and reports'. They consequently felt 'badgered and worried by untrained staff officers with but little experience and whom they naturally resent'. Harington confessed that Second Army did contain staff officers who failed to understand that 'the result of all bad staff work is that the troops themselves directly suffer'. Harington underlined the need for staff officers and battalion commanders to treat each other as friends 'out to help and not always to find fault'. He suggested that substituting personal visits for written requests would reduce paperwork and he highlighted the importance of conferences in all formations, 'to see that all parts of the machinery are working properly'. In a covering letter, Plumer himself added that the notes were being circulated to 'bring out certain things that we are all equally anxious to improve'.[44]

Practising what they preached, Plumer and Harington sought to establish trust and cultivate teamwork by means of daily personal contacts with sub-ordinate formations.[45] This policy was not confined to Plumer and Harington, for the diaries of Haig, Rawlinson and Horne show that they too devoted many hours every month to similar visits.[46] In Second Army's case, Plumer, accompanied by an ADC, would normally set off from his headquarters at Cassel immediately after the morning conference and, covering an average of 100 miles a day, visit corps and divisional headquarters in the forward areas as well as gun positions, ordnance depots, transport lines, workshops, rest billets, railheads and medical facilities. Harington would generally travel in the opposite direction so that they could call on as many formations as possible during the day. Plumer also attached a junior staff officer to every corps for liaison purposes, their duty being to get to know each battalion in that formation and to spend at least two nights a week in the front-line trenches. John Monash, commander of 3rd Australian Division, told Plumer on 4 February 1917 that 'Harington's doctrine that all staffs exist to *help* units and not to make difficulties for them is the only one that can possibly lead to success and I am constantly preaching that doctrine myself'.[47]

Thoroughness also extended to training. Before Messines, special training areas were designated at the rear of each corps sector, on ground that resembled that which would have to be crossed. Training areas were marked out with coloured flags and tapes to denote farms, strong points, woods and other objectives on the ridge. All assault brigades carried out half a dozen or more rehearsals and every aspect of the operation was practised. A huge scale model of the ridge – 'the size of two croquet lawns' – was built near Scherpenberg and was studied by parties of officers and NCOs from formations down to platoon level, while divisions taking part produced clay models of their own sectors.[48] There was nothing particularly new in all this, for careful battle drill had been a feature of the preparations of Ivor Maxse's 18th (Eastern) Division before its successful assault on Thiepval in September 1916, and many aspects had likewise been foreshadowed in the build-up to the Canadian attack on Vimy Ridge in April 1917.[49] Nonetheless, the troops taking part were deeply impressed by the care taken to brief them. Private Victor Fagence, a Lewis gunner in 11th Royal West Kents, later said: 'It was all explained to us and models were shown, models to scale showing our front line, No Man's Land, the enemy front line ... and how far our objective would be ... It was all pretty good really.'[50]

As late as 3 June 1917, Plumer was still directing Harington to bring to the attention of corps various points arising from that day's rehearsals and also that reports should be obtained from infantry units on their experience of the training.[51] Anthony Eden, then adjutant of the 21st King's Royal Rifle Corps (Yeoman Rifles), wrote of 'an intensive system of training such as we had never known ... It was typical that during the training of our battalion Plumer himself inspected us at work, while Harington visited us several times'.[52]

Second Army continued to employ such training methods for set-piece assaults. Prior to the final breakout from the Salient in late September 1918, Second Army – now with Jocelyn Percy as Plumer's MGGS – once again had a large scale model of the battlefield constructed, this time at Cassel. Plumer, however, does not seem to have enjoyed the same relationship with Percy as he had with Harington. Though the tall Percy was 'a personality to be remembered', according to Edmonds, he was not, in Charles Bonham-Carter's opinion, 'given the standing that was his due', and sometimes consequently had 'great difficulty in obtaining an essential service'.[53]

By mid-1917 the BEF had begun to master the German system of elastic defence in depth by means of limited-objective attacks based upon 'bite and hold' tactics.[54] The scale and complexity of the major set-piece assaults of 1917 made it essential for formations at all levels to engage, during the planning stages, in a continuous two-way process of consultation through liaison officers, personal contacts and regular conferences. Second Army was particularly effective at this, thanks to the command style already adopted by Plumer and Harington. Mitchell thought that one of Plumer's 'greatest and most valuable characteristics' was that, before finally deciding upon a plan, he would first make sure that everyone involved in shaping the decision was, as far as possible, in 'thorough agreement', though Mitchell admitted that the key planning conferences had 'many stiff hours and sometimes tense moments'. Plumer's conferences usually took place in a spacious room in his house at Cassel, with the participants gathered around a huge table. Once he felt that the conference had reached a satisfactory conclusion, Plumer would signal the end of proceedings with a dramatic flick of his eyeglass.[55] Lord Cavan always left these meetings 'with a clearer idea of what was required of me' than he had from any other. Plumer 'not only listened to one's difficulties but suggested remedies and then gave decisions. Tim Harington saw to it that those difficulties were overcome'.[56]

The fact that a fair proportion of the corps and divisional commanders who served under Plumer were entirely comfortable with this consultative command style was a vital element in Second Army's formula for success in limited-objective attacks. In the New Zealand Division, under the outstanding Major General Sir Andrew Russell, the conference system extended down to battalion level and below.[57] Lieutenant General Sir Arthur Currie of the Canadian Corps similarly excelled in methodical planning and close co-operation.[58] Plumer visited Monash and 3rd Australian Division at least eight times in the run-up to Messines. On 19 May, Monash recorded that Plumer had spent all afternoon of the previous day with him, 'going patiently and minutely through the whole of my plans, and said he felt sure that I had done all that was possible to ensure success'.[59] Monash, too, preferred to leave nothing to chance.[60] A good illustration of the extent of detailed planning is provided by the preliminary bombardment programme worked out for Messines by 3rd Australian Division's staff, who listed 446 targets to be shelled before 7 June.[61] Monash, in fact, tended to usurp the role of his brigade commanders. After the war, Harington remembered that, on 4 June 1917, Monash had presented him with all the division's orders and instructions relating to Messines collated into a single document some 6 inches thick. 'I never saw such a document – wonderful detail but not his job,' Harington told Edmonds.[62] However, the meticulous planning and briefing methods applied by men like Currie, Monash and Russell dovetailed neatly, in most respects, with those of Plumer and Harington, and, for several months at least in 1917, Second Army was blessed with a happy confluence of similar command philosophies at all levels.

In the absence of his personal papers, it becomes extremely difficult to assess how far the nature of the Western Front matched Plumer's pre-war expectations or to judge the extent to which Second Army's responses to the war's tactical challenges were the product of his own experience and imagination. His service in Africa and his time as quartermaster general had instilled in him a firm belief in the merits of sound administration and logistics, and the importance of meticulous planning. The value of thorough training was another conviction that he carried with him into the Great War. Crucial though these principles and beliefs were, they scarcely reflect a capacity for radical tactical innovation. Plumer's opportunities for developing new tactics and techniques had, of course, been somewhat restricted as, between May 1915 and June 1917, Second Army had not been centrally involved in major offensive operations, while the Salient offered the least suitable ground on which to experiment with the tank.

By the same token, it must be said that most of the new tactical methods that helped to define the shape and steepness of the BEF's 'learning curve' originated, or were first employed, elsewhere. The 'bite and hold' approach to offensive operations largely originated with Rawlinson.[63] The techniques necessary to mount a successful limited-objective attack had been brilliantly demonstrated – *before* Messines – by the Canadians at Vimy. Similar methods had been employed earlier by the French at Verdun and they were generally referred to as 'Pétain tactics'.[64] Thus, although Plumer is widely credited as being a master of the limited-objective attack, the concept was by no means unique to Second Army.

The same might be said of other developments that transformed the fighting capabilities of the BEF. The hugely significant reorganization of the infantry platoon early in 1917 had been driven largely by GHQ after digesting the lessons of Verdun and the Somme.[65] Creeping artillery barrages had become standard months before Messines, and Fifth Army had demonstrated the value of overhead machine-gun barrages in support of the infantry at Beaumont Hamel in November 1916. By the end of the Somme, the massive importance of effective counter-battery work had been grasped by all, as proved by the more systematic counter-battery programme implemented at Vimy the following April.[66] Finally, it was Third Army which, at Cambrai in November 1917, ushered in the 'predicted' artillery bombardment and the massed employment of tanks – tactics which helped to restore surprise and mobility to the battlefield.

Second Army did, however, contribute some tactical refinements of its own, quite apart from the unprecedented scale of its mining operations in preparation for the assault on Messines Ridge. One was the establishment, prior to Messines, of a report centre at Locre, which could receive messages from aircraft, balloons, field survey companies, anti-aircraft positions and wireless stations. It was in telephonic and telegraphic contact with Harington's office at Cassel and corps and divisional headquarters, so minimizing delays in forwarding information to counter-battery and bombardment groups.[67] In addition, a new and more complex form of multi-layered creeping barrage, comprising five belts of fire, was employed by Second Army in the Menin Road Ridge attack of 20 September 1917.[68] Strictly speaking, however, these measures should be attributed respectively to Mitchell and Buckle more than to Plumer himself.[69] There was certainly a growing recognition within Second Army in 1917 that the secret of tactical success lay in combined all-arms attacks.[70] It was simply not realistic to expect that the lengthy and extensive preparations for the Messines assault could be repeated with any frequency, but there seems little doubt that the pragmatic Plumer – an apostle of teamwork, who was at the very least endowed with sound tactical instincts and great common sense – did as much as anyone, and more than most, to encourage and develop the type of all-arms attack that proved the key to victory in 1918. In this respect, Plumer may have been a facilitator and a catalyst rather than an innovator, yet, for all that, his part in helping to produce the winning tactical formula should not be underrated.

Third Ypres

Third Ypres provides examples of both the strengths and the weaknesses of Plumer. Towards the end of June 1917, in the course of the debate as to how deep the objectives should be on the first day of the offensive, Brigadier General J.H. 'Tavish' Davidson – head of GHQ's Operations Branch – questioned the scheme submitted by Gough and recommended strictly limited objectives. According to Davidson, on 28 June, when Haig met Gough and Plumer at Cassel to discuss the matter, Plumer – much to Davidson's surprise – supported Gough's proposals rather than Davidson's step-by-step approach. Davidson recalled that, as he walked to the conference room with Plumer, the latter asked him:

> Do you think that after making the vast preparations for attack on this position over a long period of months, if not years, and after sitting in the salient all this time, I am going to agree to limiting the progress and advance of my troops at the outset ? ... I say definitely *no*, I would certainly not agree to any such limitation.

Gough later challenged this and even said that he could not remember such a conference taking place. If Davidson's version is accepted, it would seem that Plumer's reported stance may well have been a major factor in persuading Haig to swallow temporary misgivings about pursuing distant first-day objectives and, consequently, to endorse the Fifth Army scheme. It might also suggest that Plumer's belief in the limited-objective attack was perhaps not always quite so solid, deep-seated and consistent as has sometimes been supposed.[71]

Although Second Army had only a subsidiary role in the opening phases of Third Ypres, Plumer and his staff still carefully analyzed the lessons of their own initial operations, and those of Fifth Army. Thus, by 25 August, when the main burden of the offensive was transferred from Gough to Plumer, Second Army had already clarified most of the principles upon which its forthcoming attacks would be based. In a series of memoranda, Plumer and Harington highlighted the need for more flexible infantry assault formations, for more thorough 'mopping-up' at every stage of the advance and for sufficient reserves to be available to defeat both local and more organized counter-attacks. They

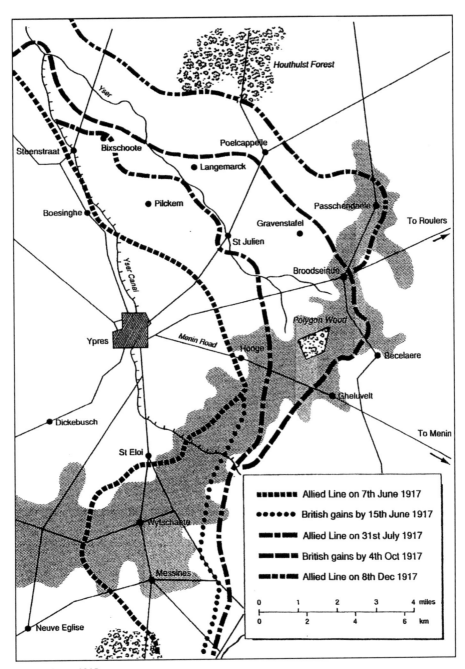

Houthulst Forest

Steenstraat

Bixschoote

Poelcappelle

Langemarck

Pilckem

Boesinghe

Gravenstafel

Passchendaele

To Roulers

St Julien

Yser Canal

Broodseinde

Polygon Wood

Ypres

Menin Road

Hooge

Becelaere

Gheluvelt

Dickebusch

To Menin

St Eloi

▪▪▪▪▪▪▪ Allied Line on 7th June 1917

●●●●●● British gains by 15th June 1917

▬ ▬ ▬ Allied Line on 31st July 1917

▬▬ ▬▬ British gains by 4th Oct 1917

▬▬ ▬▬ Allied Line on 8th Dec 1917

Wytschaete

Messines

| 0 | 1 | 2 | 3 | 4 miles |
| 0 | 2 | 4 | 6 | km |

Neuve Eglise

Third Ypres, 1917.

laid down that, where possible, fresh troops – using the 'leapfrog' method – should be employed at each stage in the advance. The distances between objectives should become shorter, and the pause for consolidation on each objective longer, as the attack progressed. It was also emphasized that the artillery barrage should have much greater depth and should not move too rapidly, while the length of each advance must be determined by the range of heavy artillery and machine-gun support and by the time required to bring guns forward to deal with counter-attacks. The 'primary importance' of counter-battery fire in neutralizing German guns was similarly underlined as 'the real road' to infantry success.[72]

These principles were embodied in the scheme which Plumer submitted to GHQ on 29 August for the capture of the Gheluvelt plateau. His plan was to secure it by four step-by-step attacks, with an interval of some six days between each in order to move supplies and artillery forward for the next bound. The distance of each step was governed by the need to meet organized German counter-attacks with fresh infantry and with an effective artillery barrage, and was therefore limited to about 1,500 yards. To avoid the problems experienced at Messines, where serious overcrowding and consequent casualties had been caused by the deployment of reserves according to a strict timetable rather than actual need, such deployment would now be left more to local commanders. A notable feature of Plumer's first set-piece assault in the series – the Battle of the Menin Road Ridge on 20 September – was the five-layered creeping barrage, 1,000 yards deep, fired by 240 machine-guns and around 738 of the 1,295 guns and howitzers available to Plumer. Standing barrages, 2,000 yards further on, were maintained to isolate the German forward positions and break up counter-attacks. The creeping barrage was described by eyewitnesses on the day as 'magnificent both in accuracy and volume', and of the six British and Australian divisions committed to the attack by Second Army, only one failed to achieve all its objectives on time.

The attack of 20 September 1917 has been judged by most historians to be an outstanding success – even given its relatively limited aims – and one that stands in marked contrast to the operations carried out by Fifth Army in August. Some, however, have pointed out that the operation was not an unqualified triumph. Prior and Wilson, for example, observe that the German artillery had not been totally subdued, either before or during the attack. They also indicate that Plumer won less ground than had Gough on 31 July and at proportionally more casualties per square mile: Gough won 18 square miles at a cost of 1,500 casualties per square mile and Plumer 6 square miles at a cost of 3,800 per square mile.[73]

Plumer's next two attacks – Polygon Wood (26 September) and Broodseinde (4 October) – employed much the same tactical formula and, ostensibly, were equally successful in broad terms, securing most of the key objectives and, as intended, smashing the expected German counter-attacks. However, the

German artillery was still able to inflict heavy losses, partly because Plumer's 'bite and hold' assaults were too shallow to capture the German guns and also because, when Second Army's own guns were being brought forward, the counter-battery programme was inevitably weakened. This time the attacking British and Australian units suffered 15,375 casualties for the capture of 3.5 square miles and a 1,250-yard advance, representing a cost of about 4,400 casualties per square mile, or 50 per cent more than on 20 September.[74] Haig, nevertheless, was greatly encouraged, feeling that 'decisive results' were now in sight.

Plumer, to be fair, did sound a note of caution on 30 September, when he warned against underestimating German morale and overestimating the possibility of immediate far-reaching strategic results. He did, however, think that German demoralization might sharply increase once the enemy had been pushed off Passchendaele Ridge. Apart from the minor dissent that he expressed on 30 September, Plumer did not otherwise seriously question the prospect presented by Haig.[75]

The results of the Broodseinde attack initially seemed to justify Haig's optimism. Second Army took more than 4,000 prisoners, and almost the whole of the Gheluvelt plateau had now been seized. Harington later judged the attack to be 'by far the best thing the Second Army ever did', and Bean described it as an 'overwhelming blow'.[76] It was also successful in securing vital ground from which the Germans had previously enjoyed good observation, but the flank operations had been costly, and over 20,000 casualties were incurred for an average gain of 1,000 yards and a maximum advance of 1 mile in the centre.[77]

For this and other reasons, some scholars have begun to challenge the validity of Plumer's 'bite and hold' methods, even as practised between 20 September and 4 October 1917. It is indeed reasonable to argue that Plumer's tactics – given the resources available to him and also the peculiar and unhelpful conditions and terrain – were, in several respects, subject to the law of diminishing returns to the point of being ultimately self-defeating. So long as Second Army's limited-objective attacks failed to capture significant numbers of enemy guns, Plumer could not achieve the full artillery dominance or increased operational tempo necessary to produce the decisive results Haig was seeking. The massive bombardments and multi-layered barrages also progressively damaged the fragile drainage system and infrastructure of the Salient, destroying the very roads and tracks required to move troops, guns and ammunition forward for the next bound and creating an almost impassable morass when the rain began to fall again in earnest on 4 October.[78]

The low point of Plumer's performance at Third Ypres was between 5 and 12 October. Both Plumer and Harington seem to have been swept along by the tide of false optimism which prevailed in the week after Broodseinde. Ignoring the steadily deteriorating conditions, Plumer permitted Second Army's cherished principle of 'thoroughness' to be temporarily cast aside, and the time granted to II Anzac Corps to prepare for the next two battles – Poelcappelle (9 October) and First Passchendaele (12 October) – was, respectively, only four and two days. There is no real documentary evidence for Edmonds's claim that, on 7 October, Plumer and Gough indicated to Haig that they 'would welcome a closing down of the campaign'. On the contrary, Plumer informed Haig the following day (8 October) that Godley of II Anzac Corps 'had specially asked that there should be no postponement' of the Poelcappelle operation. That same evening, a few hours before the attack, Harington glibly announced to assembled war correspondents that the crest of Passchendaele Ridge was 'as dry as a bone' and that, after one or two more 'bangs', the cavalry would be ready to go through. Bean, who was present, feared that the attack was 'a great bloody experiment – a huge gamble and no more than that', and concluded that Passchendaele was now an obsession with Haig. Yet Harington was at pains to point out, years later, that it was 'unthinkable' and 'inconceivable' that there had been any fundamental disagreement between Haig and Plumer during Third Ypres, especially in the first half of October 1917.[79]

Even as reports began to show that the Poelcappelle attack had been an expensive failure, Godley remained undeterred, clearly expecting the previously reliable 3rd Australian and New Zealand Divisions to do the trick again on 12 October.[80] Haig, Plumer and Godley were all rapidly disillusioned by the outcome of Poelcappelle and First Passchendaele. In each case the mud made it impossible to move sufficient artillery forward or to provide stable gun-platforms, the supporting barrages therefore being feeble, patchy and ineffective. Matters were undoubtedly made worse by the failure of Godley and his staff to pay the necessary attention to the repair of roads and tracks in their sector. While Plumer was not entirely to blame for the conditions, he cannot escape all censure for the problems encountered, as he manifestly abandoned his principle of methodical planning and preparation and signally failed to exert appropriate 'grip' on Godley. Some of the esteem in which able subordinates such as Monash had earlier held him also started to evaporate.[81]

It was only when the Canadians entered the battle and Currie insisted on being given adequate time to prepare his proposed three-step attack on Passchendaele Ridge – with each step advancing the line barely 500 yards – that Plumer reverted to first principles. Even then the Canadians lost nearly 13,000 officers and men in securing the ridge by 10 November.[82] Indeed, Second Army's casualty figures in September and up to 12 October – 69,000 for an overall gain of less than 4,000 yards – have been compared unfavourably with Fifth Army's 86,000 casualties for an advance of 3½ miles in seven weeks, thus also casting some doubt on Plumer's reputation as a 'soldier's general' who was particularly careful with men's lives.[83]

Yet to heap too much criticism on Plumer's shoulders for mistakes at Third Ypres not only is unjust but misses the main point. It is too often forgotten that Plumer defended Ypres itself successfully for three years. It should be reiterated, moreover, that the German system of defence in depth – even when strengthened after Messines – had largely failed in the face of Second Army's 'bite and hold' attacks, forcing the Germans to alter the system at least twice more before the end of October 1917. It is equally worth bearing in mind that Plumer's penchant for teamwork and consultation did much to foster the kind of devolved command that permitted more mobile operations a year later. The right combination of strategic, tactical and logistical conditions that would allow such success simply did not exist until the last months of the war. However, from August to November 1918, when circumstances did permit a rolling series of limited-objective and all-arms attacks to be conducted on an almost daily basis, then the formula proved irresistible. As a leading proponent and practitioner of the limited-objective attack and of all-arms tactics, Plumer surely deserves considerable credit for his contribution to the BEF's 'learning curve' and his part in the eventual German defeat.

Bibliography

As the bulk of Plumer's private papers were destroyed, on his own instructions, before his death, those wishing to study his military career will find it useful to begin by reading the two principal biographies of him that have been published to date. General Sir Charles 'Tim' Harington, *Plumer of Messines* (London: Murray, 1935), contains many valuable personal insights, but it inevitably suffers from its uncritical and hagiographical tone. Indeed, its declared intention is to avoid uttering 'one unkind word of either the living or the dead'. Harington's own papers have similarly been lost to history. The more recent full-length biography, Geoffrey Powell, *Plumer: The Soldier's General* (London: Leo Cooper, 1990), is much more objective, and draws upon a wider range of sources, though, curiously, Powell does not appear to have consulted the Second Army war diaries or more than a handful of published unit histories. Fortunately, some scholarly analyses of Plumer's major battles have appeared, notably Ian Passingham, *Pillars of Fire: The Battle of Messines Ridge, June 1917* (Stroud: Sutton, 1998), and Robin Prior and Trevor Wilson, *Passchendaele: The Untold Story* (New Haven: Yale University Press, 1996). Passingham's study contains much useful material on the German view of Messines, and is generally favourable to Plumer. Prior and Wilson, on the other hand, are sometimes highly critical of his conduct of operations, including those battles usually considered to be among his greatest successes. The more positive aspects of Second Army's handling of the Menin Road Ridge operation are highlighted in John Lee, 'Command and Control in Battle: British Divisions on the Menin Road Ridge, 20 September 1917', in Gary Sheffield and Dan Todman, eds, *Command and Control on the Western Front* (Staplehurst: Spellmount, 2004), pp. 119–38. However, two other recent pieces are less kind to Plumer – Rob Thompson, 'Mud, Blood and Wood', in Peter Doyle and M. Bennett, eds, *Fields of Battle: Terrain in Military History* (Dordrecht: Kluwer, 2002), pp. 237–55, and Gerald Casey, 'General Sir Herbert Plumer and "Passchendaele": A Reassessment', *Firestep*, 5/2 (2004), pp. 40–60. Relevant chapters can also be found in Peter Liddle, ed., *Passchendaele in Perspective: The Third Battle of Ypres* (Barnsley: Leo Cooper, 1997).

Notes

1 B.H. Liddell Hart, *History of the First World War* (London: Pan, 1972), pp. 323–4; *Daily Telegraph*, 18 July 1932; Arthur Behrend, *As from Kemmel Hill: An Adjutant in France and Flanders, 1917 & 1918* (London: Eyre and Spottiswoode, 1963), p. 12.

2 See the entry on Plumer in the *Dictionary of National Biography, 1931–1940* (Oxford: Oxford University Press, 1949), pp. 702–6; General Sir Charles Harington, *Plumer of Messines* (London: Murray, 1935); and Geoffrey Powell, *Plumer, the Soldier's General: A Biography of Field-Marshal Viscount Plumer of Messines* (London: Leo Cooper, 1990).

3 Richard Holmes, *The Little Field-Marshal: Sir John French* (London: Cape, 1981), pp. 209–10; Powell, *Plumer*, pp. 101–2; The National Archives (hereafter TNA), WO 33/713, French to Kitchener, 17 August 1914, and Kitchener to French, 18 August 1914.

4 Imperial War Museum (hereafter IWM), French MSS, JDPF 1/Vol.K PP/MCR/C32, French diary, 26 April 1915; Holmes, *Little Field-Marshal*, pp. 282–6; A.J. Smithers, *The Man Who Disobeyed: Sir Horace Smith-Dorrien and His Enemies* (London: Leo Cooper, 1970), pp. 282–9.

5 Brigadier General Sir James Edmonds, *Military Operations: France and Belgium, 1918* (this series hereafter *OFH*) (London: Macmillan, 1937), vol. 2, pp. 299–300; Harington, *Plumer*, pp. 161–2; Powell, *Plumer*, pp. 263–4.

6 Plumer was wearing his monocle, or eyeglass, when he posed for the war artist Francis Dodd on 19 February 1917. Dodd's charcoal portrait drawing of Plumer is held in IWM, Department of Art, IWM ART 1817.

7 Harington, *Plumer*, pp. 164–5, 310.

8 Ibid., pp. 6, 285, 287–92, 311, 326–34; Powell, *Plumer*, pp. 24, 99; Richard Holmes, *Tommy: The British Soldier on the Western Front, 1914–1918* (London: Harper Collins, 2004), p. 55.

9 Powell, *Plumer*, pp. 98, 294–5, 302, 319–20.

10 See, for example, TNA, WO 256/19, Haig diary, 7 June 1917.

11 Harington, *Plumer, passim*; Liddell Hart Centre for Military Archives (hereafter LHCMA), Edmonds MSS, II/1/163A, Harington to Edmonds, 21 November 1934.

12 LHCMA, Liddell Hart MSS, 11/1935/58, Liddell Hart, 'Talk with Edmonds', 10 January 1935; 11/1935/117, 'Talk with Edmonds', 16 December 1935; 11/1935/132, 'Note on Duff Cooper's *Haig*'.

13 Harington, *Plumer*, pp. 56–62; Powell, *Plumer*, pp. 91–7; Dudley Sommer, *Haldane of Cloan: His Life and Times, 1856–1928* (London: Allen and Unwin, 1950), p. 167; British Library, Arnold-Forster MSS, Add. MSS 50343, Arnold-Forster diary, 16 December 1905; National Library of Scotland (hereafter NLS), Haldane MSS, 5874, Haldane to mother, 15 December 1905; LHCMA, Liddell Hart MSS, II/1/163A, Harington to Edmonds, 21 November 1934; Peter Fraser, *Lord Esher: A Political Biography* (London: Hart-Davis, MacGibbon, 1973), p. 162; Ian F.W. Beckett, *Riflemen Form: A Study of the Rifle Volunteer Movement, 1859–1908* (Aldershot: Ogilby Trusts, 1982), p. 237; Edward M. Spiers, *Haldane: An Army Reformer* (Edinburgh: Edinburgh University Press, 1983), p. 74.

14 General Sir Tom Bridges, *Alarms and Excursions* (London: Longmans, Green, 1938), pp. 138, 163.

15 LHCMA, Robertson MSS, 7/6/23, Haig to Robertson, 17 February 1916; *OFH, 1916* (1931), vol. 1, pp. 162–72.

16 TNA, WO 256/8, Haig diary, 18 February 1916; LHCMA, Robertson MSS, 7/6/24 and 26, Haig to Robertson, 18 February 1916, and Robertson to Haig, 20 February 1916.

17 TNA, WO 256/9, Haig diary, 21 and 23 April 1916; *OFH, 1916*, vol. 1, pp. 177–91, 227; Colonel G.W.L. Nicholson, *Canadian Expeditionary Force, 1914–1919: Official History of the Canadian Forces in the First World War* (Ottawa: Queen's Printer, 1962), p. 147, n. 57; A.M.J. Hyatt, *General Sir Arthur Currie: A Military Biography* (Toronto: University of Toronto Press, 1987), pp. 55–6, 155, n. 24–5. Hyatt makes it clear that, although Borden adopted this view later, there is no real evidence that he had actually communicated it as such to Aitken by 23 April 1916.

18 Harington's predecessor, Hugh Bruce Williams, who had been in the post since July 1915, had left to become GOC of 137 Brigade in 46th (North Midland) Division, less than a month before its ill-fated attack at Gommecourt.

19 NLS, Aylmer Haldane MSS, Edmonds to Haldane, 17 March 1931.

20 *OFH, 1917* (1948), vol. 2, pp. 9–20, 206–7; TNA, WO 158/214, 'Army Instructions for Main Offensive on Second Army Front', 12 December 1916; LHCMA, Kiggell MSS, 4/1/129, Kiggell to Second Army, 27 January 1917; TNA, WO 158/38, Second Army to GHQ, 30 January 1917; Canberra, Australian War Memorial (hereafter AWM), Operational Records, 45/32/6, Plumer to Haig, 18 March 1917; ibid., AWM 51, Haig to Second Army (OAD 349), 3 April 1917; ibid., 45/39/4, Plumer to GHQ, 20 April 1917; Robin Prior and Trevor Wilson, *Passchendaele: The Untold Story* (New Haven: Yale University Press, 1996), pp. 45–9; Andrew Wiest, 'Haig, Gough and Passchendaele', in G.D. Sheffield, ed., *Leadership and Command: The Anglo-American Experience since 1861* (London: Brassey's, London, 1997), pp. 77–92.

21 *OFH, 1917*, vol. 2, p. 127; Prior and Wilson, *Passchendaele*, pp. 49–51; Powell, *Plumer*, pp. 166–9; John Terraine, *Douglas Haig: The Educated Soldier* (London: Hutchinson, 1963), p. 337.

22 TNA, WO 256/18, Haig diary, 22 May 1917. On 22 May, Haig visited II Corps, X Corps, 23rd Division, 24th Division, 41st Division and 47th Division.

23 TNA, WO 256/18, Haig diary, 22 and 23 May 1917; Liverpool Central Library, Derby MSS, 920 DER(17) 27/2, Haig to Derby, 28 June 1917; Powell, *Plumer*, p. 171; Liddell Hart, *History of the First World War*, p. 323; *OFH, 1917*, vol. 2, p. 388.

24 AWM, 45/32/6, Plumer to Haig, 18 March 1917; AWM, 51, Haig to Second Army (OAD 349), 3 April 1917; AWM, 45/33/1, Macmullen, Interview with Plumer, 5 April 1917; Plumer to Haig, 9 April 1917; AWM, 51, 'Note on the Messines-Wytschaete attack' (OAD 432), 5 May 1917; AWM, 26/6/187/9, Second Army Operation Order No. 1, 10 May 1917; *OFH, 1917*, vol. 2, p. 418; Prior and Wilson, *Passchendaele*, pp. 57–66; Terraine, *Haig*, pp. 315–17; Powell, *Plumer*, pp. 184–6.

25 TNA, WO 256/19, Haig diary, 7 June 1917; Brigadier General John Charteris, *At GHQ* (London: Cassell, 1931), p. 226.

26 TNA, WO 256/21, Haig diary, 25 August 1917; ibid., WO 158/250, Fifth Army Operations File, Haig to Gough (OAD 609), 28 August 1917; ibid., 'Notes of a Conference held at Cassel on Thursday, 30 August, 1917'; *OFH, 1917*, vol. 2, pp. 206–7; Prior and Wilson, *Passchendaele*, pp. 108–10.

27 TNA, WO 256/22, Haig diary, 17 September 1917. A copy of Haig's checklist of 'Questions to Corps' is attached to the diary.

28 Ibid., Haig diary, 26 and 28 September 1917; AWM, 45/33/1, Conferences at Second Army Headquarters, 26 and 29 September and 2 October 1917; ibid., Plumer to Haig, 30 September 1917; *OFH, 1917*, vol. 2, pp. 296–9, 323–7; Prior and Wilson, *Passchendaele*, pp. 133–8, 159–64; Powell, *Plumer*, pp. 221–5.

29 David Lloyd George, *War Memoirs* (London: Ivor Nicholson and Watson, 1936), vol. 5, p. 2332; Harington, *Plumer*, pp. 133–4.

30 Major General Sir C.E. Callwell, *Field-Marshal Sir Henry Wilson: His Life and Diaries* (London: Cassell, 1927), vol. 2, pp. 58–61; IWM, Wilson MSS, HHW 1/27, Box 73/1/9, Wilson diary, 9 and 15 February 1918; Royal Archives, GV F 1259/4, Note made by Stamfordham of a meeting with Lloyd George, 22 January 1918; *OFH, 1918* (1935), vol. 1, p. 88; Powell, *Plumer*, pp. 247–53; TNA, WO 256/27, Haig diary, 15 February 1918; Stephen Roskill, *Hankey: Man of Secrets*, vol. 1, *1872–1918* (London: Collins, 1970), pp. 493–6; LHCMA, Edmonds MSS, VI/9, W. Robertson to Edmonds, 31 August 1945. Lt. Col. W. Robertson was GSO1 (Operations), Second Army, 1917–18.

31 Harington, *Plumer*, p. 147.

32 TNA, WO 256/28, Haig diary, 23 March 1918.

33 TNA, WO 158/242, GHQ to Army Commanders (OAD 926/4), 25 September 1918; ibid., WO 256/36, Haig diary, 9 September 1918; *OFH, 1917*, vol. 2, p. 238; *OFH, 1918* (1947), vol. 4, pp. 427–36; *OFH, 1918* (1947), vol. 5, pp. 57–93; TNA, WO 158/218, 'Second Army Operations from 28 September to 13 October 1918'; J.P. Harris with Niall Barr, *Amiens to the Armistice* (London: Brassey's, 1998), pp. 119–202; Powell, *Plumer*, p. 273. An interesting and useful analysis of these operations has recently been produced in Dennis Williams, 'Flanders' Forgotten Army. The British Second Army in Flanders: The Final Advance to Victory, September–November 1918', unpublished MA, Leeds, 2005. I am greatly indebted to Dennis Williams for allowing me to read and refer to this dissertation.

34 TNA, WO 256/37, Haig diary, 15, 16, 24 and 26 October and 4 and 11 November 1918; ibid., WO 158/218, Reports on Second Army Operations for 14–31 October and 1–11 November and for weeks ending 18 and 25 October and 1 November 1918; Harris, *Amiens to the Armistice*, pp. 230, 242–4, 259–60; Powell, *Plumer*, pp. 276–8; *OFH, 1918*, vol. 5, pp. 283–92, 426–53. See also IWM, Film and Video Archive, Film No. 132, 'Haig and his Army Commanders on 11th November 1918'.

35 Powell, *Plumer*, pp. 153–5; Philip Gibbs, *Realities of War* (London: Heinemann, 1920), pp. 47–9, 389–90.

36 AWM, Elliott MSS, 2DRL 513, Item 42A, Elliott to Bean, n.d., circa 1930.

37 Gibbs, *Realities of War*, pp. 389–90.

38 Charteris, *At GHQ*, p. 226.

39 Harington, *Plumer*, pp. 78–9.

40 Ibid., pp. 166, 317.

41 Ibid., pp. 79–80, 166–7.

42 Ibid., pp. 164–5.

43 Private collection, Malcolm MSS, Malcolm diary, 10 June 1916.

44 Notes compiled by Harington, 5 February 1917 with a covering letter from Plumer (dated 6 February). A copy can be found in AWM, Monash MSS, 3DRL 2316, Item 23: Personal File Book 14.

45 Harington, *Plumer*, p. 80.

46 Peter Simkins, 'Haig and the Army Commanders', in Brian Bond and Nigel Cave, eds, *Haig: A Reappraisal 70 Years On* (Barnsley: Leo Cooper, 1999), pp. 94–6.

47 Harington, *Plumer*, pp. 80–82; Powell, *Plumer*, pp. 158–9. See also IWM, Parrington MSS, 76/118/1, Parrington diary, II, pp. 177–88; Peter Pedersen, *Monash as Military Commander* (Melbourne: Melbourne University Press), 1985, p. 158.

48 *OFH, 1917*, vol. 2, p. 34; Harington, *Plumer*, p. 100; Ian Passingham, *Pillars of Fire: The Battle of Messines Ridge, June 1917* (Stroud: Sutton, 1998), pp. 30–33; Christopher Pugsley, *The Anzac Experience: New Zealand, Australia and Empire in the First World War* (Auckland: Reed, 2004), p. 223.

49 Peter Simkins, 'The War Experience of a Typical Kitchener Division: The 18th Division, 1914–1918', in Hugh Cecil and Peter Liddle, eds, *Facing Armageddon: The First World War Experienced* (Barnsley: Leo Cooper, 1996), p. 301; Major General F.I. Maxse, *The 18th Division in the Battle of the Ancre* (printed report, December 1916), pp. 3–4; *OFH, 1917* (1940), vol. 1, p. 305; Bill Rawling, *Surviving Trench Warfare: Technology and the Canadian Corps, 1914–1918* (Toronto: University of Toronto Press, 1992), pp. 98–100; National Archives of Canada, RG9, V 4943, 78th Canadian Battalion, War Diary, 28 March 1917; ibid., V 4049, Folder 14, File 4, 2nd Canadian Brigade to 1st Canadian Division, 20 February 1917; ibid., V 4916, 5th Canadian Battalion, War Diary, 13 March 1917; ibid., V 4912, 1st Canadian Battalion, War Diary, 13 February and 11–24 March 1917.

50 IWM, Sound Archive, 000327/08, Recollections of Private Victor Fagence.

51 Harington, *Plumer*, p. 88.

52 Anthony Eden, *Another World, 1897–1917* (London: Allen Lane, 1976), pp. 184–85.

53 *OFH, 1918*, vol. 5, p. 64; Obituary of Percy, *The Times*, 25 August 1952; Churchill Archives Centre, Churchill College, Cambridge (hereafter CAC), Bonham-Carter MSS, Bonham-Carter Autobiography, ch. 9, pp. 29–30. Percy, who had previously served as MGGS, Fifth Army, after Neill Malcolm's departure, had changed his name from Baumgartner in 1917. I am indebted to Dr John Bourne for this information.

54 Andy Simpson, 'British Corps Command on the Western Front, 1914–1918', John Lee, 'Command and Control in Battle: British Divisions on the Menin Road Ridge, 20 September 1917', and Peter Simkins, '"Building Blocks": Aspects of Command and Control at Brigade Level in the BEF's Offensive Operations, 1916–1918', all in Gary Sheffield and Dan Todman, eds, *Command and Control on the Western Front: The British Army's Experience, 1914–1918* (Staplehurst: Spellmount, 2004), pp. 97–115, 119–38 and 141–65. See also Andy Simpson, 'The Operational Role of British Corps Command on the Western Front, 1914–1918', unpublished PhD thesis, London, 2001.

55 Harington, *Plumer*, pp. 315–17.

56 Harington, *Plumer*, p. 307; CAC, Cavan MSS, 1/3, Cavan typescript, 'Recollections Hazy but Happy', circa 1945.

57 New Zealand National Archives, WA 20/3/13, 'Report on the Capture of Messines by the 4th Battalion, 3rd New Zealand (Rifle) Brigade'; Pugsley, *Anzac Experience*, p. 222.

58 General A.G.L. McNaughton, 'The Development of Artillery in the Great War', *Canadian Defence Quarterly*, 6/2 (January 1929), pp. 162–8; Hyatt, *Currie*, p. 82.

59 Passingham, *Pillars of Fire*, p. 33; Pedersen, *Monash*, p. 166; National Library of Australia (hereafter NLA), Monash MSS, Monash to Plumer, 17 April 1917; AWM, Monash MSS, 3DRL 2316, War Letters of General Sir John Monash, Final Typed Copy, vol. 2, Monash to his wife, 19 May 1917; F.M. Cutlack, ed., *War Letters of General Monash* (Sydney: Angus and Robertson, 1935), pp. 298–300.

60 Pedersen, *Monash*, p. 168.

61 C.E.W. Bean, *Official History of Australia in the War of 1914–1918*, vol. 4, *The Australian Imperial Force in France, 1917* (hereafter *AOH*) (Sydney: Angus and Robertson, 1933), p. 578.

62 Pedersen, *Monash*, p. 165.

63 Robin Prior and Trevor Wilson, *Command on the Western Front: The Military Career of Sir Henry Rawlinson, 1914–1918* (Oxford: Blackwell, 1992), pp. 36–43, 68–73, 77–8, 137–53, 155–70, 227–37.

64 *OFH, 1917*, vol. 2, pp. 22–4; *AOH*, vol. 4, pp. 941–2; Field-Marshal Sir William Robertson, *Soldiers and Statesmen, 1914–1918* (London: Cassell, London, 1926), vol. 2, pp. 233–45.

65 See, in particular, Richard Bryson, 'The Once and Future Army', and John Lee, 'Some Lessons of the Somme: The British Infantry in 1917', both in Brian Bond, ed., *'Look to Your Front': Studies in the First World War* (Staplehurst: Spellmount, 1999), pp. 46–9, 79–84; Rawling, *Surviving Trench Warfare*, pp. 89–95.

66 General Sir Martin Farndale, *History of the Royal Regiment of Artillery: Western Front, 1914–18* (London: Royal Artillery Institution, 1986), pp. 156, 184; Rawling, *Surviving Trench Warfare*, p. 111; *OFH, 1917*, vol. 1, pp. 312–13.

67 *OFH, 1917*, vol. 2, p. 42; Harington, *Plumer*, p. 101.

68 *OFH, 1917*, vol. 2, pp. 241, 247–8, 253–4; Farndale, *Royal Regiment*, p. 206.

69 Harington, *Plumer*, p. 101; *OFH, 1917*, vol. 2, p. 247.

70 LHCMA, Spears MSS, 2/2, Haldane to Plumer, 16 April 1917; Simon Robbins, *British Generalship on the Western Front, 1914–1918: Defeat into Victory* (London: Frank Cass, 2005), p. 104.
71 IWM, Maxse MSS, 69/538A, Malcolm, 'Notes for Conference', 23 May 1917; TNA, WO 95/519, 'Notes on Conference held at Lovie Château, June 6th'; ibid., WO 158/249, Note by Malcolm, 7 June 1917; ibid., Davidson to CGS, 26 June 1917; ibid., Memorandum by Gough, 28 June 1917; ibid., WO 256/19, Haig diary, 27 June 1917; ibid., WO 158/249, Malcolm to Corps commanders, 30 June 1917; ibid., Note by Haig, 30 June 1917; ibid., CAB 45/140, Gough, margin comments on draft of Official History and Gough to Edmonds, 7 June 1944 and 27 May 1945; ibid., Notes by Wynne, 31 May 1945; Major General Sir John Davidson, *Haig: Master of the Field* (London: Peter Nevill, 1953), pp. 28–32; General Sir Hubert Gough, *The Fifth Army* (London: Hodder and Stoughton, 1931), pp. 196–7; *OFH, 1917*, vol. 2, pp. 128–31, 431–2, 436–42. The topic is examined extensively and illuminatingly by Tim Travers in *The Killing Ground: The British Army, the Western Front and the Experience of Modern Warfare, 1900–1918* (London: Allen and Unwin, 1987), pp. 203–16, and more recently by Andrew Green in *Writing the Great War: Sir James Edmonds and the Official Histories, 1915–48* (London: Routledge, 2003), pp. 161–88.
72 TNA, WO 95/275, 'Army Commander's Minute', 1 August 1917 [also in AWM, Monash MSS, 3DRL 2316 Item 25, Personal File Book 16]; ibid., Plumer to Kiggell, 12 August 1917; *OFH, 1917*, vol. 2, Appendix XXIV; TNA, WO 95/275, 'Notes on Training and Preparation for Offensive Operations', 31 August 1917 [also in AWM, Monash MSS, 3DRL 2316, Item 25].
73 *OFH, 1917*, vol. 2, pp. 142–9, 206–7, 231–79, 449–57; TNA, WO 95/275, 'Second Army Instruction of the 29th August 1917: General Principles on which the Artillery Plan Will Be Drawn'; ibid., Second Army Operation Order No. 4, 1 September 1917, and Addendum of 10 September 1917; Farndale, *Royal Regiment*, pp. 205–8; Nigel Steel and Peter Hart, *Passchendaele: The Sacrificial Ground* (London: Cassell, 2000), p. 233; Prior and Wilson, *Passchendaele*, pp. 113–23. The most recent detailed scholarly analysis of the attack is by John Lee, 'Command and Control in Battle', pp. 119–38.
74 *OFH, 1917*, vol. 2, pp. 280–95; *AOH*, vol. 4, pp. 791–832; Prior and Wilson, *Passchendaele*, pp. 125–31.
75 TNA, WO 256/22, Haig diary, 26 and 18 September 1917; AWM, Operational Records, 45/33/1, Notes of Second Army Conferences, 26 and 29 September and 2 October 1917; TNA, WO 158/250, Plumer to Haig (G 924), 30 September 1917; AWM, 45/39/4, Plumer to Corps Commanders, 2 October 1917. See also LHCMA, Maurice MSS, 3/2/7, Harington to Maurice, 9 November 1934; and Prior and Wilson, *Passchendaele*, pp. 133–4.
76 LHCMA, Maurice MSS, 3/2/7, Harington to Maurice, 9 November 1934; *AOH*, vol. 4, p. 875; *OFH, 1917*, vol. 2, pp. 296–319.
77 *OFH, 1917*, vol. 2, pp. 309, 315; Prior and Wilson, *Passchendaele*, p. 137.
78 For recent critical analyses of Plumer's 'bite and hold' tactics, see, in particular, Prior and Wilson, *Passchendaele*, pp. 138–9, and Gerald Casey, 'General Sir Herbert Plumer and "Passchendaele": A Reassessment', *Firestep* [the magazine of the London Branch of the Western Front Association] 5/2 (2004), pp. 40–60.
79 Prior and Wilson, *Passchendaele*, pp. 159–61; Harington, *Plumer*, pp. 110–11; TNA, WO 256/23, Haig diary, 8 and 9 October 1917; AWM, Bean MSS, 3DRL 606, Item 89, Bean diary, 8 October 1917.
80 TNA, WO 256/33, Haig diary, 10 and 11 October 1917.
81 *OFH, 1917*, vol. 2, pp. 323–37, 339–45; AWM, Monash MSS, 3DRL 2316, War Letters of General Monash, Final Typed Copy, vol. 2, Monash to his wife, 18 October 1917. For a stimulating recent critique of the performance of II Anzac Corps in October 1917, see Rob Thompson, 'Mud, Blood and Wood: BEF Operational and Logistico-Engineering during the Third Battle of Ypres, 1917', in Peter Doyle and M. Bennett, eds, *Fields of Battle: Terrain in Military History* (Dordrecht: Kluwer, 2002), pp. 237–55.
82 TNA, WO 95/1051, Currie to Second Army, 'Passchendaele: Causes of Success and Failure in the Recent Operations of the Canadian Corps', 20 November 1917 [also in AWM, 45/47/1]; Hyatt, *Currie*, pp. 79–86; *OFH, 1917*, vol. 2, pp. 345–59.
83 Ian F.W. Beckett, 'Operational Command: The Plans and Conduct of Battle', in Peter H. Liddle, ed., *Passchendaele in Perspective: The Third Battle of Ypres* (Barnsley: Leo Cooper, 1997), p. 112; Casey, 'Plumer and Passchendaele', pp. 40, 57.

Chapter Eight

Henry Rawlinson

First Army, 1915–1916; Second Army, 1917;
Fourth Army, 1916–1917, 1918; Fifth Army, 1918

Ian F.W. Beckett

Sir Henry Rawlinson presided over some of the most successful operations of the British army during the Great War, but also over some of its worst catastrophes. His corps undertook the first major British offensive mounted from a trench system at Neuve Chapelle in March 1915 and the first British offensive in which gas was employed at Loos in September 1915. Both were unsuccessful and, on the Somme on 1 July 1916, Rawlinson's Fourth Army suffered the greatest loss of life in a single day in British military history. He also presided, however, over the first, moderately successful use of tanks at Flers-Courcelette in September 1916, albeit it a minor one, and over innovative but ultimately abortive preparations for an amphibious assault on the Flanders coast in 1917. Then, in 1918, Rawlinson's army played a significant role in the victories of the 'Hundred Days', inflicting the 'Black Day' on the German army on 8 August and breaking the Hindenburg Line in September. His career, therefore, seemingly provides in microcosm a classic example of the nature of the learning curve on the Western Front.

The eldest son of Sir Henry Rawlinson, Bt, a noted soldier, politician, linguist and Assyriologist, who was the first translator of cuneiform, Henry Seymour Rawlinson was born in February 1864. Known to his father variously as Harry or Sennacherib,[1] young Henry was educated at Eton and Sandhurst, and commissioned in the King's Royal Rifle Corps in February 1884 and posted to India. Through his father's influence, Rawlinson became an ADC to Lord Roberts in the Third Burma War but, following his mother's death, returned to England in 1889 to nurse his ageing father. Rawlinson married in 1890 and transferred to the Coldstream Guards two years later. He attended the Staff College in 1892–3 and, under the influence of its commandant, G.F.R. Henderson, visited the battlefields of the Franco-Prussian War. Succeeding to the baronetcy on his father's death in 1895, Rawlinson was appointed a brigade major at Aldershot. In 1898 he accompanied his ailing wife

Chronology

20 February 1864	Henry Seymour Rawlinson born at Trent Manor, Dorset
	Educated at Eton and Royal Military College, Sandhurst
6 February 1884	Commissioned King's Royal Rifle Corps
March 1884	Sailed to India to join 4th Battalion, KRRC
28 November 1885	Appointed ADC to Lord Roberts
6 November 1890	Married Meredith Sophie Frances Kennard
4 November 1891	Promoted captain
1892–3	Attended Staff College, Camberley
20 July 1892	Transferred to Coldstream Guards
26 February 1895	Succeeded to baronetcy
2 January 1898	Appointed DAAG in the Sudan
25 January 1899	Promoted major
26 January 1899	Promoted brevet lieutenant colonel
16 September 1899	Appointed DAAG in South Africa
12 March 1900	Joined Robert's staff as DAQMG
6 May 1901	Took command of mobile column
26 June 1902	Promoted brevet colonel
1 April 1903	Appointed AAG at War Office and substantive colonel
5 December 1903	Appointed commandant, Staff College
1 March 1907	Appointed GOC 2 Brigade
10 May 1909	Promoted major general
1 June 1910	Appointed GOC 3rd Division
31 May 1914	Went on half pay
5 August 1914	Appointed director of recruiting at War Office
21 September 1914	Took temporary command of 4th Division
5 October 1914	Appointed GOC IV Corps and temporary lieutenant general
22 December 1915	Appointed GOC First Army and temporary general
1 January 1916	Promoted substantive lieutenant general
5 February 1916	Appointed GOC Fourth Army
1 January 1917	Promoted substantive general
10 May 1917	Assumed command of proposed Flanders amphibious operation
9 November 1917	Appointed GOC Second Army
20 December 1917	Second Army redesignated Fourth Army
17 February 1918	Appointed British military representative at Supreme War Council
28 March 1918	Appointed GOC Fifth Army
2 April 1918	Fifth Army redesignated Fourth Army
1919	Created Baron Rawlinson of Trent
4 August 1919	Appointed GOC North Russia
15 November 1919	Appointed GOC Aldershot
21 November 1920	Appointed C.-in-C. India
28 March 1925	Died at Delhi
30 April 1925	Buried at Trent, Dorset

Appointed CB 1900, KCB 1915, GCVO 1917, KCMG 1918, GCB 1919, GCSI 1924 on a trip to Cairo to regain her health at the precise moment when Kitchener was mounting the final phase of the campaign to reconquer the Sudan. He was appointed DAAG on Kitchener's staff.

Successful performance in the Sudan campaign was one of a number of factors influencing appointments to the forces sent to reinforce Natal in the summer of 1899 and, through the influence of another of Roberts's protégés, Ian Hamilton, Rawlinson found himself appointed DAAG on the staff of Major General Sir Penn Symons, though he had assumed he was actually being appointed to the staff of Lieutenant General Sir George White. In the event, another officer joined Symons in his stead and Rawlinson was trapped in Ladysmith with White's Natal Field Force.[2] Soon after the relief of Ladysmith, Rawlinson was summoned to join the staff of Roberts, who had succeeded to the South African command with Kitchener as his chief of staff. Rawlinson accompanied Roberts back to England in December 1900 but shortly rejoined Kitchener. In May 1901 he was given command of one of the mobile columns hunting down the remaining Boer commandos, later calculating that, in the course of covering 5,211 miles, his men had killed 54 Boers while capturing a further 1,376 men and 3 guns for the loss of only 12 dead and 42 wounded.[3]

Following the conclusion of the South African War, Rawlinson was appointed to the War Office Education Department together with his close friend Henry Wilson, working on the new *Manual of Combined Training*. Rawlinson and Wilson had first met in Burma, and Rawlinson introduced Wilson to the Roberts circle when both were students at the Staff College.[4] Rawlinson was then appointed commandant of the Staff College in December 1903, and he initiated a series of significant practical reforms in the syllabus. More attention was devoted to likely operations on the Franco-Belgian frontiers and on the North-West Frontier, while consideration was also afforded for the first time to amphibious operations.[5] Succeeded at Camberley by Wilson, whose candidacy he had supported, Rawlinson then held brigade and divisional commands, before going on to half pay as a major general in May 1914. While still commanding 3rd Division in March, he had unequivocally backed the then Brigadier General Hubert Gough's defiance of the Liberal government during the Curragh incident. Indeed, he and Wilson had previously sounded out Hubert's brother, John Gough, Haig's chief of staff at Aldershot, on the likelihood of the latter supporting the Ulster cause.[6]

With the outbreak of the Great War and Kitchener's appointment as Secretary of State for War, Rawlinson was made director of recruiting at the War Office. In September 1914, however, he was sent to take command of 4th Division on the Aisne after Major General T.D'O. Snow was badly injured in a fall from his horse. Then, in October, Rawlinson was given command of the hastily constituted IV Corps, intended by Kitchener for the relief of Antwerp and comprising Major General Thompson Capper's 7th Division and Major

General the Hon. Julian Byng's 3rd Cavalry Division. Too late to save Antwerp, IV Corps withdrew southwards, becoming the first British formation to enter Ypres and thereby operating on the left of the British Expeditionary Force (BEF) as it began to arrive in Flanders from the Aisne. Rawlinson was directed to attack Menin on 18 October, and his caution led to his being severely criticized by Sir John French, the commander-in-chief of the BEF, who had already expressed his irritation at Rawlinson's brief independent role at Antwerp. Subsequently, French also took exception to a pessimistic telegram from Rawlinson urging the speedy transfer of the 8th Division to Flanders and, for all practical purposes, he was sent home in late October, albeit to ensure that 8th Division was fully prepared for its introduction to the Western Front.[7]

Returning to the command of IV Corps, now comprising 7th and 8th Divisions and soon part of Haig's First Army, Rawlinson was entrusted with the first tentative attempts to solve the problems posed by the Western Front through 1915. Passed over for command of the new Third Army through French's enmity,[8] Rawlinson then assumed command of First Army upon Haig's elevation to command of the BEF in December 1915. This was only temporary, for First Army was intended for Sir Charles Monro, but in February 1916 Rawlinson received command of the new Fourth Army. During the course of the operations on the Somme, the relationship between Haig and Rawlinson cooled. Consequently, though Rawlinson anticipated that he would be given command of the planned Flanders offensive in 1917, he was effectively sidelined in May by being tasked with amphibious operations on the Flanders coast, these being finally cancelled on 14 October.[9] In the event, Rawlinson was entrusted with the final few weeks of the Passchendaele offensive and took command of Second Army when Sir Herbert Plumer was sent to command British forces in Italy in the wake of the Italian defeat at Caporetto.

Plumer's Second Army was redesignated Fourth Army, but in February 1918 Rawlinson became the British military representative on the Supreme War Council at Versailles, in which position he tended to support the view of Haig and GHQ over such issues as the control of Allied reserves rather than that of the new chief of the Imperial General Staff, Henry Wilson. When, therefore, Hubert Gough's Fifth Army was forced back by the German offensive of March 1918 and Gough relieved of his command, Henry Wilson in particular found it convenient that Rawlinson should be available to take over Fifth Army on 28 March, to be replaced at Versailles by Wilson's ally Major General Charles Sackville-West.[10] Fifth Army was redesignated Fourth Army on 2 April 1918 and Rawlinson commanded it to the end of the war. His reward in the victory celebrations was to be elevated to the peerage as Baron Rawlinson of Trent and to be given a parliamentary grant of £30,000.

Initially, Rawlinson expected Fourth Army to become part of the army of occupation in Germany but this did not come to fruition, and instead he was sent to north Russia to extract the British forces previously committed there against the Bolsheviks. In November 1919 he took the Aldershot command, but he had expressed an interest in the command in India back in November 1918 and, having turned down the Middle East command, he secured India in November 1920 through the support of Wilson and of Winston Churchill, now Secretary of State for War and Air.[11] In theory, following the retirement of Sir Charles Monro, an officer of the British army, the appointment of commander-in-chief in India should have gone to an officer of the Indian Army, Sir William Birdwood being the most obvious choice. Rawlinson benefited, however, from the fallout from the Amritsar affair, Churchill agreeing to the recall of Brigadier General Reginald Dyer only if the India Office accepted Rawlinson over Birdwood.[12]

Rawlinson faced a significant number of problems in attempting to reform the Indian Army and advance the concept of 'Indianization' within the officer corps at a time of financial retrenchment and serious unrest in Waziristan, Malabar and Iraq, the pacification of which fell within his remit. Moreover, his 'forward policy' in Waziristan and reforms in military organization both aroused opposition, the latter not least from Birdwood. Having turned down the opportunity to succeed Lord Cavan as chief of the Imperial General Staff in 1924 because he wished to see his proposals through, Rawlinson was therefore angered to learn in the following year that his eventual successor in India would be Birdwood, who would also be given field marshal's rank.[13] Within a short time, however, Rawlinson learned in March 1925 that he himself would succeed Cavan after all as CIGS. Later that month, he was taken ill with suspected appendicitis but, in view of his general fitness, surgery was delayed: indeed, he had played polo on his sixty-first birthday and cricket subsequently.[14] In mounting discomfort, Rawlinson agreed to surgery on 24 March, which revealed a strangulated intestine. He appeared to make good progress but then died suddenly and unexpectedly on 28 March 1925.

The most recent analysis of Rawlinson as a commander has suggested that, whatever might be said of his professional experiences and talents, he was 'personally of no great interest'.[15] This is a somewhat mistaken judgement since Rawlinson's personality is of some significance in the assessment of his career. He was certainly regarded as a 'lucky' soldier and with the initial advantages of his father's connections, but, while acknowledging this himself at the time of the South African War, he also wrote that 'I think I can honestly say I have done my best to deserve my luck'. Moreover, 'Rawly', as he was most frequently known, was clearly intelligent and active with a generally cheery disposition that his colleagues often found lifting. Haig, for example, noted on one occasion in October 1914 that while Rawlinson 'may have many faults as an officer ... his bright joviality is of great value to an Army when on active service', and it was also noted by Edward Louis Spears that Rawlinson 'had a way of floating over and away from his troubles'. Rawlinson was also a keen sportsman and a talented artist, whose sketches of the campaign in the Sudan had been published in the *Illustrated London News*.[16]

Yet, there was also a less attractive side of Rawlinson's personality. While it was no doubt useful and necessary to Rawlinson to be able to 'sleep like a top' at the height of the Somme battle, there was also often a certain distancing from the implications of what he was ordering his troops to attempt, despite his concern on other occasions to minimize casualties. Indeed, even his official biographer suggested Rawlinson appeared hard and cold, though arguing that he adopted this persona, as it would get the most out of others.[17] Certainly, Rawlinson's ambition was frequently apparent and his other nicknames of 'The Cad' and 'The Fox' are plainly suggestive of the widespread belief that he was an untrustworthy intriguer. Haig's director of military intelligence, Brigadier General John Charteris, for example, thought so, as did the official historian, Brigadier General Sir James Edmonds. To Hubert Gough, Rawlinson was simply 'crooked'.[18]

One historian of the Somme campaign has suggested that Rawlinson was 'an expert in laying bets on and off any project for which he was responsible'.[19] Haig had noted in April 1915 after a dispute between Rawlinson and one of his subordinates, Major General 'Joey' Davies of 8th Division, that Rawlinson's divisional commanders believed 'that if his personal interests required it, he (R.) would throw over his subordinate commanders, and that he would not hold to any verbal order which he had given'. Significantly, Haig commented to Clemenceau in February 1918 of Rawlinson's role at Versailles that 'as long as my star was in the ascendant, R. would be faithful to me'.[20] Rawlinson's capacity for intrigue was evident at the time of the Currragh incident and he was also one of those instrumental in undermining Sir John French's version of the reasons for the failure to break through at Loos in September 1915, his long friendship with the king's assistant private secretary, Clive Wigram, giving Rawlinson a highly useful contact. Rawlinson was not always discreet, however, and on occasions was warned against overt politicking by Wigram and Wilson's predecessor as CIGS, Sir William Robertson.[21]

It is in the relationship between Rawlinson and his superiors and subordinates that the defects of his personality are most apparent and, in this context, affected his conduct of operations. With respect to his subordinates, as the episode with Davies illustrated, Rawlinson was quite ready on occasion to allow them to take the blame for failure. Believing Davies responsible for failing to exploit opportunities at Neuve Chapelle by not advancing sufficiently quickly once the village was captured, Rawlinson called upon Haig to remove Davies from his command. To be fair to Rawlinson, when Davies pointed out the realities of the situation on the ground, Rawlinson forwarded Davies's letter to Haig and accepted responsibility. Haig, however, noted that Rawlinson was 'unsatisfactory in this respect', namely 'loyalty to his subordinates'. French and Robertson both wanted Rawlinson himself sent home but, on this occasion, he escaped with a warning as to his future conduct.[22]

In April 1916, during the planning process for the Somme, Rawlinson was equally critical of Major General Sir Walter Congreve of VIII Corps, who had doubts about the nature of the offensive. As a result, Rawlinson considered Congreve's plans not 'dashing enough', and two of his divisions were taken away from him and a greater role afforded to Lieutenant General Henry Horne's XV Corps. Congreve noted that 'I had expected something of the sort from the combination of Rawly & Haig both of whom consider nothing & no one of use unless from 1st Army', though Haig assured Congreve that 'it had never entered his head to consider me lacking in push'. Perhaps not surprisingly, when Rawlinson subsequently discussed the Somme plan with his corps commanders, he recorded in May that there was 'little or no cavilling or argument', and in June that 'few questions were asked'. During the Somme campaign itself, Rawlinson was also critical of Lieutenant General Sir William Pulteney of III Corps but it can be noted that Rawlinson eventually responded to the entreaties of Lord Cavan, then commanding XIV Corps, to advise Haig to abandon the attempt to capture the Transloy Ridges in October 1916. Unfortunately, after consulting with the French, Haig reversed his decision and XIV Corps took another 2,000 casualties.[23]

At other times, and not unexpectedly in view of the confused attitudes frequently displayed by British commanders, Rawlinson did not intervene in his subordinates' spheres of responsibility when he might have done so profitably. For example, he was very critical of Capper's habit of placing his trenches on forward slopes during the First Battle of Ypres in October 1914, but did nothing to prevent it. Having called for, though then rejected, Davies's advice in advance of the Neuve Chapelle offensive, Rawlinson failed to secure any advice whatsoever from Capper, leading to Haig complaining about the dissipation of the decision-making process in Rawlinson's corps.[24] Gough, who had a somewhat rigid concept of command, similarly later suggested of the Somme that Rawlinson and his staff 'had not much grasp of the situation – and that instead, under the influence of prudent general principles, which had no particular application to the situation before them, they let most valuable opportunities slip. Platitudes rather than realities, were their guide'. In a sense, of course, evidence from Gough and Fifth Army might be considered tainted. One of Gough's intelligence officers suggested in May 1918, for example, that Rawlinson was not generally liked and Fifth Army's headquarters had been 'pleasanter'.[25]

Yet, there was certainly a sense of drift in Fourth Army on the Somme between mid-July and mid-September 1916, with Rawlinson failing to exercise any real control over a piecemeal series of attacks. Indeed, at one point on 24 August, Haig, who was far from consistent in his own command attitudes, sent Rawlinson what has been characterized as a 'boy's-own guide' on command, urging closer supervision of subordinates: 'It is not "interference" but a legitimate and necessary exercise of the functions of a Commander in whom the ultimate responsibility for success or failure lies.'[26]

By the time Rawlinson had returned to active field command in 1918, the role of an army commander had been modified substantially not only by the advances of technology but also by the resulting changes in the nature of the semi-mobile warfare that increasingly became apparent. Rawlinson's reaction was to devolve more and more responsibility to his subordinates. Thus, in April 1918 he designated one of his corps commanders to co-ordinate the defensive effort across the whole front of Fourth Army. He was equally prepared to listen much more than in the past to the views of men such as the Australian, Lieutenant General Sir John Monash of the Australian Corps and his chief of staff, Brigadier General Thomas Blamey, in planning the Hamel operation in July 1918 and the breaking of the Hindenburg Line in September, and to that of the Canadian corps commander, Sir Arthur Currie, in breaking off the Amiens offensive in August 1918. Similarly, Rawlinson publicly backed the initiative of the 5th Australian Brigade in carrying out a daring attack on Mont St Quentin on 31 August 1918, even though he believed privately that this had 'spoilt a bloody good battle' already being planned. Thus, he had become a manager and facilitator of the efforts of others.[27]

It has been argued plausibly that some of Rawlinson's failures of co-ordination on the Somme reflected his lack of belief in the objectives Haig had identified, which raises the whole issue of his relationship with Haig. As noted earlier, Rawlinson had a poor relationship with Sir John French and survived being sacked in the aftermath of the Davies affair at Neuve Chapelle only as a result of Haig's support. To a certain extent, therefore, Rawlinson was dependent upon Haig, who had recommended Rawlinson succeed him at First Army in December 1915 on the grounds that though 'not a sincere man, he has brains and experience'. Indeed, the dependency appeared such that Lloyd George remarked on one occasion to C.P. Scott that every time Rawlinson failed he seemed to get promoted.[28] If Rawlinson was beholden to Haig, it has also been suggested that he was afraid of Haig, that he would not thrash out operational differences in a frank discussion with his commander-in-chief and that his 'political sense seems to have overborne his moral courage' in dealing with Haig. On at least one occasion in April 1916 Rawlinson and Monro were both sharply admonished by Haig for sending what was deemed incorrect information to Kitchener on the number of men employed on lines of communication. Equally, however, it has been pointed out that Rawlinson's diary entries do not suggest that he was living in daily fear of Haig, so that, for example, on 7 November 1916 Rawlinson anticipated a cool reception for a paper arguing for the discontinuation of the Somme offensive: 'I daresay D. H. won't like it but it is my duty to point it out to him. I think he now realises that he cannot continue the offensive all through the winter without prejudicing our chances of another big success in the spring.' The most recent judgement, however, is perhaps correct in suggesting that, within the constraints of the army's undoubted rigidly hierarchical structure, Rawlinson's resistance to Haig 'was only ever taken so far'.[29]

As in the case of Rawlinson's concept of command, however, there is a high degree of inconsistency in his approach to direction from Haig. This will become particularly apparent in the discussion of Rawlinson's conduct of the Somme offensive below, but the uncertain trend was clear from the beginning. In the preparations for Neuve Chapelle, Rawlinson got his way in arguing for an opening bombardment of 35 minutes. Moreover, for some time he ignored Haig's demands that wider objectives embracing the seizure of Aubers Ridge be set beyond the capture of the village. In the planning for the subsequent Givenchy offensive in June 1915, however, he did not convey his misgivings to Haig. When it came to Loos in September 1915, he again cast off his doubts to accept Haig's demands for wider objectives than he believed wise. While initially entrusted in early 1917 with the preliminary planning for what became the Passchendaele offensive, Rawlinson accepted some of Haig's demands but remained insistent on the need to gain the high ground on the right of the proposed advance. Removed from the process because Hubert Gough was deemed more suited to the 'pursuit', Rawlinson continued to argue for caution without success. In 1918, however, Rawlinson had rather more success in converting Haig to his views, though it has been argued that this was primarily a product of the change in the nature of the role of higher command on the battlefield mentioned earlier.[30]

One additional aspect of the relationship between Rawlinson and other authorities worth mentioning in passing is that he was generally more prepared to co-operate with the French than some of his contemporaries and, indeed, he spoke French well. Again, however, the record is mixed. There were some disagreements with Emile Fayolle commanding the French Sixth Army in the planning of the Somme offensive, but the French sided with Rawlinson rather than Haig on where to continue the main effort after 1 July 1916. By contrast, in 1918, Rawlinson had continuing problems with Eugène Debeny of the French First Army, to the extent that Ferdinand Foch, as supreme Allied commander, ordered Debeny to co-operate more with Rawlinson in April, though the difficulties actually persisted as late as November. Rawlinson also had his differences with the American commander, John Pershing, over the use of the US XXXIII Corps at Hamel in July 1918. Rawlinson generally appreciated Foch's role in 1918, though it was not the case, as the official history later claimed, that he had openly defied Foch in cancelling a projected attack on 14–15 August 1918. The actual sequence of events was that Currie made representations to Rawlinson. Rawlinson then convinced Haig, who reminded Foch that his responsibility to the British government precluded the attack.[31]

No army commander can be considered in isolation from his staff, and this needs to be considered before passing to Rawlinson's operational concepts. Initially, Haig was critical of Rawlinson's improvised staff, noting on a visit in October 1914 that it included just two regulars. In addition, there was Rawlinson's brother, Toby; Leo Amery, formerly of *The Times*; the Duke of Westminster; and two or three others connected to 'motors or polo'. From August 1915 onwards, Rawlinson's principal advisers were Archibald Montgomery (later Montgomery-Massingberd) as chief of staff, Charles Budworth as artillery adviser, and Russel Luckock as GSO1. Budworth was a capable technician. However, though also an artilleryman, to the official historian, Edmonds, Montgomery was a 'bottle washer'. Moreover, Edmonds claimed that Montgomery and Luckock had attempted to falsify the records of Fourth Army to cover up its failures. Certainly, following Rawlinson's death, it was Montgomery who penned the account recording Fourth Army's victories in 1918 and, together, Montgomery and Luckock endeavoured to defend Fourth Army's reputation so far as the compilation of the official history was concerned.[32]

In many respects the principal differences between Rawlinson and Haig arose from Rawlinson's particular concept of operational requirements, a concept usually described as 'bite and hold'. Rather than attempting an ambitious breakthrough of the German defensive zone as a whole, Rawlinson largely favoured a step-by-step siege-type operation. He had certainly often reflected on his profession. In the Sudan he had found Kitchener 'very sketchy' in his methods as regards administration and staff work. At the Staff College he had endeavoured to correct what he saw as the over-compartmentalization of the army's branches and the lack of mutual knowledge between army and navy. He had been impressed by the ability of the Boer artillerymen in the South African War and his analysis of the Russo-Japanese War suggested that, while infantry remained the arm of decision on the battlefield, co-operation between infantry and artillery was crucial to success.[33]

It was not surprising, therefore, that Rawlinson should discern appropriate lessons from his initial experiences on the Western Front. Unfortunately, however, as in much else concerning his command style and in keeping with his relationship with Haig, Rawlinson often failed to apply the lessons consistently. The first major British offensive from a trench system at Neuve Chapelle was innovative in many ways, including aerial reconnaissance, pre-registering of targets, the placement of telephone lines across open fields to try to ensure they would not be cut by counter-bombardment and the allocation of guns to specific tasks such as wire cutting. Rawlinson was also very successful in maintaining secrecy.

The short and concentrated preliminary bombardment delivered over a narrow front against a single German defensive line enabled IV Corps to break into the German defences before the other manifold problems of converting the break into the breakthrough kicked in, preventing any further advance.

Perceptively, Rawlinson recognized that artillery was the key to success and that all depended upon the range of the guns available. It might be added in passing that he was also in the forefront of the development of trench mortars. Consequently, of course, he had been quite right in attempting to limit the advance to the village of Neuve Chapelle rather than trying to seize Aubers Ridge as Haig demanded. He felt that Haig had 'looked for too much' and lost lives unnecessarily when he would have been happy to take the German front line and await their counter-attack. Thus, he wrote to Kitchener, 'Had we been content with the capture of the village & stopped at the end of the 1st day our losses would have been only 2,300 & we should have killed twice that number of Germans.'

Reflecting on the lessons, he wrote to Wigram on 25 March 1915:

> What we want to do now is what I call, 'bite and hold'. Bite off a piece of the enemy's line ... and hold it against counter attack. The bite can be made without much loss, and, if we choose the right place and make every preparation to put it quickly into a state of defence, there ought to be no difficulty in holding it against the enemy's counter-attacks, and in inflicting on him at least twice the loss that we have suffered in making the bite.

Similarly, in recognizing that he had mishandled the reserves at Neuve Chapelle, he wrote to Sir Henry Sclater that reserves intended to exploit any opportunities should be kept out of the initial assault, predicting 'we are learning the tactics which this trench warfare teaches, and on each occasion we shall improve on our methods'. Another assumption was that biting was easier than holding, Rawlinson noting in April 1915, 'The capture of a system of hostile trenches is an easy matter compared with the difficulty of retaining it'. This particular assumption, however, was unfortunate since Rawlinson appeared to give little thought thereafter to infantry tactics.[34]

Yet, as has been remarked by his most recent biographers, these insights did not inform his subsequent actions at Aubers Ridge, where Rawlinson assumed there would be sufficient guns. However, he did appreciate the lack of artillery available for the task required at Givenchy and simply hoped that the use of gas would make up for the deficiency in artillery at Loos. It was also the case that the steady widening of the frontage for offensives meant that, despite the deployment of more guns and the firing of more shells over longer periods of time, the intensity of the bombardment at Neuve Chapelle was not being reproduced. The Neuve Chapelle bombardment delivered the equivalent of 288 lb of high explosive per yard of German trench, while at Loos a greater bombardment delivered only 43 lb of high explosive per yard of trench over forty-eight hours, and the Somme only 150 lb over seven days. More will be said of the Somme below, but Rawlinson was clearly still of the view that bite and hold was the best way forward, though he always recognized that this would not bring decisive or rapid results. Others, too, thought the method sound and, indeed, Rawlinson was to receive support and encouragement from Robertson.[35]

In the event, as will be shown, Rawlinson failed to stand by his beliefs on the Somme. Back in active command in 1918, he showed once more that he was capable of appreciating the potential contribution of new developments to solving the problem of the Western Front. Significantly, in commenting on the Passchendaele plans, he had noted of Gough's intentions, 'The rule is that they must not go beyond the range of their guns or they will be driven back by counter attacks.' His advice, of course, was ignored. He has been characterized as a 'cautious progressive', and certainly called in June 1918 for 'all possible mechanical devices in order to increase the offensive power of our divisions'. Moreover, with the change in the nature of command relationships within the BEF, Rawlinson's operations were far more limited in their nature with substantially better results. He insisted the Australians employ tanks at Hamel, and, later in July, adopted a French method of attacking in depth and moving his entire force forward at once, since front line troops would invariably advance faster than the reserves. Rawlinson also attempted to demonstrate to Haig the value of infantry co-operation with tanks.[36]

The Somme

If 1918 represented something of a success for Rawlinson's operational style, 1916 had represented its nadir. Indeed, the phrase most often used to characterize the result of the dispute over operational objectives between Haig and Rawlinson is of a command 'vacuum'.[37] In beginning the planning process in February and March 1916, Rawlinson's early optimism faded rapidly and, after consulting with his corps commanders, he concluded the Somme highly suitable for bite and hold. He hoped to minimize losses by restricting the depth of advance to the range of the available artillery. Though he gave most emphasis to destroying the German defences rather than neutralizing German manpower, he believed greater losses would also be inflicted on the Germans through the seizure of points of tactical importance 'which will provide us with good observation and which we may feel quite certain the Germans will counter attack'.[38] He assumed that the guns available would enable him to attack over a frontage of 22,000 yards and to a depth of 4,000–5,000 yards, but believed that the troops would be too inexperienced to get much beyond 3,000 yards. He was also well aware of the problems encountered at Loos with German defenders surviving both the opening bombardment and the gas attack in deep dugouts, but beyond persisting with a long, steady and hopefully accurate bombardment, he could offer no other alternative solution than covering the infantry advance with smoke. As it happened, while the 'Tactical Notes' issued to Fourth Army in May 1916 favoured a creeping barrage, there was little in the notes that was actually prescriptive, and in practice it was

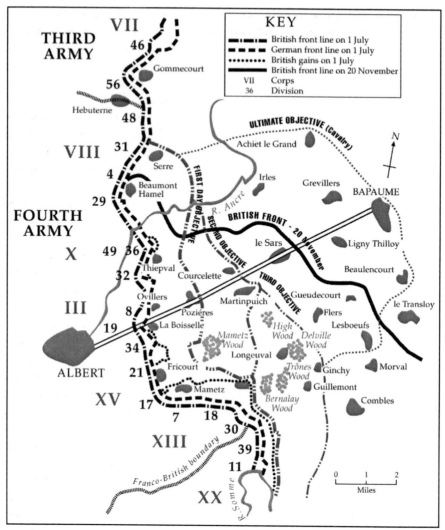

The Somme, 1916.

accepted that a fixed timetable of artillery lifts was more practicable. Moreover, Rawlinson rejected the suggestion by Brigadier General James Jardine of 97 Brigade, who had been an observer in Manchuria during the Russo-Japanese War, that infantry should hug the bombardment. Again, though there was no actual tactical uniformity displayed by British formations on 1 July, it was assumed that the infantry would advance methodically and steadily by waves at intervals of 50–100 yards, carrying the first line through a combination of energy, weight and mass. In any case, according to the official historian, Rawlinson had told his corps commanders that 'nothing could exist at the conclusion of the bombardment' and the infantry 'would only have to walk over to take possession'.

Following the actual opening of the offensive on 1 July, Rawlinson was hopeful that more howitzers and mortars could deal with dugouts, writing to Wigram on 3 July that 'with more of these weapons and with unlimited ammunition for them we shall be able to reduce our casualties considerably. Anyhow we have shown the Boche that we can break his line on a wide front and I think we shall penetrate the second line if our ammunition holds out'. In fact, there were some untenable assumptions in the artillery plan since the calculations extrapolated from earlier bombardments were being made on the basis of yards of front rather than yards of trench, the significant difference being that there was more than one German defensive line on the Somme compared to the single line the Germans had held at Neuve Chapelle. Moreover, insufficient emphasis was placed upon counter-battery work, despite Rawlinson having suggested it as a prerequisite for success in reflecting upon the lessons of Loos.[39]

With his chief of staff, Neill Malcolm, Hubert Gough, whose Reserve (later Fifth) Army was intended to exploit the opportunities achieved by Fourth Army, believed wider objectives were desirable. Not unexpectedly, Rawlinson had noted of Haig's likely reaction to his original plan, 'I daresay I shall have a tussle with him over the limited objective for I hear he is inclined to favour the unlimited with the chance of breaking the German line'. Such proved to be the case, Haig demanding a shorter opening bombardment than Rawlinson planned and a deeper initial advance, with the expectation of breaking the German second line at an early stage with a southwards advance to link to the French. Then, when the French indicated that they were unable to participate in as great a force as originally anticipated, Haig wanted to overwhelm all three German lines at the outset. Rawlinson felt his troops could reach the first objective but not break through, writing to Wigram on 26 June, 'I shall be agreeably surprised if we succeed in breaking through the line on the first day'. In keeping with other occasions on which he had disagreed with Haig, however, Rawlinson put up a new plan which has been described as a 'melange of capitulation and resistance', retaining the longer bombardment but accepting an advance to 4,000–5,000 yards. Moreover, crucially, Rawlinson did not state that his artillery was insufficient to achieve these wider objectives. Thus, while having virtually no confidence in the new plan, Rawlinson recorded at one point, 'The attack is to go for the big thing. I still think we would do better to proceed by shorter steps; but I have told D.H. I will carry out his plan with as much enthusiasm as if it were my own'.[40]

On 1 July itself, Rawlinson received 160 telegrams from his corps commanders during the course of the day but many were inaccurate. Accordingly, though he knew of the success by XIII Corps in the south by early afternoon, it was not until mid-afternoon that he became aware of the true situation on VIII Corps front in the north. Having assumed that there would be little opportunity for exploitation on the first day, Rawlinson had no disposable reserve available. He may not have believed the messages received from XIII Corps and his judgement may well have been coloured by his lack of confidence in the wider objectives. Consequently, the cavalry was not ordered to the south and even the immediate operational reserve of 9th Division was dispersed. Moreover, Rawlinson continued to lay emphasis upon increasing pressure around Thiepval in the centre rather than at Montauban in the south as Haig wished and, indeed, he continued to prove dilatory in this regard. Rawlinson had never had much confidence in the 'New Armies', and there was a tendency to blame his troops for the failures on 1 July. Rawlinson wanted Major General Sir Ivor Philipps of 38th Division removed for the failure to take Mametz, though he did not choose to blame Horne, one of Haig's favourites, for not occupying the empty wood on 3 July. Subsequently, Archibald Montgomery wrote that Rawlinson 'being further back did not feel the draught so much and kept on pressing for an advance'.[41]

As it happened, Haig had concluded that the area of operations was too large for one man to co-ordinate, and Hubert Gough was given responsibility for X and VIII Corps late on 1 July. In a reversal of roles, Rawlinson now favoured attempting to push through German second and third lines as fast as possible, while Haig favoured a more methodical approach. Nonetheless, having been prompted into taking the initiative in the south, Rawlinson was able to convince Haig of the potential of a night attack on 14 July to occupy some of those areas that had actually been within Fourth Army's grasp on 1 July. Haig had initially declared the idea of a night attack unsound, and Rawlinson 'at once, in the most broad minded way, said he would change it'. Rawlinson, however, played on Haig's desire for a breakthrough and the role accorded to cavalry in the plan devised by Rawlinson and Congreve, as well as the supposed poor German morale. Thus, the 2nd Indian Cavalry Division was made available and the artillery bombardment was more concentrated, though with only two-thirds of the number of guns used on 1 July. Once more, however, Rawlinson was not ready to exploit opportunities, holding the infantry back from entering High Wood. By the time he was ready to order the infantry into the wood, Horne, commanding XV Corps, was obliged to countermand the order as it would now leave an open flank. Moreover, Rawlinson did not again attempt the artillery concentration that had contributed to the limited success of the attack.[42]

Thereafter, and for reasons that remain unclear, Rawlinson slipped into that lack of activity noted earlier, presiding over a series of forty-one attacks over the sixty-two days between 15 July and 14 September in which, on average, only six and a half battalions out of the eighty-four available to him took part. Rawlinson became seemingly merely a conduit for orders passed from GHQ to his corps commanders, though it is possible that he simply became thoroughly confused by Haig's muddled and contradictory instructions in July and August. As also indicated earlier, Haig wanted progress, specifically in seizing

Guillemont, and ultimately reminded Rawlinson of his responsibilities as an army commander. Haig apparently also wanted Rawlinson to experiment with the French practice of small group tactics, but Rawlinson was doubtful about the efficacy of French methods. He discussed these with Major General John DuCane of XV Corps on 21 September, indicating that he thought British infantry superior to the French but the French artillery better than the British, as well as acknowledging the French criticism that the British did not take sufficient care to study ground. Rawlinson appears, too, to have felt the French control of artillery at divisional level a better system. Paradoxically, however, he also told Lord Derby on 29 September that there was little to learn from the French artillery and the French had copied the British creeping barrages.[43]

In planning the celebrated first attack by tanks at Flers-Courcelette on 15 September, Rawlinson was perfectly willing to use them, though, pre-dictably, he had less faith in them as a potential breakthrough weapon than Haig. Moreover, they had different views on their deployment, Rawlinson wishing to retain the element of keep surprise by using them at night before being withdrawn. At Haig's insistence, Rawlinson was compelled to recast the plan for an advance in daylight. Rawlinson envisaged the tanks advancing ahead of the infantry, only for Haig to intervene once more by insisting that tanks and infantry must start together. On this occasion, Rawlinson held his ground and it was agreed, but with the tanks only 50 yards ahead of infantry. Unfortunately, too, Rawlinson's desire to give the tanks better going by leaving gaps in the creeping barrage through which they could advance subsequently proved fatal to the infantry assault. Rawlinson showed in the further attack at Morval on 25 September that he had learned the lesson, the tanks now being held in reserve and a continuous creeping barrage being employed to cover the infantry. Yet, further attacks by Fourth Army on 7, 12 and 18 October were only poorly supported by artillery. Rawlinson showed grasp of the problems when summarizing the reasons for the first two failures at a conference of his corps commanders on 13 October but then, following the third, still accepted Haig's demands to press ahead with a fourth on 23 October when nothing had changed.[44] As suggested earlier, in late October and early November, Rawlinson wanted the offensive to be continued to secure higher ground before the winter but Cavan objected and, in the end, Rawlinson was able to persuade Haig to suspend the Somme offensive on 7 November.[45]

What, then, can be said of Rawlinson as an army commander? In theory, Rawlinson was well suited by his background and intellect to rise to the challenges posed by warfare on the Western Front. Indeed, he displayed early and significant understanding of the problems. No doubt as a result primarily of his character and ambition, however, Rawlinson did not demonstrate the kind of moral courage required to stick by his operational principles in the face of opposition from Haig. Also, in common with many others, he failed to maintain any consistency in those principles. More often than not there was a tendency to allow subordinates to exercise their own judgement but with the proviso that Rawlinson was rarely prepared to stand by his subordinates when things went wrong. In many respects, it was difficult for any army commander to control events on the battlefield in 1915 and 1916 but, as it happened, Rawlinson's relatively informal approach to command was well suited to the more mobile and technologically advanced warfare that emerged in the summer of 1918. In that regard, he continued to be a 'lucky' soldier.

Bibliography

The standard biography is Fredrick Maurice, *The Life of General Lord Rawlinson of Trent* (London: Cassell, 1928). While not a new biography in a conventional sense, Robin Prior and Trevor Wilson, *Command on the Western Front: The Military Career of Sir Henry Rawlinson 1914–1918* (Oxford: Blackwell, 1992), was a major re-evaluation of Rawlinson as a battlefield commander, which also made a significant contribution to the understanding of the nature of the 'learning curve' on the Western Front. Earlier, Tim Travers, *The Killing Ground: The British Army, the Western Front and the Emergence of Modern Warfare, 1900–1918* (London: Allen & Unwin, 1987), devoted considerable attention to Rawlinson's role on the Somme, and Travers is also illuminating on the changing nature of warfare and of Rawlinson's role in *How the War Was Won: Command and Technology in the British Army on the Western Front, 1917–1918* (London: Routledge, 1992). The most recent studies of Rawlinson and the Somme are Gary Sheffield, *The Somme* (London: Cassell, 2003), and Robin Prior and Trevor Wilson, *The Somme* (New Haven: Yale University Press, 2005), while one particular aspect of Rawlinson's command is analysed in Peter Simkins, 'For Better or Worse: Sir Henry Rawlinson and his Allies in 1916 and 1918', in Matthew Hughes and Matthew Seligmann, eds, *Leadership in Conflict, 1914–1918* (Barnsley: Leo Cooper, 2000), pp. 13–37. An exhaustive account of Fourth Army's final campaign is to be found in Major General Sir Archibald Montgomery, *The Story of the Fourth Army in the Battle of the Hundred Days, August 8th to November 11th, 1918* (London: Hodder & Stoughton, 1931). Rawlinson's later career in India is well covered by Mark Jacobsen, ed., *Rawlinson in India* (Stroud: Sutton, 2002). Rawlinson's father has also been the subject of a recent biography, Lesley Adkins, *Empires of the Plain: Henry Rawlinson and the Lost Languages of Babylon* (London: Harper Perennial, 2004).

Notes

1 Lesley Adkins, *Empires of the Plain: Henry Rawlinson and the Lost Languages of Babylon* (London: Harper Perennial, 2004), p. 345.

2 Ian F.W. Beckett, 'Buller and the Politics of Command', in Gooch, ed., *The Boer War: Direction, Experience and Image* (London: Frank Cass, 2000), pp. 41–55.

3 Major General Sir Frederick Maurice, *The Life of Lord Rawlinson of Trent GCB, GCVO, GCSI, KCMG from His Journals and Letters* (London: Cassell, 1928), p. 77.

4 Keith Jeffery, ed., *The Military Correspondence of Field Marshal Sir Henry Wilson, 1918–1922* (London: Bodley Head, 1985), pp. 2–3, 339.

5 Brian Bond, *The Victorian Army and the Staff College, 1854–1914* (London: Eyre Methuen, 1972), pp. 196–9.

6 Ian F.W. Beckett, ed., *The Army and the Curragh Incident, 1914* (London: Bodley Head, 1986), pp. 5, 23, 28, 38, 263–4, 272–3; idem, *Johnnie Gough VC: A Biography of Brigadier-General Sir John Edmund Gough VC, KCB, CMG* (London: Tom Donovan, 1988), p. 164.

7 Ian F.W. Beckett, *Ypres: The First Battle, 1914* (London: Pearson Education, 2004), pp. 24, 61, 94, 148; Maurice, *Rawlinson*, pp. 110, 113–14.

8 Robin Prior and Trevor Wilson, *Command on the Western Front: The Military Career of Sir Henry Rawlinson, 1914–18* (Oxford: Blackwell, 1992), pp. 95–6.

9 Andy Wiest, 'Haig, Gough and Passchendaele', in Gary Sheffield, ed., *Leadership and Command: The Anglo-American Military Experience since 1861* (London: Brassey's, 1997), pp. 78–83; idem, 'The Planned

Amphibious Assault', in Peter Liddle, ed., *Passchendaele in Perspective* (Barnsley: Pen & Sword, 1997), pp. 201–12.

10 David Woodward, *Lloyd George and the Generals* (Newark: University of Delaware Press, 1983), pp. 287–9; Tim Travers, *The Killing Ground: The British Army, the Western Front and the Emergence of Modern Warfare, 1900–1918* (London: Allen & Unwin, 1987), p. 241.

11 Maurice, *Rawlinson*, pp. 251–3.

12 Mark Jacobsen, ed., *Rawlinson in India* (Stroud: Sutton, 2002), pp. xx–xxi.

13 Ibid., pp. 1–6, 31–4, 73–80, 125–8, 175–6, 189–90; Partha Sarathi Gupta, 'The Debate on Indianization, 1918–39', in Partha Sarathi Gupta and Anirudh Deshpande, eds, *The British Raj and Its Indian Armed Forces, 1857–1939* (New Delhi: Oxford University Press, 2002), pp. 228–70.

14 Maurice, *Rawlinson*, p. 341.

15 Prior and Wilson, *Command*, p. 5.

16 Jacobsen, *Rawlinson in India*, p. xviii; Maurice, *Rawlinson*, pp. xiii–xiv; Bond, *Victorian Army*, pp. 196–9; National Library of Scotland (hereafter NLS), Haig MSS, Acc. 3155/99, Haig diary, 18 October 1914; David Woodward, ed., *The Military Correspondence of Field Marshal Sir William Robertson, CIGS 1915–18* (London: Bodley Head, 1989), p. 343; Peter Harrington, 'Images and Perceptions: Visualising the Sudan Campaign', in Edward Spiers, ed., *Sudan: The Reconquest Reappraised* (London: Frank Cass, 1998), pp. 82–101.

17 Churchill Archives Centre, Churchill College, Cambridge, Rawlinson MSS, CC 1/5, Rawlinson diary, 20 July 1916; London, National Army Museum (hereafter NAM), Rawlinson MSS, 5201-33-27, Rawlinson short diary, 30 September 1917; Maurice, *Rawlinson*, p. xiii.

18 John Charteris, *At GHQ* (London: Cassell, 1931), p. 87; King's College, London, Liddell Hart Centre for Military Archives (hereafter LHCMA), Liddell Hart MSS, 11/1935/107, Conversation with Hubert Gough, 28 November 1935; ibid., 11/1937/4, Conversation with Edmonds, 5 February 1937.

19 Anthony Farrar-Hockley, *The Somme* (London: Pan, 1966), p. 66.

20 Robert Blake, ed., *The Private Papers of Douglas Haig* (London: Eyre & Spottiswoode, 1952), pp. 91, 289.

21 Royal Archives, PS/Geo V. Q.832/2, Rawlinson to Stamfordham, 28 September 1915; NAM, Rawlinson MSS, 5201-33-66, Wigram to Rawlinson, 26 April 1915; ibid., 5201-33-73, Wigram to Rawlinson, 2 January 1918 and 25 September 1918; Beckett, *Curragh*, pp. 38, 42; idem, *Johnnie Gough*, p. 199; idem, 'King George V and His Generals', in Matthew Hughes and Matthew Seligmann, eds, *Leadership in Conflict, 1914–1918* (Barnsley: Leo Cooper, 2000), pp. 247–64; Woodward, *Lloyd George*, p. 276; idem, *Military Correspondence of Robertson*, p. 115.

22 Blake, *Private Papers*, pp. 88–9.

23 Travers, *Killing Ground*, pp. 105–6, 168, 186; Congreve MSS, Congreve diary, 5 and 7 April and 9 May 1916; Gary Sheffield, *The Somme* (London: Cassell, 2003), p. 141; Robin Prior and Trevor Wilson, *The Somme* (New Haven: Yale University Press, 2005), pp. 276–7.

24 Beckett, *Ypres*, pp. 91–2, 121; Prior and Wilson, *Command*, p. 29.

25 Imperial War Museum (hereafter IWM), A.J.H. Smith MSS, 84/22/1, Smith to mother, 16 May 1918; The National Archives, Public Record Office (hereafter TNA), CAB 45/134, Gough to Edmonds, 16 June 1938; Ian F.W. Beckett, 'Hubert Gough, Neill Malcolm and Command on the Western Front', in Brian Bond, ed., *'Look to Your Front': Studies in the First World War* (Staplehurst: Spellmount, 1999), pp. 1–12.

26 IWM, Fourth Army Papers, OAD 123, GHQ to Rawlinson, 24 August 1916; Prior and Wilson, *Command*, pp. 205, 223, 226; idem, *Somme*, p. 168.

27 Tim Travers, *How the War Was Won: Command and Technology in the British Army on the Western Front, 1917–1918* (London: Routledge, 1992), pp. 94, 131, 146; Prior and Wilson, *Command*, pp. 297–8, 300, 335, 357.

28 Blake, *Private Papers*, p. 116; Trevor Wilson, ed., *The Political Diaries of C.P. Scott, 1911–18* (London: Collins, 1970), pp. 217–19.

29 Travers, *Killing Ground*, pp. 178–82; Shelford Bidwell and Dominick Graham, *Fire-Power: British Army Weapons and Theories of War, 1904–45* (London: Allen & Unwin, 1982), p. 87; Blake, *Private Papers*, p. 141; Peter Simkins, 'Haig and his Army Commanders', in Brian Bond and Nigel Cave, eds, *Haig: A Reappraisal 70 Years On* (Barnsley: Leo Cooper, 1999), pp. 78–106; Prior and Wilson, *Somme*, p. 47.

30 Prior and Wilson, *Command*, pp. 30–31, 97–9, 105–6, 270, 305–6, 333–4; Wiest, 'Haig, Gough and Passchendaele', pp. 77–92; Travers, *How the War Was Won*, pp. 14–15, 17.

31 Prior and Wilson, *Command*, pp. 277, 335–6; Peter Simkins, 'For Better or Worse: Sir Henry Rawlinson and His Allies in 1916 and 1918', in Hughes and Seligmann, *Leadership in Conflict*, pp. 13–37; NAM, 5201-33-73, Rawlinson to Wigram, 6 September 1918.

32 Beckett, *Ypres*, p. 59; LHCMA, Liddell Hart MSS, 11/1931/3 and 11/1937/4, Conversation with Edmonds, 22 January 1931 and 5 February 1937; private collection, Hubert Gough MSS, Edmonds to Malcolm, 27 May 1930; Travers, *Killing Ground*, pp. 166, 204–5; Andrew Green, *Writing the Great War: Sir James Edmonds and the Official Histories, 1915–48* (London: Frank Cass, 2003), pp. 52, 66–7; Major General Sir Archibald Montgomery, *The Story of the Fourth Army in the Battle of the Hundred Days, August 8th to November 11th, 1918* (London: Hodder & Stoughton, 1931).

33 Ian F.W. Beckett, 'Kitchener and the Politics of Command', in Spiers, *Sudan*, pp. 35–53; Prior and Wilson, *Command*, pp. 6–9.

34 NAM, 5201-33-17, Notes on Neuve Chapelle, 18 February 1915; ibid., 5201-33-25, Rawlinson short diary, 28 January 1915; ibid., 5201-33-17, Rawlinson to Kitchener, 21 April 1915; ibid., 5201-33-70, Tactical Notes, 11 April 1915; Bidwell and Graham, *Fire-Power*, pp. 74–9; Prior and Wilson, *Command*, pp. 42, 78; Maurice, *Rawlinson*, pp. 129–30; Travers, *Killing Ground*, pp. 133–4.

35 Prior and Wilson, *Command*, pp. 80, 88, 97, 105, 112, 166–7; Woodward, *Military Correspondence of Robertson*, pp. 72–3.

36 NAM, 5201-33-73, Rawlinson to Wigram, 7 July, 25 September, 2 October and 16 October 1918; Travers, *How the War Was Won*, pp. 8, 14–15; 113–18, 125, 141, 170; Prior and Wilson, *Command*, p. 291.

37 Travers, *Killing Ground*, pp. 97, 142, 166; Andy Simpson, *The Evolution of Victory* (London: Tom Donovan, 1995), p. 59.

38 Travers, *Killing Ground*, pp. 134–5, 138; Prior and Wilson, *Somme*, pp. 39–41; TNA, WO 158/233, Fourth Army Plan, 3 April 1916.

39 Prior and Wilson, *Command*, pp. 143–4, 160, 164–5, 168–9; Travers, *Killing Ground*, pp. 133, 141–5; NAM, 5201-33-18, Rawlinson to Wigram, 3 July 1916; Sir James Edmonds, *Military Operations: France and Belgium, 1916*, vol. 1 (London: Macmillan, 1932), p. 288; Prior and Wilson, *Somme*, pp. 53–6, 67–9.

40 Private collection, Malcolm MSS, Malcolm diary, 19 June 1916; Maurice, *Rawlinson*, pp. 154–8; Prior and Wilson, *Command*, pp. 141, 149, 395; idem, *Somme*, pp. 45–7, 50–52; Travers, *Killing Ground*, pp. 131–2; NAM, 5201-33-18, Rawlinson to Wigram, 26 June 1916.

41 Prior and Wilson, *Command*, pp. 182–4, 217–19; Sheffield, *Somme*, pp. 65–8; Travers, *Killing Ground*, pp. 160, 168; TNA, CAB 45/136, Montgomery to Edmonds, 7 December 1937.

42 Sheffield, *Somme*, pp. 78–9, 160–61; NLS, Acc. 3155, Haig diary, 11 July 1916; Travers, *Killing Ground*, p. 107; Prior and Wilson, *Command*, pp. 191–2; idem, *Somme*, pp. 133–6.

43 Prior and Wilson, *Command*, p. 205; idem, *Somme*, pp. 123–4, 154, 171; Simkins, 'For Better or Worse', pp. 13–37; Maurice, *Rawlinson*, pp. 172–3.

44 Travers, *Killing Ground*, pp. 74–5; Prior and Wilson, *Command*, pp. 229, 232; idem, *Somme*, pp. 270–77; Sheffield, *Somme*, pp. 126, 137.

45 Prior and Wilson, *Command*, pp. 255, 259; Travers, *Killing Ground*, p. 186.

Chapter Nine

Horace Smith-Dorrien

Second Army, 1914–1915

Steven J. Corvi

Brigadier General Colin Ballard and A.J. Smithers[1] in their respective biographies create effective and lucid portraits of Horace Smith-Dorrien's early career. The many generals who rose to high rank in the British army before 1914 were his contemporaries. Unlike many of his contemporaries, Smith-Dorrien was not a political intriguer. He was concerned with the men who served under him. Compassion for the troops can be a blessing or a curse depending on one's own ambition. Certainly, Smith-Dorrien did not lack ambition, finally rising to one of the highest ranks in the British army. The engaging ambition that drove him was derived from a practical and genuine interest in soldiering. This dedication permeated the Smith-Dorrien family and made an impression on his sons. The youngest son, David, attests to this professionalism, 'he was a dedicated and consummate soldier'.[2]

Horace Lockwood Smith-Dorrien was born to Colonel Robert Algernon Smith-Dorrien and his wife, Mary Anne, on 26 May 1858 in Haresfoot, Berkhampstead, Hertfordshire. He attended Harrow and, encouraged by his father, studied for the army exam and passed it, entering the Royal Military College at Sandhurst on 26 February 1876. He passed out from Sandhurst as a subaltern and joined the 95th Sherwood Foresters, an infantry regiment that was not his first choice: he had hoped for the 95th Rifle Brigade of Peninsular fame.[3] Smith-Dorrien's first combat duty, a forging element that clearly presaged his career, was in South Africa in 1878–9.

The Battle of Isandlwana, at which Smith-Dorrien was present as a transport officer, has been endlessly debated since 1879. The underlying point about Smith-Dorrien's experiences was his ability to connect the operational aspects of war with the soldier's plight on the battlefield. It was conveniently maintained long after the battle that ammunition shortages on the firing line caused the defeat and massacre of the five companies of the 1st and one company of the 2nd Battalion, 24th Foot. This is now widely accepted as being highly doubtful, but it was clearly a Zulu victory and should be so viewed.[4]

Chronology

26 May 1858	Horace Lockwood Smith-Dorrien born at Haresfoot, Berkhampstead, Herts
	Educated at Harrow and Royal Military College, Sandhurst
26 February 1876	Commissioned Lieutenant, 95th Foot (later 2nd Battalion, Sherwood Foresters)
1 November 1878	Proceeded to South Africa on special service
1 April 1882	Promoted captain
22 August 1882	Appointed assistant chief of police at Alexandria
3 September 1882	Given command of Mounted Infantry in Egypt
1 February 1884	Seconded to Egyptian Army
1887–89	Attended Staff College, Camberley
1 May 1892	Promoted major
1 April 1893	Appointed DAAG Bengal
27 October 1894	Appointed AAG Bengal
1897	Served in Tirah campaign
20 May 1898	Promoted brevet lieutenant colonel
16 July 1898	Appointed CO, 13th Sudanese Battalion
16 November 1898	Promoted brevet colonel
1 January 1899	Appointed CO, 1st Battalion, Sherwood Foresters, and substantive lieutenant colonel
2 February 1900	Appointed to command 19 Brigade, South Africa
11 February 1900	Promoted major general
6 November 1901	Appointed adjutant general in India
3 September 1902	Married Olive Croton Schneider
30 June 1903	Appointed GOC 4th Indian Division
9 April 1906	Promoted lieutenant general
1 December 1907	Appointed GOC Aldershot
1 March 1912	Appointed GOC Southern Command
10 August 1912	Promoted general
21 August 1914	Appointed GOC II Corps
26 December 1914	Appointed GOC Second Army
6 May 1915	Resigned command
22 June 1915	Appointed GOC First Home Army
22 November 1915	Appointed GOC East Africa
13 January 1916	Compelled by ill health to return to England
29 January 1917	Appointed lieutenant of the Tower of London
7 September 1918	Appointed governor of Gibraltar
September 1923	Retired
12 August 1930	Died as result of motor accident at Chippenham, Wiltshire

Appointed DSO 1886, KCB 1904, GCB 1913, GCMG 1915

On 22 January 1879 the British camp was caught off guard by a Zulu impi[5] of about 20,000 warriors. It is now generally supposed that the British firing became over-extended and, once outflanked, the British troops were forced to fight hand-to-hand with some of the best close-combat soldiers in the world. Interestingly, it was the testimony of Smith-Dorrien – in his later memoirs rather than in his contemporary correspondence – that contributed much to the survival of the traditional explanation of a failure in the ammunition supply.[6]

Smith-Dorrien had an epic hair-raising escape from the Zulu over 20 miles of rough terrain, with twenty warriors in hot pursuit.[7] Finally, he was able to escape by jumping into the Buffalo River, which was 80 yards across. He managed to swim to the other side against the heavy current by grabbing hold of the tail of a loose horse. He was able to help wounded soldiers and even gave up his broken-kneed pony in the mêlée. He was able to hold off the twenty warriors with his revolver and managed to save a colonial commissariat officer named Hamer. His intrepid conduct during the battle gained him the nomination for the Victoria Cross for these incidents.[8]

Smith-Dorrien was assigned to Egypt in 1882 under the command of Sir Garnet Wolseley. Smith-Dorrien, however, was initially given police duties under Evelyn Wood in the city of Alexandria, while Wolseley fought the Battle of Tel-el-Kebir, captured Arabi and seized Cairo. Smith-Dorrien moved to the now secure Cairo to further his duties under Wood before resuming his duties with his regiment in India.

Smith-Dorrien subsequently joined the Egyptian army under Evelyn Wood's command, the army being reconstituted under British officers, with Wood made its commander-in-chief or Sirdar. Smith-Dorrien was deployed to Cairo in early 1884 and met Major General Charles Gordon at this time, 'I had the good fortune to meet him more than once at the Sirdar's house'.[9] Smith-Dorrien, however, was not part of the subsequent Gordon relief expedition, 'as my bad knee kept me at base'.[10] Nonetheless, he did serve in the Suakin expedition, which played an important role in limiting Mahdist expansion in the wake of the Khartoum debacle. Moreover, Smith-Dorrien began his long professional relationship with an engineer officer named Captain Herbert Kitchener, who had served as an intelligence liaison between Gordon and Wolseley. This became a lasting friendship that would endure through the early phases of the Great War.

Smith-Dorrien's first independent command came on 31 December 1885, consisting of a mixed force of 150 men drawn from hussars, mounted infantry, Egyptian Camel Corps and Egyptian cavalry supported by a 50-man infantry reserve. His mission was to pursue nine sailing nuggars (Arab river supply boats) within a set geographic area bounded by the small village of Surda. When he reached the village he had only captured one nuggar, so he decided to exceed his orders to apprehend the other vessels. This entailed a 60-mile journey on horseback in 24 hours! In a sharp action, Smith-Dorrien was able to capture the remaining eight nuggars in a dashing and bold action that earned him the new decoration for gallantry, the DSO: 'The fact that I had exceeded my instructions by going beyond Surda was overlooked, and only the success-ful results were referred to.'[11]

Smith-Dorrien attended the Staff College from 1887 to 1889 but was not particularly shaped by his experience there, the college still not being as yet respected as an institution of military learning.[12] He stated: 'I enjoyed every minute of my two years there. I do not think we were taught as much as we might have been, but there was plenty of sport and not too much work.'[13] However, his training at the Staff College later influenced him to be the impetus behind the creation of a new Staff College at Quetta in India.

In 1896 the British agent and consul general in Egypt, Lord Cromer, with Prime Minister Lord Salisbury's approval, decided to abandon the previously cautious attitude toward a campaign of reconquest in the Sudan. One factor that propelled Britain to take this path was the upswing in the Egyptian economy and finances. A second was the defence and security of upper areas of the Nile against French usurpation.[14] Another reason was to avenge the humiliating defeat of General Gordon. Securing command of the 13th Sudanese Battalion for the campaign, Smith-Dorrien fought at Omdurman in September 1898. He was able to keep up a steady fire on the advancing enemy from entrenched positions, witnessing the destructive firepower of the Maxims against Dervish forces advancing in open order. The victory at Omdurman was to create the persona of Kitchener, a portrait that would endure until his death in 1916.[15]

Soon, however, the British were to face a greater challenge in South Africa in 1899. The execution of the war by the British high command during the first year was marked by overconfidence and incompetence. There was poor logistical planning because the consensus was that the war would be short in duration. Soldiers and horses, for example, were not allowed enough time to acclimatize to the hot and dry weather, which caused illness and, in the case of horses, disease that crippled mobility.[16] By this point it should have been obvious that the rifle and artillery technology available greatly favoured the defender over the attacker. Boer marksmanship skills were excellent, resulting in horrific losses for the British in the opening bouts of the war. Moreover, as the war progressed, logistical overburdening exacerbated the military situation.

As a result, reputations were made and destroyed in South Africa. After Smith-Dorrien's repeated pleas to Evelyn Wood, now adjutant general at the War Office, his unit received orders to ship out to South Africa on 31 October 1899.[17] What a fitting day – All Hallows Eve – to receive orders to go to war. He arrived at Durban on 13 December 1899 during the disaster of 'Black Week' with the triple defeats of Stormberg, Magersfontein and Colenso, but was forced into a period of inactivity after his long voyage: 'I was very cross because I was forced to observe Christmas Day as a holiday, and am afraid I made some pointed remarks to the effect that we were not out there to observe Christmas day.'[18]

Arriving to take command, Field Marshal Lord Roberts, with Kitchener as his chief of staff, at once converted one company from every battalion to mounted infantry, a wise precaution since the majority of the Boer forces were mounted.[19] Another decision that would personally affect Smith-Dorrien occurred on 2 February 1900, when Roberts offered him command of 19 Brigade. Smith-Dorrien optimistically leaped at the opportunity and, in his own words, 'after a long day, the fatigue was knocked bang out of me by a wire from Lord Roberts, offering me a Brigade'.[20]

Smith-Dorrien assumed command and was promoted to Major General (11 February 1900), making him one of the youngest generals in the British army. It was a harsh time, for he had witnessed poor tactics that uselessly squandered lives. He resisted dubious orders at Paardeberg (20 February 1900) given to him by Major General Sir Henry Colvile and Kitchener to assault an entrenched laager over open ground. He fully understood the collective firepower of the rifle and the power of entrenched defensive positions. Logic prevailed and his ideas on bombardment, on sapping trenches forward to a closer assault and on the importance of fire support were accepted. The exposure of troops to modern weapons on open ground produced horrific casualties that could not be endured over a prolonged period. Another incident of Colvile's ineptitude that Smith-Dorrien endured occurred during an attack on Sannah's Post (31 March 1900). He was ordered to withdraw his brigade from its position immediately, leaving wounded and a great amount of equipment under the protection of a small party of cavalry and a few batteries of the Royal Horse Artillery: 'I shall never forget the indignation of General Porter and his men when they heard of this inhuman order. So leaving the Shropshire as a support just behind the position, and remaining myself, I sent the other battalions back by slow stages to camp.' This allowed the wounded and equipment to be withdrawn in a steady and orderly retreat that did not endure a single casualty.[21] Smith-Dorrien 'went to report my return, but was told the Divisional General was snugly asleep in a farmhouse, and that the orders were not to disturb him; and perhaps it was just as well, for I was boiling with indignation, and might have said more than was discreet.'[22]

Smith-Dorrien was also very concerned with the logistics of an army in the field. He spent many hours overseeing the supply of equipment and food to his men. A satirical telegram he sent on 1 March 1901 to the director of supplies at Pietretief proves his aptitude in this area: 'Many thanks for bread; one sort is excellent, the other is causing heavy casualties. You might use your influence with the Lieutenant-General to send large quantities of the latter to all Boer laagers, for I am convinced that such a measure would hasten termination of the war, as long as they don't use the bread as projectiles.'[23]

Later, many attested to the leadership qualities of Smith-Dorrien during the South African War. Ian Hamilton recalled, 'As for Smith-Dorrien he was my Brigadier in South Africa and when he and I differed he usually turned out to be right. I never knew anyone who had a better flair for the morale of T. [Tommy] Aitkens.'[24] Thus, Smith-Dorrien was one of the few who emerged from the war with an enhanced reputation. Roberts also thought that

Smith-Dorrien was one of the best major generals during war. Thus, at Paardeberg, Smith-Dorrien was summoned:

> During this morning I was sent for by Lord Roberts and asked, in the presence of Lord Kitchener, General French and Colvile whether I thought I could at once carry the laager by direct assault. Kitchener and Colvile seemed to be in favour of such action, but I deprecated it strongly, saying the losses would be great and our chances of success small. I urged a bombardment for a few days with our fine force of artillery, and constant harassing on all sides, whilst I pushed my trenches nearer every night, until I was satisfied that an assault must succeed. My views were accepted, and, as I mounted to ride back, Lord Kitchener came up to me, saying that if I would attack them at once, I should be a made man. To which I, with a smile, replied: 'You heard my views, and I shall only attack now if ordered to.'[25]

This is a good example of Smith-Dorrien's adherence to his principles and beliefs in fire and movement tactics, and also of his ability to go against his superior's wishes if he felt they were wrong. His concern for the men that fought under his command was also highly commendable. A week later, his assertions proved correct and success was gained as Smith-Dorrien's brigade took the Boer laager after his careful preparation and attack. Even Sir John French complimented him, 'Selfishly I often wish you were back again. I would give anything to have you helping me direct these operations.'[26] Indeed, Smith-Dorrien's brigade provided effective covering fire at Klipsdrift for French's cavalry division. This undoubtedly saved many casualties and was a contributing factor to the cavalry charge's success. These objective observations from a cross-section of general officers and mention on three different occasions in the *London Gazette*[27] confirmed Smith-Dorrien's intrepidness in combat, his coolness under fire and his tactical skill in handling infantry on the battlefield.

Smith-Dorrien received orders on 22 April 1901 to become adjutant general[28] of the Indian Army under its new commander-in-chief, Kitchener.[29] Except for the commander-in-chief, Smith-Dorrien's was the most important post in the Indian Army. It was an example of the confidence Kitchener had in Smith-Dorrien at a time when the Indian Army was judged in need of reform. On a more personal note, when Smith-Dorrien was on leave in England after his service as adjutant general in India, he married Miss Olive Croton Schneider, whom he had known for some years, on 3 September 1902. It was a quick marriage and honeymoon, and he and his new wife were in Simla by 23 October 1902.[30]

Smith-Dorrien was then appointed to command the 4th Division in Baluchistan. It provided ample opportunity for him to implement many of his ides on modernization. Among the many innovations during his tenure was the 'staff ride', the results of which were published and distributed throughout the

Indian Army.[31] This is a major element of training in most armies in the world today and can be attributed to Smith-Dorrien's innovative and tactically sound doctrines.

Smith-Dorrien was notified in early January 1907 that he would succeed Sir John French in the Aldershot command.[32] French had made few innovations there.[33] A proponent of the *arme blanche*, French saw the cavalry as the superlative weapon of the British army and consistently trained it for mass knee-to-knee mounted charges. Indeed, he laid so much stress upon the *arme blanche* that other forms of training were either ignored or held in outright contempt. During the farewell dinner, French made reference to Smith-Dorrien taking up the reins at Aldershot: 'There was no soldier for whom he possessed a greater regard or esteem, and that it was with the utmost confidence that he handed over the command to him [Smith-Dorrien].'[34]

Smith-Dorrien went to work straight away and made reforms in training, discipline and creature comforts for the men under his command. He wanted to create a reciprocal bond of trust and respect between the officers and the men.[35] Smith-Dorrien also encouraged physical activity in the form of sports. He felt it dovetailed well with a soldier's training and duty. Thus, he provided facilities for sports throughout the sprawling grounds of Aldershot.[36] His great efforts to improve the men's comfort and recreation would pay dividends in the future.

Trust was the essential bond between soldier and commander in the heat of battle and Smith-Dorrien understood this from actual battlefield experience. One of his radical reforms was to abolish the piquet's duties, which involved an NCO and four to six men who would patrol the roads and streets in the district surrounding the Aldershot camp to maintain order and quell any military disturbances. Smith-Dorrien published an order saying 'that I did so as I trusted the men to behave, but that if events proved I had formed too high an appreciation of the characteristics of the British solder I should cancel the order'.[37]

Smith-Dorrien also turned his attention to two areas sorely lacking in the British army, musketry skills and the employment of machine-guns. He did not just pay lip-service to marksmanship, which many contemporary British generals did, but instituted training to make it a reality. Current training methods were outdated and not practised often enough to obtain the proper skill levels. Targets were static and at fixed distances, and this Smith-Dorrien determined to change.[38]

Smith-Dorrien increased the ammunition allotment and training frequency. He also encouraged the men to compete in marksmanship contests and supported the adoption of more realistic targets in the form of upper torso target, which is employed in military and law enforcement training today. Moving targets were instituted, which sharpened the soldier's skill at quick, instinctive snap-shooting.[39] Indeed, the marksmanship of the British soldier was to prove legendary at Mons and Le Cateau in 1914.[40] Smith-Dorrien decided to implement his marksmanship training for the cavalry as well:

> I was, therefore, not at all pleased to find that the Cavalry Brigade at Aldershot were low down in the annual musketry courses, and further on field days and manoeuvres, hardly ever dismounted, but delivered perfectly carried out, though impossible, knee-to-knee charges against infantry in action ... I gave them my views pretty clearly, with the result that dismounted work was taken up seriously and the improvement in musketry was so marked that the cavalry went nearly to the head of the lists in the annual musketry.[41]

Smith-Dorrien also wanted to upgrade the quality of the machine-guns in use at that time. His argument centred on the replacement of the older Maxim models with the newer Vickers-Maxim guns.[42] The latter cut the weight of the much older Maxim models by nearly half, which increased their mobility and flexibility. The water-jacket cooling system was also improved, and this cut down on overheating and jamming. In the event, the War Office did not approve the financial expenditure and deemed it superfluous in the then current military situation.

Smith-Dorrien's training protocols were to prove the main source of French's increasing dislike and mistrust of him. French felt his beloved cavalry was being turned into auxiliary infantry soldiers by an infantry officer who, French felt, had no true understanding of cavalry training. This rivalry was to become a cancerous impediment in 1914. It might be added, however, that Smith-Dorrien himself had a ferocious temper, which also contributed to the uneasy relationship.

Following his tenure at Aldershot, Smith-Dorrien was offered the Southern Command at Salisbury. This differed greatly from Aldershot in that it covered twelve counties, many regimental depots, and a large coastal defence area that included the important ports of Plymouth and Portsmouth. It also put Smith-Dorrien in touch with Territorial divisions[43] for the first time, and he soon realized that a short period of sharp training would make these part-time soldiers very useful in a combat situation. The following memorandum was circulated by Smith-Dorrien at Salisbury on 20 June 1914, presaging in many ways the retreat at Mons and Le Cateau and clearly illustrating his comprehension of fire and movement tactics:

> I want rather more attention paid to the following points with regard to infantry attack and retirement:-
> Retirements. I do not think the troops are skilfully trained at retirement.
> The essence of a good retirement is that it should be unseen by the enemy, the full front of fire should be maintained as long as

possible, and that the new fire position should be reached as rapidly as possible.

To carry this out, instead of commencing a retirement by alternative sections or platoons, a commencement should be made by thinning the whole line. Under the instructions of the several commanders, named men should wriggle back out of the firing line so as to hide the rearward move from the enemy, and as soon as they have reached a point where they cannot be seen by the enemy they should rush back to the next firing position.[44]

Smith-Dorrien held the Southern Command until the outbreak of war in 1914, whereupon he took command of the Home Defence Army, part of the Home Defence Central Force commanded by his friend and fellow infantryman Ian Hamilton. Smith-Dorrien desperately wanted to be part of the BEF (British Expeditionary Force) being dispatched to France. On 17 August 1914 his wish came true under the most grave of circumstances: Lieutenant General Sir James Grierson, commander of II Corps, died from a heart attack en route to the front:

> On the 17th of August came the sad news of the death of the commander of our II Corps – poor Jimmy Grierson, the man who was heart and soul a soldier, who, once a *persona grata* with the Kaiser, and a welcome guest in the German Army, had of late years seen through their wily machinations, and devoted himself to preparing the Army and himself for the day when the Germans should unmask. *Der Tag* had arrived, and Grierson landed in France, bursting with enthusiasm and thirsting for the fray, when the cruel blow fell and the nation lost an unrivalled leader in the very hour of her need.[45]

The resulting problem had to be solved with the greatest economy of time and with the most qualified and experienced officer. Sir John French, commanding the BEF, wanted Lieutenant General Herbert Plumer, but Kitchener thought otherwise.[46] Kitchener may have felt obligated to Smith-Dorrien because of the latter's devotion and loyalty in past service. Consequently, he offered the command to Smith-Dorrien. Another reason may stem from Kitchener's mistrust of French and his desire for an officer who would offer resistance to any outright foolish plans. According to Smith-Dorrien,

> Lord Kitchener's first words to me, when I entered his room at the War Office that afternoon, expressed grave doubts as to whether he was wise in selecting me to succeed Grierson, since the C.-in-C. in France had asked that General Sir Herbert Plumer should be selected to fill the appointment . . . However after thinking the matter over, he adhered to his decision to send me.[47]

The BEF comprised two army corps and one cavalry division, along with various ancillary units.[48] However, II Corps was not as well staffed or equipped as I Corps. It was short of important portions of its artillery, medical units and Royal Engineers Field companies. Nor was it in the best of physical condition since it was made up of many reservists, who also lacked the discipline that I Corps had from its Aldershot training. Smith-Dorrien inherited Grierson's small staff when he arrived at Bavai, and his first priority was to meet with French at Le Cateau. In a suggestion of French's animosity, Smith-Dorrien was received in an unprofessional manner, with gruffness and with a minimally communicative report on the current condition of II Corps.

The situation demanded a calm, intrepid and objective command style that would place the needs of the army above one's own personal feelings. Smith-Dorrien noted in his autobiography that he was received 'pleasantly' and was briefed on the general situation. This notation seems to have been an effort to quell rumours of bad blood that coloured the reactions to the debate that had by now ensued between French and Smith-Dorrien. Smith-Dorrien's contemporary diary makes no note on how he was received, merely stating, 'I motored into Le Cateau and saw the Commander-in-Chief.'[49] This omission of commentary is suspicious in light of Smith-Dorrien's generally keen and detailed observations and probably reflects his desire to avoid negative comments on superior officers. Contextualizing this lapse could indicate that Smith-Dorrien was met with coolness or even nervous hostility for three reasons. First, Smith-Dorrien was not French's first choice to replace Grierson. Second, French had disapproved of Smith-Dorrien's command style at Aldershot and now also took offence at Kitchener's imposition of someone whose tactics so violated his own views. Third, the king had asked Smith-Dorrien to keep him directly informed on II Corps. This would involve writing a special diary for the king, which would require Smith-Dorrien to request permission of French. Whatever his private views, French was in no position to refuse it. The king had already asked Douglas Haig his opinion of French, Haig explaining that he had 'grave doubts'[50] about French in such a position.[51]

Smith-Dorrien ignored these political pitfalls, instead focusing his attention on the duty at hand, the tactical deployment of his soldiers on the battlefield, but the snake-pit atmosphere at French's headquarters only created problems within the BEF's high command. Haig served to aggravate rather than alleviate the tension, and there was also long-standing animosity between Haig's chief of staff, John Gough VC, and Smith-Dorrien's chief of staff, George Forestier-Walker. Smith-Dorrien was viewed by both French and Haig as a rival, since he was the most senior ranking officer after French. In addition, Smith-Dorrien was from the infantry branch, and this further alienated him from both Haig and French.

Major General Lord Loch[52] was liaison officer between II Corps and GHQ. His unique position allowed him to witness both sides of the interchange between them. His diary entry was an accurate assessment of the situation: '21st August Friday . . . Le Cateau – the situation is intensely interesting. Please God it will turn out in our favour.'[53] Loch continued:

> 22nd August Saturday, I went out to 2nd Corps headquarters this morning in a car – Saw Smith-Dorrien and went with him to the 3rd Division: the head of which now reaches Mons. They were not opposed – We hear tonight that the Cavalry had a small fight today in which our people think they had the best of it – At last they think they are man for man better than the Germans which is a good thing.[54]

The plan was to advance to the left of the French Fifth Army on the Belgium–France border. The French anticipated that the German army's right wing facing the British would not reach Mons. Therefore, if the British were in a defensive position, they would be ready to envelop the German army once the French Fifth Army had threatened the German army's left wing and centre. A plausible plan, it relied on suppositions and not factual information of the German army, including size and location. In fact, of course, the initiative had passed into the hands of the Germans. The French Fifth Army and the BEF were actually facing two full German armies (First and Second German Armies). Moreover, the Germans had a two to one manpower advantage over the British and French. What started out as a plan for attack and envelopment had turned into a defensive holding action.

As the situation disclosed itself, Sir John French, while still hoping that an offensive action might be possible, began to realize the necessity, in view of the isolated position of his force, of being prepared for any kind of move, either advance or retreat.[55] Facing a larger force than they had expected, the French had begun a retreat without informing British GHQ. Smith-Dorrien, however, was soon aware of the situation.

II Corps took the brunt of the German assault, the BEF having begun a concentration at Mons where the cavalry at the north-east end created a small salient.[56] Smith-Dorrien and Haig organized a hasty defence that resulted in a sharp action that delayed the German advance. Mons, along with Le Cateau, would act as important delaying actions that would permit the French to gather correct intelligence and assemble their forces for the pivotal Battle of the Marne. Smith-Dorrien noted on 22 August 1914, 'The Mons salient, which is held by the 8th Brigade, is almost an impossible one to defend, but I gather it is not expected that this is to be treated as a defensive position.'[57] There is an interesting omission in Smith-Dorrien's war diary, however, which attests to his loyalty and aversion to derisive comments on fellow officers. According to Sir James Edmonds, at a meeting of corps commanders at GHQ on 22 August, French said to Smith-Dorrien, 'The British Army will give battle on the line of the Conde Canal.' When Smith-Dorrien asked, 'Do you mean take the offensive or stand on the defensive?', French retorted, 'Don't ask questions. Do as you are told.' Edmonds, a staff officer at the time, felt that this illustrated the 'true facts, which were omitted from history'.[58]

Unfortunately, the Germans would not allow II Corps to build a better defensive line. The German First Army attacked en masse in the early afternoon of 23 August. Smith-Dorrien was not a general who avoided the personal dangers of combat and he wanted to assess the situation himself: 'I went out to the outpost in a motor, and in going along a shell just missed the car. The Germans apparently were firing high explosives of a very virulent nature. In order to cover a certain withdrawal from the untenable salient at Mons, I had an entrenchment made in rear of it to prevent the enemy debouching to the south.'[59]

Smith-Dorrien's account is worth quoting at length:

> At this period the 5th Division, which was on my left, was not so heavily attacked, but in the afternoon the enemy's infantry worked forward across the Canal, although we had blown up a good many of the bridges, and about 7 p.m. I heard they had penetrated our lines in the neighbourhood of Frameries. Directly I heard this information, as I had not a single man to put in to support my left, I motored straight to Haig's Headquarters about four miles off and asked for the help of the 5th Infantry Brigade, which was within 5,000 yards of the point where the Germans were penetrating my line. This he readily gave, and they got up so quickly that the Germans were forced back and the whole line was cleared again. This was how matters stood about two hours after dark. During the night, there was some very heavy street fighting in the neighbourhood of Frameries. The whole of the position we were occupying, especially from Frameries, Westward from the 5th Division portion, is a series of mines and miners' houses, very broken country indeed, and very difficult to fight in. However, I was quite happy after the result the days [*sic*] fight, and from what I heard of the men's spirits and from the number of Germans who had been killed, and that we had held our own well so long as our flanks were not turned. It was during the afternoon, when the fight was going on, that Allenby's Cavalry Division had been moved across our rear to our left flank, in the neighbourhood of Thulin, a very difficult operation requiring excellent staff work, and it was most successfully accomplished.[60]

This was the juncture at which GHQ began to lose control over and comprehension of the tactical situation: 'the retreat of 1914 was not, as is now imagined, a great military achievement, but rather a badly bungled affair only prevented from being a disaster of the first magnitude by the grit displayed by the officers and men'.[61]

Le Cateau, 1914

The eventuality of a retreat had not been discussed with the respective commanders by French and therefore there were no contingency plans. Smith-Dorrien understood that retreat was not ideal, but, if an army was prepared for such an eventuality, then the loss could be minimized. He, of course, had underlined the basic requirements for a proper retreat in his 'Memorandum on Infantry Training' in the spring of 1914 and this understanding was undoubtedly one of the main reasons for II Corps's survival at Le Cateau. Haig, meanwhile, made a fateful decision when he consulted French at GHQ. Haig was concerned with the survival of his own corps and French did not seem to take into consideration the needs of the whole BEF in approving Haig's movement:

> I pointed out strongly to Sir John French that if we halted for a day at Bavai the whole force would be surrounded by superior numbers. He agreed and ordered the force to continue its retreat. By Murray's request I arranged roads for retirement of my Corps on Landrecies giving the direct route to Le Cateau to the Second Corps.[62]

This assessment of the tactical situation and the determination of next steps were undertaken entirely without Smith-Dorrien's knowledge or consent. The BEF's chief of staff, Sir Archibald Murray, had noted on 25 August 1914, 'Withdrawal from Le Cateau to St Quentin. 1st Corps heavily engaged by night'.[63] The absence of any reference to II Corps was reflective of the disorganization at GHQ and its basic misunderstanding either of the whereabouts of II Corps on 25–26 August, or the position of the French – not to mention that of the Germans.

French and Haig assumed that the left flank of II Corps was being covered by the French. This was not true since the French had already retired beyond the Le Cateau line by the night of 25 August. Smith-Dorrien, however, understood and expected mutual support from I Corps. Thus, when Smith-Dorrien was informed of these decisions he realized that the unilateral decision by French and Haig abandoned II Corps to fight the entire German army. The major geographic feature that was ignored by Haig and French was the Forest of Mormal, which effectively split I Corps from II Corps. Major General Snow of 4th Division reported: 'I also gathered that the I Corps had had little or no fighting, but were tired out with marching and were separated from the II Corps by the Forêt de Mormal, a huge forest about 10 miles through from east to west, and so no hope could be expected from that quarter.'[64]

During the retreat, Haig recorded, 'In two actions, the casualties were [at] Maroilles 2 killed, 41 wounded and 101 missing [and at] Landrecies 17 killed 86 wounded and 23 missing.'[65] I Corps was not heavily engaged with the advancing Germans as indicated by the relatively light casualties. Thus, Smith-Dorrien was perplexed by Haig's decision, supported by French, to continue

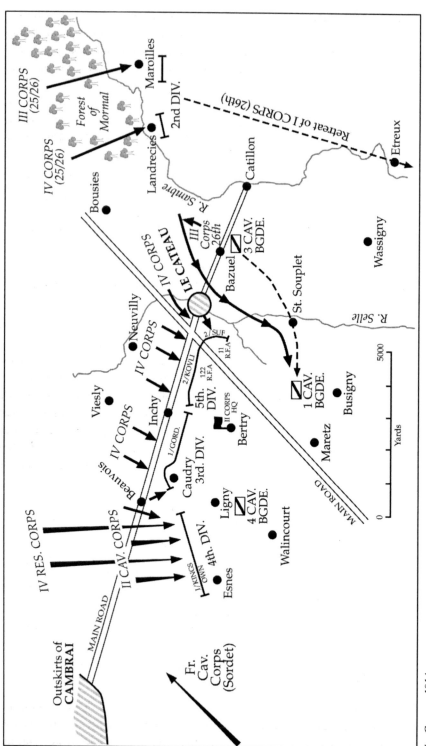

Le Cateau, 1914.

the retirement without the knowledge of the condition and whereabouts of II Corps: 'A lot of fighting took place this day, and Haig's Army – in some ways of which I have no knowledge – instead of coming back in to line with my own, kept much further East and North and halted, leaving a gap of some ten miles between us.'[66]

This created a dangerous situation for II Corps and would allow the German advancing army to concentrate its forces on a single British corps. Smith-Dorrien was aware of the condition of his men and the amount of ground that had to be covered to reach Le Cateau:

> 25th August Moving all impediments off 2 a.m., the retirement was ordered to a line running about East and West through Le Cateau, a very long march considering the state of the troops of over 20 miles, and in many cases 30. It will be noticed from the map that what makes the operation a still more difficult and complicated one is the fact that we are not retiring moving straight to our rear, but diagonally away to the West, thus making our West flank very much more difficult to cover, as well as complicating the movement of our impediments.[67]

Smith-Dorrien outlined the situation of the night of 25 August very clearly and appreciated the timely arrival of the 4th Division. Major General Snow even commented in his diary that 'I will say that it was very lucky it arrived when it did and it was pure luck'.[68] Another illustration of GHQ's complete misunderstanding of II Corps's tactical situation was a further comment from Snow's diary, 'No pressure was brought to bear from G.H.Q., France, or the War Office to hurry up the Divisions neither, when the Division embarked, was there any reason to believe that its presence was so urgently required'.[69] Smith-Dorrien on the other hand stated the urgent need of the 4th Division and its timely arrival on the battlefield:

> The 4th Division (General Snow), fresh from England, had taken up a position to the West of Le Cateau to help the retirement which it did most nobly – remaining out and allowing our tired rearguards to come through, and acting as a pivot for our Cavalry to fall back on, and indeed in some cases behind. It was very difficult to realise the situation of all one's troops, and it was not until 1.30 a.m. on the 26th that I fully realised the state of affairs, which was that the troops in this theatre of operation consisted of the whole of the Cavalry Division under Allenby, the 4th Division under Snow, and the 19th Brigade under Drummond (who had gone sick) besides my own Corps, consisting of the 3th and 5th Divisions.[70]

The Battle of Le Cateau (26 August 1914) that ensued was on an impromptu defensive line that halted the full force of the Germans in Belgium for twenty-four hours.[71] GHQ was not aware of the German forces facing Smith-

Dorrien's II Corps, the Cavalry Corps or the 4th Division, or the condition of these units or their exact locations. Accordingly, only Smith-Dorrien on the spot was capable of making a tactical decision that would avert disaster or complete the annihilation of II Corps and a possible rout of the whole BEF: 'I had received distinct Orders to continue the retirement at dawn. The position of all the troops in this area was very scattered, the men were very tired, there was a very large force of the enemy in close touch with us all along the line, and a very good chance of the retirement developing into a rout.'[72]

Smith-Dorrien was faced with a momentous decision to either stand and fight (in direct violation of his orders) or continue the retreat. He made his decision on the basis of the tactical situation, the morale and physical condition of his men, and his combat experience.[73]

Smith-Dorrien was able to take command of the situation because of his experience and intrepid attitude towards combat. He was able to overcome the atmosphere of defeatism, which was evident, by concentrating on the tactical situation at hand and the best means to slow or stop the German advance. At the same moment, GHQ and I Corps had little or no confidence and feared the worse outcome. Haig can be quoted on the eve of Le Cateau, 'If we are caught, by God, we'll sell our lives dearly'.[74] Indeed, the situation of desperation weighed heavily in the air and permeated all levels of command from GHQ to I Corps.[75]

The decision of Smith-Dorrien to stand and fight was based on a sound tactical assessment of the situation. He wanted to halt or delay the German advance. Therefore, a defensive counter-attack employing lightly entrenched troops was the course of action that he determined. He also was adamant on artillery support and the use of machine-guns. A defensive action employing the tools of a modern army brought into high relief the heretofore implicit contradiction between effective technology integration and traditional military doctrine. Smith-Dorrien summed up his command decision as follows:

> I therefore decided to assume command of all the troops and I told General Allenby and General Snow that the Cavalry and 4th Divisions respectively would come under my command, and that I had decided to send all baggage away at once in the direction of the line Beaurevoir–Le Catelets. I had received orders yesterday generally as to the position to be taken up, some of which had already been lightly entrenched. The line generally was from the South side of Le Cateau through the villages of Troisvilles–Audencourt–Caudry, with the left thrown back on Hautcourt; the 5th Division on the right, 3rd Division in centre, and 4th Division on left. The Cavalry Division which was tremendously scattered early that morning – 2½ Brigades being at Catillon, East of Le Cateau, and 1½ Brigades near Caudry – I arranged with General Allenby that the Caudry lot should fall back

on Ligny and try and guard my left flank, and the others from Catillon should guard my right flank.

The French Cavalry Corps, under General Sordet, which was moved across South of us from East to West the previous day, promised to help us in the neighbourhood of Cambrai. The situation was not a pleasing one.[76]

Snow was also given orders by GHQ to create a defensive reserve line on the Le Cateau–Cambrai position since it was not realized that Snow's 4th Division was being put into action rather than 'reserve': 'I was also told that the idea was to fall back on Le Cateau–Cambrai position and there accept battle, and that the position was being prepared by impressed labour, and that the position of my Division would be about Beaurevoir and Cattenieres.'[77]

When Smith-Dorrien accepted battle on the Le Cateau line, his subordinates were fully in agreement with his decision.[78] The Le Cateau front, however, was rapidly becoming untenable, and the soldiers of II Corps were exhausted beyond human capacity. Smith-Dorrien saw that a quick offensive action would slow the German advance and allow II Corps, 4th Division and the Cavalry Division to retreat in safe order. He prepared for the worst and informed GHQ of the situation, employing a defensive retreat similar to what he had proposed in his peacetime training. His coolness and intrepidness under fire saved Le Cateau from becoming a rout. The individual fighting ability of the men involved was well documented in the official history: 'There can be little doubt but that the comparative ease with which the first stages of the retreat were accomplished was due to the tenacity of the units [of 3rd and 4th Divisions] which, having received no order to retire, clung with all their strength to the positions they had been ordered to hold.'[79] The merit of the achievements cannot be understated, since in many cases only a handful of men held a line of 8,000 yards and threw two German army Corps into a temporary retreat.[80]

Despite the heavy fighting that ensued, Smith-Dorrien was able to continue the retreat of the main body of II Corps: 'While this handful of men was thus hampering the German Advance, the main body of General Smith-Dorrien's force was in full retreat.'[81] In fact, Smith-Dorrien's troops had done what was thought to be impossible. With both flanks more or less in the air, they had turned upon an enemy of at least twice their strength, had struck him hard and had withdrawn, except on the right front of the 5th Division, practically without interference, with neither flank enveloped. Losses were certainly severe, but, considering the circumstances, by no means extravagant. The men looked upon themselves as victors; some indeed doubted whether they had been in a serious action.[82]

The official history summed up the Le Cateau action very concisely: 'So far Smith-Dorrien had everywhere held his ground successfully for some six hours: and except immediately to the west of Le Cateau, his line was not only unbroken but unshaken.' The men of the 3rd, 4th, 5th and Cavalry Divisions stood their ground remarkably well, and employed firepower tactics that held the advancing German army. The rapidity of fire and accuracy from the British was so intense that the German advance faltered. This was remarkable since the Germans had an overwhelming superiority in numbers. In fact, some German eyewitness reports overstate the number of machine-guns in the British units because of the rapidity and accuracy of their rifle fire. Marksmanship was clearly a decisive factor in the success of the British soldiers at Le Cateau. Smith-Dorrien also highly praised the intervention of the French cavalry under Sordet, which held his left wing so that his troops could retreat in an orderly fashion.

It was recognized by the British press and Sir John French at the time that the actions that Smith-Dorrien took at Le Cateau were responsible for saving the BEF, and delayed the Germans enough to allow for the pivotal Battle of the Marne in early September. This cannot be understated and was reflected in the following statement by Smith-Dorrien's chief of staff, Forestier-Walker:

> I was, as you may be aware, Sir Horace Smith-Dorrien's chief staff officer (B.G.G.S.), and in that capacity was asked by him for my opinion as to whether we should try to get away [as were the standing orders of the C.-in-C. Field Marshal French at British GHQ], or stay and fight. I did not hesitate in the answer which I gave. I do not for a moment suppose that had I given any other answer, he would have even hesitated to act as he did, for no other course of action was really possible to a soldier in possession of the facts. I only mention the incident to show that I may be held prejudiced in the views which I now put forward.

I hold that, had there been no Le Cateau, there would almost certainly have been no Marne, and even the man in street realizes that the battle of the Marne was the turning point of the war. But the connection between Le Cateau and the Marne has as yet only been grasped by the few. And even the official history of the war does not emphasize it.[83]

French wrote in his dispatches of 7 September 1914, 'I say without hesitation that the saving of the left wing of the army under my command on the morning of the 26th August could never have been accomplished unless a commander of rare and unusual coolness, intrepidity, and determination had been present to personally conduct the operation.'[84]

Smith-Dorrien's decision at Le Cateau is now well understood to have been right. Looking beneath that fact reveals that the prevailing conditions and the rather unco-operative nature of GHQ and I Corps made this achievement all the more remarkable. Smith-Dorrien was able to use a discretion not common in the prevailing 'system' to execute a military decision based on the tactical situation and then implement battlefield doctrine that was considered contrary to standard operating procedures of the British army. This action can be considered an example of a sound understanding of modern warfare and an implementation of tactics and strategies that was rarely repeated in the dead-locked battles of the next four years.

Following the Marne, Smith-Dorrien's corps fought on the Aisne and, with the remainder of the BEF, was transferred to Flanders in October 1914. At First Ypres in October and November 1914, his corps held the southern sector of the front around Armentières and La Bassée, being effectively broken up to reinforce I Corps in late October, the move partly a reflection of the continuing difficulties between French and Smith-Dorrien. Nonetheless, when the size of the BEF expanded sufficiently to warrant a new organization, Smith-Dorrien received command of the new Second Army on 26 December 1914. The new year began with some reflection by Smith-Dorrien. He had made observations on the progress of the war and noted them officially in his War Office reports. What is clear from these was his comprehension of the military realities of the battlefield in 1915. His notes show an understanding of the changing nature of warfare and that the pre-1914 notions of the war and its execution were completely false.

The impact of the new technologies on the battlefield was recognized by Smith-Dorrien and was reflected in his comment, 'No words could exaggerate the magnificent work performed by aeroplanes, their information being extra-ordinarily correct'.[85] At this stage, he saw aircraft as a tool of reconnaissance only; he did not see its potential as a weapon platform. He understood the emerging nature of mechanized warfare and that the manpower solution, summarized by Tim Travers as the 'frame of mind that saw the decisive offensive as a kind of overwhelming human solution to modern war conditions',[86] was essentially becoming obsolete as a doctrinal solution to process this war. Furthermore, the elements of the battlefield emerging on the Western Front in 1915 reflected a fundamental change in the execution of war, which now relied on a flexible paradigm that increasingly focused on the technological rather than the human elements of war.[87] Smith-Dorrien had emphasized the moral and physical effect of modern artillery on soldiers in the trenches: 'Perhaps the most unexpected feature of the present war has been the arresting power of modern artillery, and especially of howitzers and heavy artillery, both as regards their material and moral effect.'[88]

The conduct of warfare had changed dramatically by 1915, and it was apparent that artillery and the machine-gun were dominant features that produced the highest proportion of casualties and deaths. The isolation of GHQ expanded the gulf between the preconceived offensive tactical doctrine of the pre-war days and its practical application on the Western Front. Its formal execution of war was very resistant to change and its interpretation of the war to that point only reinforced the manpower principles of warfare and the conviction that the moral effect produced by a strong offensive doctrine would prevail over any circumstances. This would necessarily result from an orderly execution of a campaign that employed artillery in support of infantry and cavalry offensives that would bring victory. But when that changed under the realities of the war thus far, the doctrine did not. French and Haig understood war to be executed in four stages: manoeuvre, the preparation, the decisive attack and the cavalry exploitation. These stages properly executed would result in victory.[89] The battles in 1915 did not follow this pattern and became, instead, a long and continuous siege along static defensive lines.

Smith-Dorrien understood these strategic assumptions but became disillusioned with their tactical implementation as the way to achieve victory. He felt that the modern battlefield did not follow this predetermined order and that artillery and machine-guns needed to work in conjunction with infantry and cavalry to create a tactical manoeuvre that employed fire and cover and minimized casualties. He stated, 'The closest co-operation between infantry and artillery is an absolute necessity.'[90] He often displayed tactics that were contrary to GHQ thinking and even questioned orders that seemed to be contrary to the actual situation on the ground or the practical tactical considerations of battle. He felt the consistent ordering of offensives by GHQ was demoralizing and did not achieve any real tactical victories. GHQ stressed the intangible elements of warfare, the moral factor and strong discipline to achieve the battlefield objectives. Smith-Dorrien wanted to employ fire and movement tactics and was even a proponent of defensive retreat. This was viewed by GHQ as even defeatist in nature, and contributed to French's declining confidence in Smith-Dorrien, fuelling the antagonism that had begun in 1909.

In April 1915 Second Army was fighting in a very untenable salient on the Ypres front. On 22 April it was struck with a poison gas attack.[91] This surprised the French and British GHQ, but seven days earlier Smith-Dorrien noted in his diary the possibility of this type of attack:

> The prisoners described how they had arranged in their trenches batteries of enormous tubes of asphyxiating gas, and a battery of 16 of these tubes to every 40 metres, and how, at a given signal when the wind was in the right direction, all these tubes were to be opened, and after a decent pause to allow our men to become completely insensible from the arrival of the gases in their trenches, the Germans were to charge forward and mop them up! One prisoner even produced a packet of wool, which he said he had been given along with all the other attackers, and which at the right moment was going to be soaked in oxygen to be applied to their own noses to prevent them from being asphyxiated.[92]

Smith Dorrien had passed this on to GHQ but it was to no avail. The gas attacks exacted some heavy casualties on the British line, but fortunately the Germans did not fully comprehend the destructive nature of their attack, and therefore failed to truly exploit this surprise element on the battlefield. GHQ wanted to regain the initiative through a strong counter-attack, but Second Army was demoralized and Smith-Dorrien wanted to retreat to a more defensible line and abandon the untenable salient. This was a sound tactical judgement and would allow a desperately needed consolidation of forces along the line after the gas attacks. French felt this was defeatist and sufficient reason to dismiss Smith-Dorrien. The latter had written a letter to French outlining his withdrawal plan from the Salient:

> If the French are not going to make a big push, the only line we can hold permanently and have a fair chance of keeping supplied, would be the G.H.Q. line passing just east of Wieljte and Potijze to join our present line about 1,000 yards north-east of Hill 60. This of course, means the surrendering of a great deal of trench line, but any intermediate line, short of that, will be extremely difficult to hold, owing to the loss of the ridge to the east of Zonnebeke, which any withdrawal must entail.
>
> It is very difficult to put a subject such as this in a letter without appearing pessimistic – I am not in the least – but as an Army Commander I have, of course, to provide for every eventuality, and I think it right to let the Chief know what is running in my mind.[93]

The letter's tone was considered fatalistic and French felt that a new commander, Lieutenant General Sir Herbert Plumer (whom he had requested at the war's outset), would be more appropriate. Smith-Dorrien noted in his diary that the casualties were much higher than predicted by GHQ and that the ordered counter-attack was a complete failure: 'Further reports go to show that our casualties on Hill 60 and last night were very much heavier than we thought.'[94] Smith-Dorrien received word of his dismissal from Murray's successor as the BEF's chief of staff, 'Wully' Robertson (in his distinct pronunciation), ''Orace, you're for 'ome'. Smith-Dorrien noted in his diary without any malice, 'During the evening, I received a letter from the Adjutant General, telling me to hand over Command of the Army to Sir Herbert Plumer, and to proceed to see Lord Kitchener in England'. When Plumer arrived and assessed the situation, he adopted Smith-Dorrien's plan and carried out the withdrawal without interference from French.

This episode effectively ended Smith-Dorrien's career since ill health prevented him from assuming the command in East Africa offered him subsequently. His frank letter had displayed his method of thought and how he applied his ideas on the battlefield. In the end, doctrinal rigidity and the 'system' with its inherent personalized command structure destroyed his career. French himself was relieved of duty in December 1915. If Smith-Dorrien had continued to command Second Army until December 1915, he would have been the next senior commanding officer after French and might have taken his place. Edmonds had no doubt why Smith-Dorrien had been removed, remarking later that he 'was got rid of by French because he stood in Haig's way of the commander in chiefship'.[95] According also to Edmonds,

> It was Henry Wilson, too, who in the war, by his influence on French, got rid of Smith-Dorrien. One day he dropped a hint of this to Robertson, whose office he was in . . .
>
> . . . Edmonds didn't think French would have done it on his own, but he was vain and jealous, and Wilson played on these qualities by reminding him that if anything happened to him Smith-Dorrien was the next senior.
>
> Under the Army system these sort of evils would only be removed by having an Independent Selection Board.[96]

While the future of the cavalry was the strongest bond between Haig and French,[97] there was a simple incompatibility between Smith-Dorrien and French on the prosecution of the war. French would have wanted a like-minded cavalryman to replace him if the need arose. Who better than Haig? As Tim Travers concluded:

> when Smith-Dorrien saved the situation a few days later at Le Cateau, against Sir John French's orders, it might be predicted that Smith-Dorrien would be removed. This became fact at Ypres in 1915. Smith-Dorrien himself claims that starting in February 1915, Sir John French began to inflict 'pin pricks' on him, for example the removal of Lieutenant General Forestier-Walker as his II Corps Chief of Staff because Sir John French said Forestier-Walker could not be spared as he was wanted immediately to command a division training in England. But two months later Forestier-Walker was still waiting to command the division . . . it is now impossible to untangle the primary reasons for this rivalry, but it did exist and it did have consequences in terms of operations and efficiency.[98]

Bibliography

Smith-Dorrien's own autobiography, *Memories of Forty-Eight Years' Service* (London: John Murray, 1925) devotes only five chapters out of twenty-nine to his experiences in 1914 and 1915, and largely eschews controversy. However, the memoranda in defence of his command, based on his extensive diaries and journals, which he circulated privately in 1919, have been published in Ian F.W. Beckett, ed., *The Judgement of History: Sir Horace Smith-Dorrien, Lord French and 1914* (London: Tom Donovan, 1993). There are two biographies, Brigadier General Colin Ballard, *Smith-Dorrien* (London: Constable, 1931), and A.J. Smithers, *The Man Who Disobeyed: Sir Horace Smith-Dorrien and His Enemies* (London: Leo Cooper, 1970), the latter primarily based upon Smith-Dorrien's 1919 memoranda. More recently, Smith-Dorrien has been the subject of two dissertations, Richard A. Siem, 'Forging the Rapier among Scythes: Lieutenant-General Sir Horace

Smith-Dorrien and the Aldershot Command, 1907–1912', unpublished MA thesis, Rice University (Houston), 1980, and Steven J. Corvi, 'General Sir Horace Lockwood Smith-Dorrien: Portrait of a Victorian Soldier in Modern War', unpublished PhD thesis, Northeastern University (Boston), 2002. Nikolas Gardner, *Trial by Fire: Command and the British Expeditionary Force in 1914* (Westport: Praeger, 2003), deals with the 1914 campaigns as a whole; among many studies dealing with individual battles, see John Terraine, *Mons: Retreat to Victory* (London: Batsford, 1960); Ian F.W. Beckett, *Ypres: The First Battle, 1914* (London: Longman/Pearson, 2004); and John Dixon, *Magnificent But Not War: The Second Battle of Ypres* (Barnsley: Pen & Sword, 2003).

Notes

1 Brigadier General Colin Ballard, *Smith-Dorrien* (London: Constable, 1931), and A.J. Smithers, *The Man Who Disobeyed: Sir Horace Smith-Dorrien and His Enemies* (London: Leo Cooper, 1970).
2 Interview with David Smith-Dorrien, 20 August 1996.
3 The 95th Rifle Brigade was a popular infantry regiment that earned its reputation during the Napoleonic Wars.
4 Among many accounts of Isandlwana, see Ian Knight, 'Ammunition at Isandlwana: A Reply', *Journal of the Society for Army Historical Research*, 73, 296 (1995), pp. 237–50.
5 Impi was the Zulu fighting unit or army.
6 General Sir Horace Smith-Dorrien, *Memories of Forty-Eight Years' Service* (London: John Murray, 1925), p. 14.
7 He was one of only five regular officers (Essex, Cochrane, Gardner, Curling and Smith-Dorrien) to survive the Zulu assault.
8 Smith-Dorrien never received the Victoria Cross, since the nomination did not go through proper channels. In retrospect he felt that his actions did not warrant the highest commendation for bravery in the British army.
9 Smith-Dorrien, *Memories*, p. 47.
10 Ibid., pp. 48–50. Smith-Dorrien had hurt his knee badly in an injury incurred during equestrian activities.
11 Ibid., p. 65.
12 Brian Bond, *The Victorian Army and the Staff College, 1854–1914* (London: Eyre Methuen, 1972), pp. 134, 141, 162–3; Smithers, *Man Who Disobeyed*, pp. 24–5.
13 Smith-Dorrien, *Memories*, p. 68.
14 The French involvement became an issue in imperial defence after the defeat of the Italians by the Abyssinians at Adowa in March 1896, which left East Africa open to French ambition to forge an east–west axis from Chad to Djibouti.
15 Philip Magnus, *Kitchener: Portrait of an Imperialist* (London: John Murray, 1958), pp. 125–8.
16 Steven J. Corvi, 'Men of Mercy: The Evolution of the Royal Army Veterinary Corps and the Soldier–Horse Bond During the Great War', *Journal of the Society for Army Historical Research*, 56, 308 (1998), pp. 274–5.
17 Richard A. Siem, 'Forging the Rapier among Scythes: Lieutenant-General Sir Horace Smith-Dorrien and the Aldershot Command, 1907–1912', unpublished MA thesis, Rice University, 1980, p. 27.
18 Smith-Dorrien, *Memories*, p. 141.
19 Ibid., p. 142.
20 Ibid., p. 143.
21 Ibid., p. 179.
22 Ibid., pp. 179–80.
23 Ibid., p. 284.
24 Liddell Hart Centre for Military Archives (hereafter LHCMA), Edmonds MSS, II/1/55, Hamilton to Edmonds, 11 December 1933.
25 Smith-Dorrien, *Memories*, p. 155.
26 The National Archives, Public Record Office (hereafter PRO), WO 105/8, French to Smith-Dorrien, Spring 1902, in Smith-Dorrien's letter file.
27 *London Gazette*, 11 February and 16 April 1901, and 29 July 1902.
28 During this period the adjutant general was the senior staff officer for both training and discipline of the Indian Army.

29 Trevor Royle, *The Kitchener Enigma* (London: Michael Joseph, 1985), p. 143.

30 Smith-Dorrien., *Memories*, pp. 314–16.

31 Erroneously, Haig has been credited for the development of the 'staff ride' by John Terraine, but Haig was not its original author. See Siem, 'Forging the Rapier', p. 38.

32 Smith-Dorrien, *Memories*, p. 339; Siem, 'Forging the Rapier', pp. 33–4; Imperial War Museum (hereafter IWM), Smith-Dorrien MSS, Haldane to Smith-Dorrien, 18 December 1906 and 28 January 1907.

33 Siem, 'Forging the Rapier', p. 34.

34 *National Military Review*, 5 December 1907, p. 307; Siem, 'Forging the Rapier', p. 60.

35 PRO, WO 105/47, Smith-Dorrien, 'Note for the Improvement of the Intelligence and Comforts of the Men'.

36 Smith-Dorrien, *Memories*, p. 356.

37 Ibid., p. 355.

38 Ibid., p. 358.

39 Siem, 'Forging the Rapier', p. 76; *National Military Review*, 17 August 1910.

40 The rapid delivery of accurate rifle fire at Mons and Le Cateau was so devastating that the German command had thought they were facing British machine-guns.

41 Smith-Dorrien, *Memories*, p. 359.

42 Anthony Smith, *Machine Gun: The Story of the Men and the Weapon That Changed the Face of War* (London: Piatkus, 2002), p. 144.

43 For the Territorials, see Ian F.W. Beckett, 'The Territorial Force', in Ian F.W. Beckett and Keith Simpson, eds, *A Nation in Arms: A Social Study of the British Army in the First World War* (Manchester: Manchester University Press, 1985), pp. 127–64.

44 IWM, Reynolds MSS, 74/136/1, General Sir Horace Smith-Dorrien, 'Memorandum on Infantry Training', Salisbury, 20 June 1914.

45 Smith-Dorrien, *Memories*, p. 375.

46 Kitchener was appointed secretary of state for war on 5 August 1914. He had the initial benefit of popular iconographical appeal to the public as the ultimate imperial hero.

47 Smith-Dorrien, *Memories*, p. 375.

48 National Library of Scotland (hereafter NLS), Haig MSS, Acc. 315, Diary, 11 August 1914.

49 IWM, Smith-Dorrien MSS, 87/47/10, Diary, 21 August 1914.

50 NLS, Haig MSS, Acc. 3155, Diary, 11 August 1914.

51 Smithers, *Man Who Disobeyed*, p. 165.

52 See IWM, Loch MSS, 71/21/1.

53 Ibid., Diary, 21 August 1914.

54 Ibid., 22 August 1914.

55 Brigadier General Sir James Edmonds, *Military Operations ... France and Belgium, 1914*, vol. 1, History of the Great War (London: Macmillan, 1925), pp. 53–4, 59.

56 Ibid., p. 47.

57 IWM, Smith-Dorrien MSS, 87/47/10, Diary, 22 August 1914.

58 LHCMA, Liddell Hart MSS, 11/1933/26, Conversation with Edmonds, 7 December 1933.

59 IWM, Smith-Dorrien MSS, 87/47/10, Diary, 23 August 1914.

60 Ibid.

61 IWM, Snow MSS, 76/79/1, August–September 1914.

62 NLS, Haig MSS, Acc. 3155, Diary, 24 August 1914.

63 IWM, Murray MSS, 79/48/2, Diary, 25 August 1914.

64 IWM, Snow MSS, 76/79/1, p. 16.

65 NLS, Haig MSS, Acc. 3155, Diary, 24–5 August 1914.

66 IWM, Smith-Dorrien MSS, 87/47/10, Diary, 25 August 1914.

67 Ibid., Snow MSS, 76/79/1, p. 4.

68 Ibid., p. 14.

69 Ibid., p. 15.

70 IWM, Smith-Dorrien MSS, 87/47/10, Diary, 25 August 1914.

71 Edmonds, *Military Operations*, p. 132.

72 IWM, Smith-Dorrien MSS, 87/47/10, Diary, 26 August 1914.

73 John Terraine, *Mons: The Retreat to Victory* (New York: Macmillan, 1960), pp. 184–5.

74 NLS, Haig MSS, Acc. 3155, Diary, 26 August 1914.

75 This point is further noted in Liddell Hart's talk with Edmonds on 7 December 1933. Edmonds stated, 'Haig lost his head at Landrecies … Exactly. He was standing on his doorstep, revolver in hand saying, "We must sell our lives dearly" … "It was his first test as a commander in war and he was rattled."' See LHCMA, Liddell Hart MSS, 11/1933/26, Conversation with Edmonds, 7 December 1933.

76 IWM, Smith-Dorrien MSS, 87/47/10, Diary, 26 August 1914.

77 IWM, Snow MSS, 76/79/1, August 1914, p. 16.

78 Ibid., p. 25.

79 *Official History*, p. 186.

80 IWM, Smith-Dorrien MSS, 87/47/10, Diary, 26 August 1914.

81 *Official History*, p. 190.

82 Ibid., p. 182.

83 PRO, WO 95/629, Letter from Forestier-Walker, 27 February 1934.

84 Terraine, *Mons*, p. 154.

85 PRO, WO 79/63, Smith-Dorrien, 'Some Lessons of the War', January 1915.

86 Tim Travers, 'The Offensive and the Problem of Innovation in British Military Thought, 1870–1915', *Journal of Contemporary History*, 13/3 (1978), pp. 540–41.

87 Ibid., pp. 546–7.

88 PRO, WO 95/629, Smith-Dorrien, 'Notes Based on the Experience Gained by the Second Corps during the Campaign and Tactical Points'. Recent studies have confirmed that artillery was the major killer of soldiers in World War One.

89 Tim Travers, 'A Particular Style of Command: Haig and GHQ, 1916–1918', *Journal of Strategic Studies*, 10/3 (1987), pp. 363–4.

90 PRO, WO 95/629, Smith-Dorrien, 'Notes Based on the Experiences Gained by the Second Corps during the Campaign and Tactical Points', p. 4.

91 IWM, Smith-Dorrien MSS, 87/47/10, Diary, 22 April 1915.

92 Ibid., 15 April 1915.

93 Ibid., 27 April 1915; Ballard, *Smith-Dorrien*, pp. 292–4.

94 IWM, Smith-Dorrien MSS, 87/47/10, Diary, 6 May 1915.

95 LHCMA, Liddell Hart MSS, 11/1933/26, Conversation with Edmonds, 7 December 1933. French had a unique relationship with Haig, in that the latter had loaned him £800 to secure one of his debts. See NLS, Haig MSS Acc. 3155, Haig to Henrietta, 16 May 1899.

96 LHCMA, Liddell Hart MSS, 11/1937/30, Conversation with Edmonds, 22 April 1937.

97 Ian F.W. Beckett, 'Haig and French', in Brian Bond and Nigel Cave, eds, *Haig: A Reappraisal 70 Years On* (London: Leo Cooper, 1999), pp. 53–4.

98 Tim Travers, *The Killing Ground: The British Army, the Western Front and the Emergence of Modern Warfare* (London: Allen & Unwin, 1987), pp. 15–16.

Appendix One

Temporary Army Commanders

Haking, Sir Richard Cyril Burne (1862–1945)

A noted exponent of the 'offensive spirit', Haking commanded First Army from 7 August to 29 September 1916. Born at Halifax on 24 January 1862, Haking was educated at the Royal Military College, Sandhurst, and commissioned in the 67th Foot on 22 January 1881. He attended Staff College in 1896–7 and returned as a member of the directing staff from 1901 to 1906. After a succession of staff appointments, he became GOC of 5th Infantry Brigade in September 1911; he took it to France in August 1914, and was wounded on the Aisne in September. He received command of 1st Division on 21 December 1914 and of XI Corps on 4 September 1915. Elements of his corps were the reserve component at Loos in September 1915, the location of which became a key factor in the dismissal of Sir John French from command of the BEF in December 1915. Haking, indeed, was one of those who voiced his views of French to King George V when the latter visited the Western Front in October 1915. Despite the catastrophic failure of his attack on Fromelles on 19 July 1916 – leading to heavy losses in 61st Division and the Australian 5th Division, and Haking becoming known as 'Butcher' – Haking retained Haig's confidence. Accordingly, Haig appointed Haking to succeed Monro at First Army in August 1916. Haking, however, was unacceptable to the War Council and to the CIGS, Sir William Robertson. Sir Henry Horne, therefore, was appointed instead. Haking took his corps to Italy in November 1917, returning with it to the Western Front in March 1918.

After the armistice, Haking was chief of the British Section of the Armistice Commission. Subsequently, he was head of the British Military Mission to the Baltic in 1919, oversaw the plebiscites in East Prussia and Danzig in 1920 and was high commissioner for the League of Nations in Danzig from 1921 to 1923. His last post was as GOC in Egypt from 1923 to 1927. Haking died at Bulford on 9 June 1945. He was appointed CB 1910, KCB 1916, KCMG 1918 and GBE 1921.

There is no study of Haking, but aspects of his command have been covered. On his role at Loos and in its aftermath, see Peter Bryant, 'The Recall of Sir John French', *Stand To*, 22/23/24 (1988), pp. 24–9, 32–8, 22–6 respectively, and Ian Beckett, 'King George V and His Generals', in Matthew Hughes and Matthew Seligmann, eds, *Leadership in Conflict, 1914–18* (Barnsley: Leo Cooper, 2000), pp. 247–64. On Fromelles, see Mike Senior, *No Finer Courage:*

A Village in the Great War (Stroud: Sutton, 2004), pp. 120–77; Peter Pederson, *Fromelles* (Barnsley: Pen & Sword, 2003); and Robin Corfield, *Don't Forget Me, Cobber: The Battle of Fromelles* (Rosanna: Corfield, 2000).

Peyton, Sir William Eliot (1861–1931)

Peyton commanded Fifth Army from 8 April to 23 May 1918. The son of a colonel, he was educated at Brighton College but then enlisted as a ranker in the 7th Dragoon Guards in 1885 after failing the Sandhurst entrance examination. He received a commission on 18 June 1887 and transferred to a captaincy in the 15th Hussars in April 1896, though he then served in the Egyptian army from 1896 to 1898, and was appointed DSO. He also served in the South African War, having been promoted to major in October 1899, gaining his brevet lieutenant colonelcy in November 1900. He commanded the 15th Hussars from 1903 to 1907 and then the Meerut Cavalry Brigade from 1908 to 1912. He became military secretary to the C.-in-C. India and acted as Delhi herald of arms extraordinary at the Delhi durbar.

Promoted major general in October 1914, Peyton commanded the 2nd Mounted Division at Gallipoli and the Western Frontier Force in its operations against the Senussi in 1916. In May 1916 he became Haig's military secretary at GHQ and this explains the somewhat unexpected, albeit brief, appointment to Fifth Army as a temporary lieutenant general in April 1918, though for all practical purposes it was only a reserve army headquarters. It was followed by command of X Corps from May to July 1918, again in rear areas, and then command of 40th Division for the remainder of the war. Peyton commanded a cavalry division in the Rhine Army in 1919 and then the 3rd Indian Division from 1920 to 1926, and became military secretary to successive secretaries of state for war, Lord Derby, Stephen Walsh and Sir Lamington Worthington-Evans, from 1922 to 1926. He was promoted substantive lieutenant general in August 1921 and general in 1927. His last post was GOC at Scottish Command, 1926–30. He died on 14 November 1931. He was appointed DSO 1898, CB 1913, KCB 1917 and KCVO 1917.

There is no study of Peyton.

Appendix Two

Army Commanders and Chiefs of Staff

First Army

GOC

26 December 1914	General Sir Douglas Haig
22 December 1915	General Sir Henry Rawlinson, Bt
4 February 1916	General Sir Charles Monro
7 August 1916	Lieutenant General Sir Richard Haking (temp.)
30 September 1916	General Sir Henry Horne

MGGS

26 December 1914	Major General John Gough VC (died of wounds)
21 February 1915	Major General Richard Butler
26 December 1915	Major General George Barrow
4 February 1917	Major General Hastings Anderson

Second Army

Note: Second Army was redesignated Fourth Army on 20 December 1917 and renamed Second Army on 17 March 1918.

GOC

26 December 1914	General Sir Horace Smith-Dorrien
7 May 1915	General Sir Herbert Plumer
9 November 1917	General Sir Henry Rawlinson
18 March 1918	General Sir Herbert Plumer

MGGS

26 December 1914	Major General George Forestier-Walker
23 February 1915	Major General George Milne
15 July 1915	Major General Hugh Bruce Williams
13 June 1916	Major General Charles Harington
29 April 1918	Major General Jocelyn Percy

Third Army

GOC

13 July 1915	General Sir Charles Monro
23 October 1915	General Sir Edmund Allenby
9 June 1917	General the Hon. Sir Julian Byng

MGGS

13 July 1915	Major General A.L. Lynden-Bell
21 October 1915	Major General Louis Bols
21 May 1917	Major General John Vaughan

Fourth Army

GOC

5 February 1916	General Sir Henry Rawlinson, Bt
21 February 1918	General Sir William Birdwood (temp.)
2 April 1918	General Sir Henry Rawlinson, Bt

MGGS

5 February 1916	Major General Archibald Montgomery

Fifth Army

Note: Fifth Army was originally designated Reserve Army on 22 May 1916, then redesignated Fifth Army on 30 October 1916. It was redesignated Fourth Army on 2 April 1918. It was then reconstituted on 23 May 1918.

GOC

22 May 1916	Lieutenant General Sir Hubert Gough (general from 7 July)
28 March 1918	General Sir Henry Rawlinson, Bt
8 April 1918	Lieutenant General Sir William Peyton
23 May 1918	General Sir William Birdwood

MGGS

22 May 1916	Brigadier General Neill Malcolm (major general from 7 July)
23 December 1917	Major General Jocelyn Percy
1 June 1918	Major General Brudenell White

Index